TURNING POINTS

The Role of the State Department in
Vietnam (1945–1975)

Ambassador Thomas J. Corcoran

Edited by
Stephen Sherman

CASEMATE
Philadelphia & Oxford

A Vietnam Veterans for Factual History (VVFH) Book

Published in the United States of America and Great Britain in 2023 by
CASEMATE PUBLISHERS
1950 Lawrence Road, Havertown, PA 19083, USA
and
The Old Music Hall, 106–108 Cowley Road, Oxford OX4 1JE, UK

Copyright © 2023 Vietnam Veterans for Factual History

Hardcover Edition: ISBN 978-1-63624-367-2
Digital Edition: ISBN 978-1-63624-368-9

A CIP record for this book is available from the British Library

All rights reserved. No part of this book may be reproduced or transmitted in any form or by any means, electronic or mechanical including photocopying, recording or by any information storage and retrieval system, without permission from the publisher in writing.

Printed and bound in the United Kingdom by CPI Group (UK) Ltd, Croydon, CR0 4YY
Typeset in India by DiTech Publishing Services

For a complete list of Casemate titles, please contact:

CASEMATE PUBLISHERS (US)
Telephone (610) 853-9131
Fax (610) 853-9146
Email: casemate@casematepublishers.com
www.casematepublishers.com

CASEMATE PUBLISHERS (UK)
Telephone (0)1226 734350
Email: casemate-uk@casematepublishers.co.uk
www.casematepublishers.co.uk

Front cover image: A CIA map of Indochina and seal of the U.S. Department of State. (NCpedia and Wikimedia)

Contents

Introduction by Andrew R. Finlayson (Col., USMC, Ret.)   v
About the Author   xi

Part I   The Beginnings (1945–1954)   1
Part II   Beginnings of United States Involvement (1955–1963)   43
Part III   Deepening U.S. Involvement (1964–1968)   85
Part IV   Conclusion of U.S. Involvement (1968–1975)   127

Appendix A: The Path to Viet-Nam   167
Selected Bibliography   189
Endnotes   191
Index   207

To the Author, Ambassador Thomas J. Corcoran, and to William Lloyd Stearman (Head of National Security Council's Indochina Staff in 1973), both of whom saw the importance of recording and preserving this history.

Introduction

Ten years after the end of the American involvement in the Vietnam War, a career Foreign Service officer, Thomas J. Corcoran, set down in writing his thoughts on the history of U.S. State Department policy during our nation's involvement with South Vietnam. He produced a thoughtful, unbiased, objective, and well-researched manuscript that followed in chronological sequence the key policy decisions made by our national leaders that ultimately led to the first war our nation lost. As an ambassador and with over 30 years of diplomatic experience, which began in 1950 when he was assigned to Hà Nội and involved other postings in Southeast Asia, he brought to his analysis a long and rich personal experience with events in Laos, Cambodia, and Vietnam. Like many Americans of his generation, he was perplexed by the failure of America to achieve its goals in South Vietnam and so he embarked on an extensive study of why we made the decisions we made that led to the first lost war in our history. His work tells the story of the role played by the U.S. State Department throughout the entire period from 1945 to 1975.

For those who expect to read a story that conforms to the "orthodox" or "conventional" history of U.S. involvement in the Vietnam War, they will be sorely disappointed since Corcoran does an excellent job of exposing many of the myths and falsehoods found in these interpretations, many of which are still held as sacrosanct by some influential historians. Unfortunately, the "orthodox" interpretation of the war, one that attributes evil intent to the American involvement and heaps abuse upon our South Vietnamese ally, as well as describing the war as "unwinnable," will not find any evidence in Corcoran's work to support such claims. These false claims are still prevalent in much of the literature on the war and they have done lasting damage to the credibility of the United States and our ability to forge effective national strategies for dealing with aggression.

The central themes of the book are contained in the first and last pages. On the first page, he quotes from a reviewer of President Nixon's book, *Memoirs*, "to present a picture of Machiavellian scheming when it would be equally easy and certainly equally fair, to present a picture of bewildered men trying to find a solution to a difficult situation." What he is conveying is his opinion, while not absolving American decision makers of fault, that a careful analysis of the facts at play at the time decisions were being considered informs us that the policy blunders were made by well-intentioned and intelligent men, but they were woefully ill-informed or poorly informed when those decisions were made.

On the last page, Ambassador Corcoran sums up the dilemma that faced the American leaders, from Truman to Nixon, by identifying why the decisions taken were flawed and ultimately led to our nation's defeat. He quotes Henry Kissinger's assessment, "... no policy could succeed unless it had national opinion behind it." While many may view this opinion as simplistic and self-serving, it echoes the injunction of Carl Von Clausewitz who warned that for any war policy to be successful it requires the support of the government, the military, and the people. In this regard, it is difficult to argue that our leaders were able to successfully align these three elements of our society in support of the war. This division, which is apparent in every policy consideration outlined by Ambassador Corcoran, led to decisions made that did not enjoy broad support in any of the three key elements of our society and were often opposed or sabotaged by bureaucratic or ideological interests within these three elements.

The book is divided into four chronological parts, beginning with 1945 and ending with 1975. In Part I, The Beginnings (1945–1954), Corcoran examines the policy debates within the Truman and Eisenhower Administrations regarding the conflict between the French and the Việt Minh. The tensions between the French desire to reestablish control over their Vietnamese colony after World War II and the anti-colonial position of the United States are explained, and he demonstrates how these were exacerbated by the fear of communist expansion in Europe, the success of the communists in China in 1949, and the Korean War. Corcoran tells us that American policy makers were clearly aware from the very beginning that Hồ Chí Minh was not the idealistic nationalist so often portrayed by many historians, but a Comintern operative and founding member of the French Communist Party who systematically and ruthlessly murdered or betrayed to the French security services other non-communist, Vietnamese nationalists.

With the defeat of the French at Điện Biên Phủ in 1954, America found itself in a very delicate position where the French withdrawal from Indochina created a power vacuum that would only benefit the communists and threaten several other Southeast Asian nations confronting communist-led insurgencies. He also points out, "The Geneva Agreements did not end the war in Indochina, nor did they impose political or territorial settlements. They were, in fact, cease fire agreements." He clearly points out the Geneva Agreements were only between two parties, the Việt Minh and the French, and were not signed by either the United States or the Republic of South Vietnam, another fact overlooked by many authors of books on the war.

In Part II, Beginnings of United States Involvement (1955–1963), Corcoran begins with an examination of the Geneva Agreements and why they posed many significant obstacles for United States policy. He provides insights into why "free" elections on the unification of Vietnam were impossible in 1956, since neither the leaders of North Vietnam and the Republic of South Vietnam were prepared to accept them, and he gives the reasons why. The various debates over the efficacy of President Johnson's policy of "gradual response" and bombing halts, designed to show restraint and at the same time force the communists to the negotiating table, are covered. The conflicts in opinion on the proper courses of action, and the influence of public opinion and the national press on decision making, are explained, as well as the divergent views of LBJ's (Lyndon Baines Johnson) own National Security staff, the U.S. State Department, the CIA, and the Department of Defense. The State Department role in the disastrous coup of President Diệm is somewhat glossed over by Corcoran but he clearly demonstrates the removal of Diệm was not well thought out and led to several years of instability in South Vietnam which created the situation where it was necessary to use American military forces to save our ally.

In Part III, Deepening U.S. Involvement (1964–1968), Corcoran examines the various efforts by President Johnson and his advisors to find a substitute for President Diệm and stem the tide of communist success his removal facilitated. The Gulf of Tonkin resolution is explained as well as the dilemma facing LBJ by the expanding role played by North Vietnamese Army conventional forces infiltrating down the Ho Chi Minh Trail. The debate of how best to employ American military forces is covered, especially the use of bombing North Vietnam and the various bombing pauses that never led to any substantive peace negotiations. It is evident Corcoran views this period of U.S. involvement as one of failure after failure. However, he is also honest when he details the role the State Department played in approving many of the policies that led to failure during this period. No viable alternatives to the actions of LBJ were offered by the State Department, and in some cases they endorsed actions that proved to be based more on wishful thinking than a grasp of reality. Of particular note was the pig-headed insistence of the State Department (and, to a lesser extent, the CIA) to adhere to the 1962 Geneva Accords that prevented the introduction of American military forces into Laos, despite the flagrant disregard by the North Vietnamese to adhere to these accords. The State Department was instrumental in vetoing any plan to invade Laos to cut the Ho Chi Minh Trail using U.S. ground forces, thus allowing the North Vietnamese to continue to use the trail to send their conventional military forces and military equipment and supplies into South Vietnam along that county's long western border.

In Part IV, Conclusion of U.S. Involvement (1968–1975), Corcoran covers the efforts of the Nixon Administration to salvage a "just peace" in South Vietnam, and to do so without suffering international humiliation and the erosion of allied faith in America's commitment to its treaty obligations. He informs us that Kissinger and Nixon did not trust the State Department and provides ample evidence to support this view. He quotes Henry Kissinger on this, "Many in the State Department shared the outlook advocated by the leading newspapers or the more dovish figures in the Congress partly out of conviction, partly out of fear." This led to Secretary Rogers often attempting to thwart the policies and actions recommended by Nixon and to leak his opposition to a friendly press. Corcoran also examines the impact Watergate had on Vietnam policy, which, Kissinger explained, "The one circumstance we could not foresee was the debacle of Watergate. It was that which finally sealed the fate of South Vietnam by the erosion of executive authority, strangulation of South Vietnam wholesale by reducing aid, and legislative prohibitions against enforcing the peace agreement in the face of unprovoked North Vietnamese violations."

If there is one failing in Corcoran's story of the State Department's role in the policy decisions made prior to and during the Vietnam War, it is his inability to explain why so many intelligent and experienced foreign-service professionals and foreign-policy experts failed to understand that the North Vietnamese communists were never going to agree to and then observe a negotiated end to their aggression against South Vietnam. This was a key mistake and the one that ultimately led to disaster for both the United States and its South Vietnamese allies.

This book is valuable since it reflects the views of a career American diplomat with many years of firsthand experience in both the State Department and Southeast Asia. The reader must keep in mind that the book was written before 1994 and since that time more information about the role of the State Department and other instruments of national policy formulation during the Vietnam War have come to light. However, that does not diminish in any way the importance of this book or the keen insights of its author. It is a compelling tale of how the State Department attempted, and failed, to save South Vietnam from North Vietnamese aggression and the powerful domestic political influences that ultimately led to America's defeat. It is not an apologia, but rather a clear eyed and accurate examination of well-intentioned actions that were seriously flawed. It is a cautionary tale worthy of careful consideration by anyone interested in United States foreign policy during the Vietnam War.

Andrew R. Finlayson
Colonel, U.S. Marine Corps (Ret.)

x • TURNING POINTS

Tom Corcoran (right) was consul in Hué during the 1966 Buddhist Struggle movement there. He and Jim Bullington (left) were awarded Superior Honor Awards by Ambassador Lodge (middle) for their service during that time. (Nguyễn Văn Nghĩa, FSN political assistant)

From left to right: Ambassador Larry C. Williamson, acting director general of the Foreign Service at the time; Rev. James Blackburn, interim rector of St. John's Church, Georgetown Parish; and Ambassador Thomas J. Corcoran, secretary and chair of the Memorial Committee of Diplomatic and Consular Officers Retired, at their annual Memorial Day ceremony at the DACOR Memorial Section of Rock Creek Cemetery, May 28, 1990. (Courtesy of DACOR, an organization of foreign-affairs professionals)

About the Author

Thomas J. Corcoran was born in New York in 1920. He graduated from St. John's University. During World War II, he served in the Navy and was stationed aboard a supply ship in the Black Sea during the meeting of Allied leaders at Yalta in the Crimea.

He began his Foreign Service career in 1948. His first assignments abroad were in Spain and then, in 1950, in Hà Nội in Vietnam, which was then under French control. He became the chargé d'affaires in Vientiane, Laos, and then Phnom Penh, Cambodia, in 1952 before returning to Hà Nội from the beginning of September 1954 until about December 12, 1955. He was there about 14 months. Mr. Corcoran later served in Upper Volta, Haiti, and in Quebec, Canada. He was chargé d'affaires ad interim (Laos) from August 1975 to March 1978 and ambassador to Burundi from 1978 until retiring from the State Department in 1980. He talked about his career in some detail in an interview for the Association for Diplomatic Studies and Training Foreign Affairs Oral History Project, which can be found on their website: https://adst.org/OH%20TOCs/Corcoran,%20Thomas%20J.toc.pdf

Mr. Corcoran graduated from the Armed Forces Staff College in Norfolk and the National War College in Washington. He was a secretary and governor of DACOR (Diplomatic and Consular Officers Retired) and a member of the City Tavern Club. He died of heart ailments on November 27, 1994, at his home in Washington.

In his retirement, he created this manuscript. Prior to his death, he turned it over to William Lloyd "Bill" Stearman, a State Department colleague, with whom he had shared a villa in Sài Gòn in 1966. Before Bill passed away in 2021, he directed his wife to pass the manuscript to Vietnam Veterans for Factual History, with which he had become involved during the preceding decade.

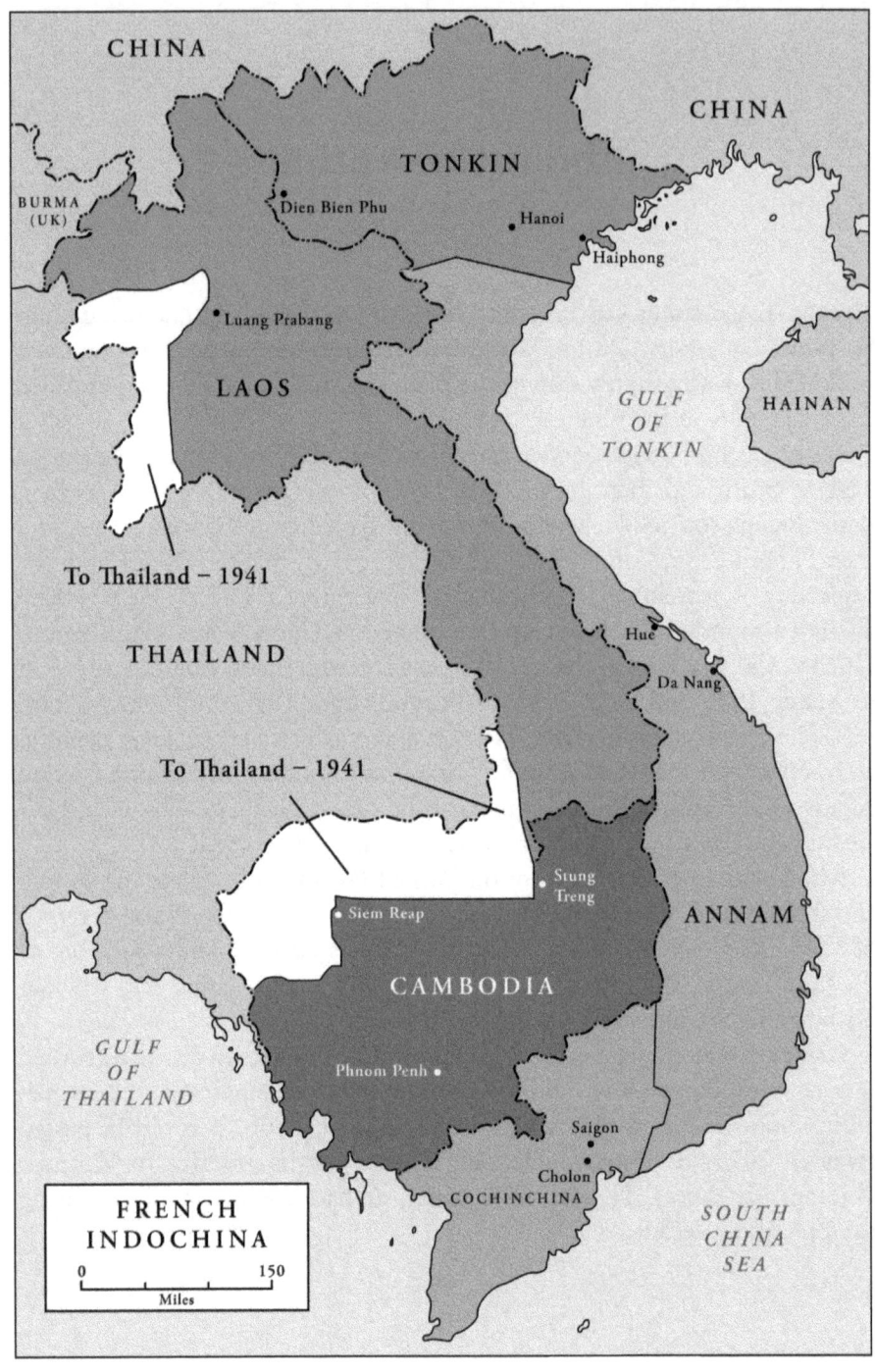

PART I

The Beginnings (1945–1954)

Before World War II, few Americans knew or cared much about Indochina or, as the maps then styled it, French Indochina. No American university offered a course of Indochinese or, for that matter, of Southeast Asian studies.[1] When events in Indochina began to dominate the news, few Americans possessed what the 19th-century historian Lord Macaulay called knowledge of "the plot of the preceding acts" sufficient to permit a full understanding of these events. The plot was complicated and the players temperamental. Some of the most important action took place off stage, at least off the Indochinese stage. It is easy, as a book reviewer remarked about Indochina in 1954, "to present a picture of Machiavellian scheming when it would be equally easy and certainly equally fair, to present picture of bewildered men trying to find a solution to a difficult situation."[2]

Americans concerned about the Far East before the war were interested in China, the Philippines and, of course, Japan, all of them in those days far away but somewhat familiar through commercial, military, and missionary contacts. The wartime alliance with China and the liberation and independence of the Philippines seemed as natural then as did the war with Japan. However, none of this knowledge went very deep. The details of "how the Americans conquered the Philippines in 1898–1902 at the cost of 250,000 lives" had, for example, faded from the American memory.[3]

The great mobilization and the massive deployment for war in the Pacific shrank oceanic distances and sharpened the interest of Americans in all the countries on the opposite shore of the great ocean. Nevertheless, those countries were still relatively far away and regarded from the point of view of distant spectators. The spectators saw colonialism as bad and the end of the European colonial empires as good. They welcomed the new governments that succeeded the former colonial regimes just as they welcomed the independence of the Philippines. They assumed relations with the new states would be good and trade with them would expand. They took it for granted that China would survive, that it would cooperate more or less with the United States, and that it would coexist with the new indigenous regimes taking form in the postcolonial era. They became aware, only slowly and painfully, of the power vacuum created in the Far East by the termination of the European colonial presence, the collapse of Japanese wartime dominance, and the consequent destabilization of the region.[4]

The effects of World War II on Indochina were considerable and lasting. However, as French scholar Bernard Fall was to point out, there were practically no American observers on the scene at the time and the French were not talking very much about developments concerning which they were neither proud nor happy.[5] Many of the French in Indochina—having been forced to live with, and to cope with, the combined results of defeat in Europe and Japanese dominance in the Far East—were inclined to blame their troubles at least in part on the acts or omissions of their American allies or, sometimes, of the "Anglo-Saxons" jointly. They were quick to recall the inconclusive Anglo–French naval talks in Singapore in June 1939 (which the Americans and the Dutch did not attend), the American disinclination to act against Japanese aggression in the 1930s, the American decision not to sell aircraft to General Catroux, governor general of Indochina in 1940, and Lord Halifax's counsel of moderation when Catroux indicated his intention to respect the Anglo–French alliance after the fall of France.[6] They recalled their early impression that the United States understood their situation and would tolerate a certain degree of acquiescence in the face of Japanese demands for military facilities. They recalled that on June 30, 1940, Under Secretary of State Welles told the French ambassador the United States Government did not believe it could enter into conflict with Japan and that should Japan attack Indochina the United States would not oppose such action. They remembered Secretary of State Hull's statement that America's policy in the Far East at that time should be limited to encouraging "countries like Indochina to delay and parlay."[7]

After the fall of France, the Armistice with Hitler on June 25, 1940, and Japanese recognition of the Vichy Government, the French administration in Indochina had little room for maneuver in any event. To complicate things further, the Thais, with Japanese advice and consent, attacked Indochina on June 12, 1940. Although the French won at Koh Chang, in the Gulf of Siam—what Admiral Decoux, Catroux's successor as governor general, called the only pitched battle fought by French naval forces in two world wars[8]—the Japanese eventually imposed a settlement which cost three Cambodian and two Lao provinces. The victorious allies forced Thailand to give back these provinces at the end of the war but the United States, mindful of the importance of Asian nationalism and the appeal of anticolonialism in this case, protected Thailand from any further punishment. The French remembered that too.[9]

Americans had entertained high expectations for the postwar period in Asia and in these they were sorely disappointed. They had intended to act in the new situation in concert with a peaceful China. Failure of American efforts to reconcile the Kuomintang Government in China and the Chinese Communists completely changed the postwar situation. The United States, for all its benevolent intentions, found itself the political and propaganda target of the Chinese Communists. In the face of the new situation, the United States found it necessary to switch from emphasis on economic assistance, such as it was applying in Europe, to an effort to organize against the particular Asian threat.[10] It saw this threat as an attempt to sweep United States influence out of Asia, thus making immense resources available to the Soviet Union. Great changes were going on in China but the Sino–Soviet ideological split was still in the future and the United States required a valid interlocutor and ally to replace the old China in the Far East. Japan was the obvious choice. Japan's economic recovery, the San Francisco Peace Treaty, the United States–Japan Defense Treaty, and acceptance of United States forces stationed in Japan all consolidated this selection.

The North Korean invasion of South Korea in 1950, and the United Nations' response, tangled the broad United States role in containment of communist expansion in the Far East with its specific role as United Nations agent in containing the invasion.[11]

As the United States sent forces to Korea, it began developing the concept of a security defense line running from the Aleutians through Japan and Taiwan to the Philippines. Not surprisingly in this context, it also began sending supplies to the French forces fighting a communist-led opponent in Indochina.[12]

United States military actions in response to both the Chinese Communist assumption of power in China and the North Korean invasion of South Korea produced a peculiar and lingering side effect.[13]

The United States' actions, dampening the feeling of insecurity in and concerning Southeast Asia, made certain Asian nations, notably India, freer to express disapproval of aspects of U.S. policy. These Asians were disinclined to accept the American analysis of the global power situation once the situation near their own area seemed to have achieved a sort of equilibrium consequent upon the United States' forward strategy. Their own analysis, in their own view quite objective, projected a power struggle and a simultaneous ideological conflict between the United States and the Soviet Union with neither good nor evil confined to one side or the other. They saw United States aims regarding the right of nations to determine their own destinies, and the organization of a world in which nations might live without war, as potential meddling in national affairs and potential limiting of national freedoms. Some of them, reflecting uneasily on the Japanese past, appeared to have some doubts about the choice of Japan as America's partner in the region.[14]

Nevertheless, the United States' perception of Indochina was an idealistic one flowing from the benevolent American attitude towards Asia in general. From 1945 to 1954, it pretty much remained so under three presidents and five secretaries of state. Global and European considerations impinged on Indochina policy during these years as they had during World War II. In the postwar period, these considerations operated to strengthen the negotiating position of the former colonial power and to inhibit the American effort to bring about genuine independence for the Indochina states. This delay was no doubt a key factor influencing the eventual communist victory in Indochina 21 years later but by no means the only one.

As early as August 1942, President Franklin D. Roosevelt had decided he did not want to see a reestablishment of French colonial presence in Indochina after the war.[15] He expressed his opinion in strong language to the effect that the French had milked Indochina for one hundred years, the people were worse off than they were at the beginning, and they were entitled to something better than that. Officers in the Department of State were set to work drafting and clearing position papers incorporating the president's views and including studies of schemes for independence and self-government of the countries of Indochina to be achieved under international supervision. Various alternative timetables were suggested.[16] This was the first specific American policy decision on Indochina, and it clearly remained policy until after the reestablishment of the French military and political presence at the end of 1945 and the beginning of 1946. On March 27, 1943, President Roosevelt suggested to British Foreign Secretary Anthony Eden the establishment of a postwar trusteeship for Indochina rather than the return of the area to France.[17] Subsequently, in obvious pursuit of the same general line of policy, Roosevelt forbade the provision of American air support and air supply to French elements who began fighting the Japanese in Indochina near the war's end.[18]

In January 1944, President Roosevelt told British Ambassador Lord Halifax that he had, for over a year, expressed the opinion that Indochina should not go back to France but that it should be administered by an international trusteeship.[19] Roosevelt again raised the trusteeship at Yalta in February 1945, suggesting the inclusion of one or two Indochinese and "even a Frenchman" in the Trusteeship Council, balancing them by a Filipino, a Chinese, and a Russian.[20] General Claire Chennault of the Fourteenth Air Force later wrote he had had orders from Theater Headquarters (General Wedemeyer) that no arms and ammunition would be provided to French troops under any circumstances. Chennault reluctantly obeyed these orders, which he understood came directly from the War Department. He concluded it was American policy that French Indochina would not be restored to the French and that "The American Government was interested in seeing the French forcibly ejected from Indochina so the problem of postwar separation from their colony would be easier ..."[21] At about the same time, various United States teams made their way from Southern China into North Vietnam and established contacts with the communist-led Việt Minh. The teams included representatives of the Office of Strategic Services (OSS), the Army Air Forces, the Army and Navy Intelligence Services, and the U.S. Combat Section of South China Command. The Việt Minh even formed a Vietnamese American Friendship Association on October 17, 1945.[22] An American official who visited both Hồ Chí Minh and Bảo Đại in Hà Nội in February 1946 found them quite familiar with the Roosevelt policy.[23]

Jean Sainteny, the French Government's representative in Hà Nội in 1945–46 and again in 1954–55, told the BBC in 1974 that the American OSS Mission under Major Archimedes L. A. Patti had endorsed the 1945 takeover of power by the Việt Minh in Hà Nội by standing alongside Võ Nguyên Giáp at the takeover ceremony. Sainteny speculated that, while Patti was operating very much on his own, he was not acting spontaneously in his opposition to the French return to Indochina but in accordance with general directives issued much higher up. However, Sainteny thought Patti might have exceeded his instructions somewhat.[24] Patti, in turn, told the BBC his mission was an anti-Japanese one, that he was not supposed to become involved in Indochinese–French politics, but that he was specifically ordered by General Donovan (head of OSS) on the president's instructions that he was not to assist any French objective to re-enter Indochina with American or Lend-Lease equipment. He was "not to support the French objective of retaking their former colony, nor necessarily to assist the Vietnamese in achieving their independence."[25] The BBC interviewer concluded, "The fact is that it was the Americans who literally took revolution by the hand and accompanied it into Hà Nội. The visible support of the Americans and their apparent benediction upon the proceedings gave Ho Chi Minh [sic] the political initiative, an apparent legitimacy and a hold on power he never let go."[26]

Of course, the Việt Minh did represent the most active and really the only important anti-Japanese insurgent group in Indochina. It was natural therefore that, after the Japanese *coup de force*, they got most of the American arms, transmitters, and other equipment the OSS parachuted into the area. Adding this materiel to the Japanese and French weapons taken over after the Japanese surrender on August 15, 1945, the Việt Minh were able to equip an army that could easily deal with the French military remnants in the North as well as with rival, non-communist, nationalists.[27] This tangible advantage in military hardware would seem to have had as much to do with Hồ Chí Minh's capture of the political initiative in the existing circumstances as any laying on of hands by the Patti Mission.

At any rate, all these contacts at this period seem to establish pretty clearly that the Việt Minh believed the United States supported independence for the countries of Indochina. The French and Americans on the scene appeared to have a similar understanding of American policy and their impressions inevitably aggravated Franco–American frictions and misunderstandings which persisted into subsequent eras of Franco–American cooperation. The Việt Minh, for their part, were later able to claim, on the basis of these early encounters, that the Americans had let them down.

Former Secretary of State Dean Rusk, in his BBC interview in 1977, offered an interesting analysis of what was happening in regard to United States policy on Indochina as World War II ended. Mr. Rusk recalled the Americans had believed the great colonial areas of Asia were going to become independent but that Churchill had never agreed with Roosevelt on this. When some Americans in India during the war had tried to explain to the Indians they were there solely to fight the Japanese and were not involved in postwar British–Indian relations, considerable British–American friction had resulted. Roosevelt had the idea that India, Burma, Ceylon, Malaya, Indonesia, and Indochina should all come out of the war as independent nations. At some point, perhaps around January 1945, he seemed to lose interest in this idea. Mr. Rusk was not sure whether age and fatigue or the pressure of other preoccupations caused this loss of interest. President Truman was so involved in taking over the office of president, and in dealing with the occupation of Germany and the continuation of the war against Japan, that "he did not pick up the same policy attitude and press it forward." Rusk also noted the Combined Chiefs of Staff had delegated command responsibility for the area including Indochina to the British Chiefs of Staff and "when an American President lost interest in pressing matters of this sort then the command responsibility really rested with Mr. Churchill."[28] Rusk speculated that, with the coming of Clement Atlee to the prime ministership, it might have been assumed the colonial problem in regard to the British areas was going to be solved. It might have been assumed the French were no more likely to be able to stay in Indochina than the Dutch were to stay in Indonesia. Rusk noted that "governments in France during too much of this period were too weak to make the tough decisions with respect to Indochina."[29]

It could also be noted the French, unlike the Dutch, did have a military instrument which they could use, not conclusively but at least temporarily, to try a comeback.

French resentment of American contacts with the Việt Minh was intensified by what they considered the low priority the Allies accorded to taking over from the Japanese occupation forces in Indochina, the political activities of the Chinese Kuomintang (KMT) forces taking over north of the 16th Parallel, and the weakness of the British forces taking over south of the 16th Parallel. Many of the French in Indochina were extremely anxious to wipe out the memory of the early World War II defeat and the last-minute Japanese *coup de force* by quickly reestablishing the French presence.[30]

It is necessary to describe these French resentments not for purposes of recrimination but simply to underline how they affected the future course of events in Indochina. It is equally important to an understanding of future events not to go off the deep end in the other direction. Hồ Chí Minh, whatever his other attributes, was hardly a "nationalist first" or a benevolent, avuncular leader of an agrarian revolution. His biography is now well known. It is sufficient to recall here that he was a co-founder of the French Communist Party on December 30, 1920, and that while he was apparently cooperating with the French in 1945–46, in his capacity as head of a broadly based nationalist movement (Việt Minh of that period), his deputies were systematically killing off or scaring away the non-communist nationalist leaders.[31] Hồ Chí Minh was in Hà Nội by August 19, 1945, four days after V-J Day, and on September 2 the nominally nationalist, but communist-dominated, Việt Minh seized power there, establishing the Democratic Republic of Vietnam.[32]

The month of September 1945 saw a great deal of activity including the arrival of British Indian forces under General Douglas D. Gracey in Sài Gòn, the arrival of Chinese (KMT) forces under General Lu Han in Hà Nội, the French *coup* which reestablished French authority in Sài Gòn, the retaliatory massacre of French civilians at the Cité Héraud housing development, and the death of Lieutenant Colonel A. Peter Dewey of the OSS, son of Congressman Charles S. Dewey of Illinois and the first of a long line of American casualties in the Indochina wars. Some eight years later, during the dedication of a small memorial to Lieutenant Colonel Dewey, a local district official attributed his death to "the progressive youth of those times" (*La Jeunesse avancée de cette époque*).[33] At the end of September, the Japanese formally surrendered in Hà Nội and the Indochina story properly began to unfold.

Officially, President Roosevelt's determination that the United States wanted to see the states of Indochina become independent still governed American policy. As a practical matter, events had already begun to erode the prospects for its execution. Secretary of State Cordell Hull had earlier pointed out to the president that the United States could not get the closest cooperation of the colonial powers in Europe in the prosecution of the war if it alienated them in the Orient.[34] In fact Petain, Giraud, and de Gaulle had all been assured at various times that the United States supported their return to their empire. Obviously, the United States was trying to balance two conflicting policies.[35] As Secretary Rusk reminded his BBC interviewer, Roosevelt's death caused some of the priority accorded the anticolonial issue to evaporate, as did the Combined Chiefs of Staff's delegation of authority to the British Chiefs of Staff. The 1945 military conference at Potsdam had agreed Great Britain would disarm Japanese forces south of the 16th Parallel in Indochina while the Chinese disarmed those to the north. The arrival of a British general in Sài Gòn at the head of a small British Indian force more or less coincided with the return of French colonialism.[36]

Writing in 1972 in a special issue of *Paris-Match* [or *Historia*], Sainteny observed:[37]

> In the south, in Cochinchina, our British allies, under the command of General D. D. Gracey, assigned to disarm the Japanese, accomplished their mission scrupulously, requiring the Japanese staff to maintain order, for which they held it responsible, and put an end to the riots which, in the days preceding their arrival had already caused some victims among the French population. The British returned to the French the responsibility for services essential to the normal life of the country. They never seemed to cast doubt on the legitimate rights of France.
>
> On the other hand, north of the sixteenth parallel, the Chinese, strengthened by the commitments obtained from the Roosevelt administration, seemed to have a very different concept of their mission.

In his interview with the BBC in 1977, Secretary Rusk pointed out the U.S. had not taken the view in 1945 that it was really its choice to order the French to stay out of Indochina, the British to stay out of India, Burma, Ceylon, and Malaya, or the Dutch out of Indonesia. Furthermore, the Cold War was beginning. The Russians were failing to live up to the Yalta agreements on free elections. Stalin was setting up new governments unilaterally in Eastern Europe and demanding the return of refugees. In short, Western Europe had first claim on American attention. Nevertheless, Secretary Hull had underlined for President Roosevelt the issue that was to vitiate United States efforts in Indochina for years.[38] Most of the French on the ground in Indochina who were, in the American view, to provide the surrogate forces to cover the Indochina states while leading them to true independence simply could not drop the idea they were being asked to make sacrifices while the Americans, through covetousness or simple naïveté, were out to supplant the French economic and cultural presence in the peninsula.

Without venturing too deeply into the tortuous history of Franco–Vietnamese negotiations and maneuvers, it is useful to cite a few developments which opened the way to American participation in the Indochina story. By October 25, 1945, General Leclerc had begun a mopping-up operation.[39] It later became clear he had serious doubts about the possibility of a military solution of the Indochina problem given its political complexity and the limited military resources available to the French. One French observer had him describing the French reoccupation effort as a repetition of Napoleon III's inglorious Mexican campaign.

Leclerc was by no means soft headed on dealings with the Vietnamese. Sainteny noted Leclerc had understood arms alone could not produce a real solution. Another French observer (Raymond Dronne) remarked that Leclerc was convinced it was impossible to reestablish the old order and it was necessary to seek a new liberal solution, along the lines of the French governmental declaration of March 24, 1945, on the basis of elected assemblies but that this solution was not, and could not be, abandonment of Indochina.[40] On the other hand, Leclerc himself, in a letter to Maurice Schumann on the eve of the Fontainebleau Conference, stressed the importance of sticking with a solution based on an Indochinese Federation within the French Union. He warned that Hồ Chí Minh was a great enemy of France whose consistent aim was to get the French out of Indochina. Leclerc warned he was responsible for the continuation of the civil war and the assassinations of pro-French "Annamites." He stressed it would be dangerous for the French representatives at the negotiations to be taken in by sympathy and by tricks of language (democracy, resistance, New France) that Hồ Chí Minh and his team knew how to use to perfection.[41]

Under Admiral d'Argenlieu as high commissioner (replacing the title of governor general) and General Leclerc, French policy initially appeared unclear. The French of Cochinchina, the southernmost and most French part of Indochina, exercised their considerable influence towards a restoration of the *status quo ante*. In this they were supported by elements of the Vietnamese middleclass of the region.⁴² In the north, the French criticized the Americans for failing to save French sovereignty. Võ Nguyên Giáp spoke of close relations with the United States and China but began to accuse the French of planning a reconquest. Meanwhile, diplomatic moves took place. On January 7, 1946, the French signed an agreement with the Cambodians. On February 28, General Salan signed an agreement with the Chinese (KMT) in Chongqing by which France gave up her extraterritorial rights and concessions in China and China agreed to remove its troops from Indochina by March 31.⁴³ On March 6, Jean Sainteny signed an agreement with Hồ Chí Minh and non-Communist Vũ Hồng Khanh (Việt Nam Quốc Dân Đảng [VNQDD], the Vietnamese Nationalist Party) by which France recognized the Democratic Republic of Vietnam and pledged a referendum on the unity of the three regions (kys) of Vietnam including Cochinchina, and Hồ Chí Minh agreed not to oppose the landing of French troops.⁴⁴

This March 6 Accord consisted of a preliminary convention and an annex. In the convention, France recognized the Republic of Vietnam as a free state belonging to the Indochinese Federation and the French Union. The annex provided for a force of 10,000 Vietnamese and 15,000 French troops to replace the Chinese and limited the retention of the French troops to five years. It is probable Hồ Chí Minh agreed to the landing of the French troops principally because of his anxiety to get rid of the Chinese troops. As long as the Chinese remained in force, they not only inflicted a ruinous economic burden but presented the constant danger of a sudden military intervention to impose a regime of their own choosing. On July 14, 1946, General Leclerc left Indochina and the following month the French signed a *modus vivendi* with Laos. Meanwhile, fighting continued in Cochinchina, to which the Sainteny–Hồ agreement of March 6 was never applied and which the French recognized as an independent republic on June 1, 1946. The Dalat Conference, which opened in April, served only to illustrate the basic disagreement between French and Vietnamese. The Fontainebleau Conference (July 6 to September 14, 1946) produced a *modus vivendi* confined to economic and cultural questions and, in effect, postponed any political agreement.⁴⁵

Faced with the fact of the return of the French presence, and increasingly preoccupied with Europe, the United States tacitly made its second decision on Indochina. This was essentially a decision to stand aside. As Secretary of State George Marshall put it, America hoped "... a pacific basis of adjustment could be found."⁴⁶

This did not of course mean the United States had abandoned the idea that the old European colonies in Asia should be free. As late as 1948, when a wave of communist attacks on foreign installations occurred in Burma, Malaya, and the Philippines, and the United States Government dispatched quantities of small arms to the area, journalists asked Secretary Marshall if this action signified a change in policy. They wanted to know, in particular, if the landing of a planeload of arms at Kuala Lumpur meant it was United States policy to help the colonialists to reestablish themselves. Marshall had it made clear to the press conference there had been no change in policy. The arms had been sent only to permit Americans on rubber plantations to see to their own defense.[47]

A good many people have criticized the decision to stand aside in the face of the French return to Indochina. They have argued the United States could have pressured the French to set Vietnam on the path to early independence at Fontainebleau using Marshall Plan aid to France as a means of applying that pressure. Looking back at the situation that existed at the time and considering subsequent experience with the French and, for that matter, with the Vietnamese, it seems unlikely such pressure would have achieved the desired result. The Marshall Plan really only became effective two years later, too late for the purpose suggested. French sensitivities were, in any event, too great to permit a French government to cave in on that particular issue at that time.[48] Furthermore, other considerations entered into the balance. The United States was not yet as deeply concerned over the strategic position of Indochina in Southeast Asia as it later became. The absence of major United States investments in Indochina dictated a more reserved approach than in Indonesia where such investments existed and required protection. The United States still saw France as the key to the defense and economic recovery of Europe. It feared that the overthrow of the third force in France would lead to the accession to power of either General de Gaulle on the one hand or the communists on the other. The key role the communists were playing in the Vietnamese resistance to the French was another important factor considered.[49]

One experienced American diplomat aptly described the years from 1946 to 1950 as the period of the French Colonial War, as distinguished from the communist war of liberation that developed from 1950 onwards.[50] During this period, military and political developments in Indochina, in France, and on the world scene all tended to lay the groundwork for the third United States decision on Indochina.

A French commentator has observed that "In the days following the March 6 Accords each side accused the other of evading it." He noted that France, divided, dealing with many difficulties of all kinds, led by precarious governments, making do while awaiting a constitution, floated in uncertainty and could only feel its way. But one thing was sure, he found, and that was the heart of the problem; in 1946, the French were much more sensitive about the question of the empire they were soon to become and nobody could or would support a solution that would amount to the total expulsion of France and her interests and the takeover by a communist regime in Indochina.[51] It was in this climate that the "frank and friendly" negotiations foreseen by the March 6 Accords were to begin.

The year 1946 began with the appearance at least of Franco–Vietnamese cooperation. It even seemed the French found the Việt Minh more agreeable to deal with than the more openly anti-French nationalists.[52] Giáp moved against the leadership of the latter elements and also doubled and armed his army, militia and youth elements. Việt Minh extremists attacked the French at Bắc Ninh after the breakdown of the Fontainebleau Conference. Meanwhile, the French had recognized the Cochinchinese Republic and banned the Việt Minh from operating in that area. November saw the adoption of a new constitution and Hồ's selection of a cabinet with a communist majority. Continuing tensions and clashes between French and Vietnamese forces led to the French bombardment at Hải Phòng on November 23, with heavy Vietnamese casualties. By December 2, Sainteny in Hà Nội found his negotiations stalemated. On December 19, the French demanded the disarmament of the Vietnamese militia. The Vietnamese attacked the French in Hà Nội that night and two days later Nguyễn Bình attacked the French in the south. Sainteny was severely wounded in the fighting in Hà Nội when his armored car was ambushed.

In explaining this complete breakdown of Franco–Việt Minh negotiations, some observers have suggested Admiral d'Argenlieu was following a policy contrary to that of the French Government by obstructing the March 6 Agreement, pushing the independence of Cochinchina, "wrecking" the Fontainebleau Conference, and "pacifying" Hải Phòng by bombardment. Others have suggested Hồ Chí Minh was playing a double game and only pretending to prefer the path of negotiations. Still others attribute the double game to some of Hồ's associates.[53] Wherever the truth may have lain, it seemed clear that, since both the French and the Việt Minh, at that time, lacked the military means sufficient to force a solution, a continuation of negotiations was indicated. As it turned out, however, the events of December 1946 had greatly complicated things.

It seems a little strange now to recall that the French Government, whose forces the Việt Minh attacked on December 19 and 21, was headed by Léon Blum, "a Socialist and long-time critic of French colonialism ..."[54] Blum had not changed his ideas, but his party was weak and divided. He also had to cope with pressure from the communists for peace and negotiations to keep Indochina within the French Union, and from the center and right against a policy of weakness and dishonor. In the circumstances, he had no choice but to fight just like any other French premier and to take the position that "Before all, order must be reestablished, peaceful order which is the basis for the execution of contracts."[55]

French historian Philippe Devillers thought the French Government was trying to find a solution that would reconcile autonomy for Vietnam with French interests and to do this while its expeditionary corps was carrying on a difficult fight in an immense country with insufficient means. Admiral d'Argenlieu and his advisors considered that, by his attack in Hà Nội in December 1946, Hồ had disqualified himself as interlocutor. The administration in Sài Gòn recommended, therefore, that the government "Vietnamize" the conflict, particularly by calling in the ex-Emperor Bảo Đại. The idea survived the admiral's departure and led to endless discussions with Bảo Đại.[56] Blum's successor, Paul Ramadier, sent High Commissioner Émile Bollaert to Indochina to offer independence within the French Union and a cease-fire. Running into opposition from the French military, he made a later offer, not including either a truce or independence which was rejected by the Việt Minh and by the group around Bảo Đại. To make a long story short, Bảo Đại, eventually on December 7, 1947, at Hạ Long Bay, signed a statement of terms which fell far short of independence. Bảo Đại no doubt hoped to maneuver towards better terms, but, if so, his hopes were excessively optimistic. The Hạ Long Bay Agreement, ratified by the French on August 19, 1948, was, essentially, a rehash of the earlier December 7 agreement with Bảo Đại, and the subsequent Elysée Accords of March 9, 1949, and consecrated the Bảo Đại solution which, many people thought, had failure built into it. Bảo Đại had really accepted the terms rejected by the Vietnamese delegation at Fontainebleau in 1946. If Bảo Đại had received genuine independence and been accorded genuine unity, he just might have been able to broaden his base among peasants, intellectuals, and youth. He could hardly achieve this result against Việt Minh opposition when he himself believed the continued presence of French troops and French officials signified he did not yet have independence.

Meanwhile, the Việt Minh, clearly opposed to the Bảo Đại solution, had begun for several reasons to move openly over to the world communist camp.[57] Since August 1945, the communists had antagonized many of the non-communist nationalists. By 1949, the international situation had become strained and western sensitivity to Communism had become intensified. The arrival of Marshall Plan dollars in France had made francs available for support of the Indochina War. By June 1949, the Department of State had welcomed the formation of the new unified state of Vietnam (the three kys in one state) and had expressed the hope the Elysée Accords would form the basis for the progressive realization of the legitimate aspirations of the Vietnamese people.

According to Devillers, the French General Staff had decided by the spring of 1949 that it could no longer hope to "win" in Indochina without American military and financial aid. He indicated they also understood they could obtain such aid only by placing the war in Vietnam in the American strategic plan while giving to Vietnam at least the appearance of an independent state. This they recognized as a risky undertaking because the conservative Vietnamese were split into two basic groups. One, which the French considered pro-French, counted on patience and negotiation to win power and independence. The other, considered pro-American, distrusted the French and counted on the Americans to apply increasing pressure to the French which would permit this second group to seize power and exercise it thanks to American aid.[58] This summary "appreciation" presents a pretty good, if rather abbreviated, analysis of a cluttered political and diplomatic situation whether or not it represents the views of the French General Staff of the period. It does not address, however, what was going on inside the Việt Minh organization, or, in Europe.

At this time, the Việt Minh still had in being a national movement. They had played down the class struggle for tactical reasons. Now they saw the French winning friends in the United States. More importantly, they saw the communist accession to power in China. They prepared, in the light of these developments, to exchange their old policy of internal union and independent diplomacy for a new one of adherence to the Peking line. In November 1949, the Việt Minh sent a delegation to the Trade Union Conference in Peking at which Liu Shaoqi laid down the communist line for Southeast Asia. Peking recognized the new Democratic Republic of Vietnam regime early in January 1950, the first country to do so. The Soviet Union followed suit on January 30.[59]

Dean Acheson's biographer reminds us that, in the fall of 1949, Acheson, President Truman's secretary of state, "found the United States severely restricted in its ability to influence international events."[60] The Berlin blockade had been lifted but it had been a close scrape and had not improved the Western power position. The first Soviet atomic test in August had followed closely on the communist victory in China; the Soviet Union was threatening Yugoslavia and conducting purges in other satellites; Austrian peace treaty talks had stalled; and nationalist divisions in Europe persisted. The American recession, by reducing

British dollar earnings, had contributed to the British decision to devalue the pound sterling. The British Labor Government resented American pressure for European Economic integration. The French ambassador thought the British devaluation coming in the course of Anglo–American financial talks was an indicator "of the existence or re-establishment of a 'special relationship' between the United States and Britain and the Commonwealth at the expense of the Atlantic Community and of European economic integration."[61] The French had to follow the British lead on devaluation with a consequent sharp increase in the French cost of living, the fall of the Queuille Government, and a time of uncertainty in France. Meanwhile, on the other hand, the North Atlantic Treaty Organization alliance had been signed and just over the horizon was the Schuman Plan which "bore within it the seed of a much more comprehensive and tightly knit union of the European states."[62]

At about the same time, a review of Asian policy ordered by Acheson in the autumn of 1949 led to National Security Staff Paper NSC 48/2, approved by President Truman on December 31.[63] This paper, while calling for continued American efforts to end colonialism and strengthen nationalism in Asia, also described Southeast Asia as the "target for a coordinated offensive directed by the Kremlin." It called for American "political, economic and military assistance and advice where needed to supplement the resistance of other governments in and out of the area which are more directly concerned."[64] "Acheson was even conjecturing that if the French effort in Indochina collapsed the United States might find itself compelled to intervene in their place. It was not a pleasant thought, but it was what underlay his final decision to give the French what political and military support they needed to keep going."[65] Stalin was still alive and the threat of a communist conspiracy directed from Moscow was pretty real. "But quite apart from Stalinism, Acheson was primarily concerned with the impact a Communist victory in Indochina would have upon the uncertain situation in Asia and on opinion at home."[66]

When the United States Government announced recognition of Vietnam, Laos, and Cambodia on February 7, 1950, it based its action on the formal establishment of those countries as independent states within the French Union and described it as consistent with the fundamental policy of giving support to the peaceful and democratic evolution of dependent peoples toward self-government and independence. It anticipated the full implementation of these basic agreements, and of supplementary accords, would promote political stability and the growth of effective democratic institutions in Indochina. Again, when on May 8, 1950, Acheson announced the extension of military and economic aid to the Associated States and France, he said that

"The United States recognizes that the solution of the Indochinese problem depends both upon the restoration of security and upon the development of genuine nationalism and that United States assistance can and should contribute to these major objectives."[67]

In commenting on the Soviet recognition of Hồ Chí Minh's Government, Acheson said that it should remove "... any illusion as to the nationalist nature of Ho Chi Minh's [sic] aims and reveals Ho in his true colors as the mortal enemy of native independence in Indochina."[68] The secretary had said earlier, in the summer of 1949, that "Should the (Chinese) Communist regime lend itself to the aims of Soviet Russian imperialism and attempt to engage in aggression against China's neighbors, we and the other members of the United Nations would be confronted by a situation violative of the principles of the United Nations Charter and threatening international peace and security."[69]

The Việt Minh had taken a step which they certainly knew would antagonize the United States. We had seen our role as helping towards an Indochina solution that would satisfy nationalist aims and minimize the strain on our European allies, while supporting a French presence as a guide and help to the three states moving towards genuine independence. The French had balked at moving swiftly. They had their reasons which had to do with the extent to which they believed French interests and French opinion would continue to support the war in the absence of any clear prospects for a continued presence. The non-communist Vietnamese pressed for control in areas in which, in Acheson's view, they could least effectively exercise it, the field of foreign affairs.[70] They, of course, had their reasons which had to do with the extent to which they believed Vietnamese interests and Vietnamese opinion would support the war in the absence of any evidence that genuine independence was to be theirs.

Inside the Department of State, the Office of Southeast Asian Affairs doubted the Elysée Accords would work out as written. The Bureau of European Affairs doubted pressure on the French could do anything except stiffen their position on Indochina and antagonize them in regard to other issues of mutual concern.[71] The United States, meanwhile, was coming to see the French stand in Indochina as part of a general attempt to repel communist military adventures. All these considerations laid the groundwork for the third United States decision on Indochina which was taken in the spring of 1950. The department recommended economic and military supplies be furnished to France and the Associated States.[72] These recommendations were eventually approved and formalized in the Pentalateral Agreement on Military Defense Assistance of 1950 and in the bilateral Economic Assistance Agreements of

1951 with Cambodia, Laos, and Vietnam. These developments indicated to some observers, Devillers for example, that the "Vietnamization" of the war, or the "Bảo Đại solution" to give it its other name, was going to lead not to the retention of Vietnam (and Laos and Cambodia) in the French Union but rather to a Sino–American conflict conducted through surrogate forces (as in Korea).[73]

Some people in the Department of State maintained that, even with economic and military assistance, the French and Bảo Đại would be defeated in the field. All in the department, according to Acheson, considered such a defeat was probable unless France moved quickly to transfer authority to the Associated States and set up indigenous military forces.[74]

Anticipating in a way what eventually happened in 1954 when the French went to Geneva, Acheson, as we have noted, became inclined to view the French role in Indochina as an indispensable one. If the French were not encouraged to stick with it, rather than pull out and turn the whole thing over to the United States, the latter would be faced with a burden it was really unprepared to take on.[75] So the French had to be handled very carefully, not only in the context of German rearmament and European economic recovery, but also in the light of what the United States had come to view as a worldwide struggle against communist aggression in which it needed all the help it could get.

A new study group under R. Allen Griffin went to Sài Gòn in April 1950 and recommended in favor of military and technical assistance, and the Joint Chiefs of Staff recommended in favor of military assistance. On May 1, 1950, President Truman approved a $10,000,000 military assistance item for Indochina. On May 8, Truman, after talks with Robert Schuman and Ernest Bevin (Acheson's opposite numbers in the French and British Governments respectively), and after consultation with Congressional groups and committees, approved economic support and military supplies. The French agreed to the presence of a Special Technical and Economic Mission (STEM), but aid was to be arranged through Paris and very little of it arrived in 1950.[76]

The outbreak of the Korean War on June 24 naturally generated considerable support for Acheson's view—that a communist conquest of Indochina would present an unacceptable danger for Southeast Asia. Acheson's biographer claimed, "Acheson was never able to surmount the contradiction between the real nature of the French effort, which was to restore colonialism and his belief that Communism could only be defeated by according genuine autonomy to a government representative of Vietnamese nationalism."[77] As the United States share of the cost of the war increased, the French became less, rather than more, willing to grant the Associated States more genuine independence. Chinese intervention in Korea served to link the two wars more closely as aspects of a global effort to resist communist aggression. General de Lattre de Tassigny publicly espoused this line the next year when he visited Washington with Schumann (September 1951). NSC 124/2 of June 1952 put it that "the danger of an overt military attack against Southeast Asia is inherent in the existence of a hostile and aggressive Communist China." It added, "In the absence of effective and timely counter-reaction, the loss of any single country would probably lead to the relatively swift submission to or an alignment with Communism by the remaining countries of this group."[78]

Considering what should be done if the French asked for direct United States military involvement in Indochina, Acheson:

> ... presented a broad strategy for consideration by the American military establishment, the French and the British ... It included recognition of the fact that the war could not be won without large well-trained native armies which the United States stood ready to pay for and help train. Only air and naval actions against China should be contemplated and it should be made clear that we were acting only against their intervention and were not out to destroy their regime. No American ground troops were to be used in Indochina. It would be futile and a mistake to defend Indochina in Indochina.[79]

It is interesting to look at an article in *Time Magazine* for August 28, 1950, entitled "Special Report: Indo-China."[80] After spending six weeks in Indochina, the magazine's Paris Bureau Chief had some thoughtful observations. He found Bảo Đại still commanded great respect (only some of which had been lost by his neglect of public affairs), that his government was weak, without credit in the country, without a social policy, and without social sense. He found the French were paying a heavy penalty for past mistakes and that French unwillingness to take generous chances, and the French legalistic mind, gave the French Union a rigidity which threatened to strangle it at birth. Nevertheless, he found the French in Indochina were buying time for the West and that the first axiom of United States policy in Indochina had, therefore, to be aid for the French Army. If the French handed over total independence to Bảo Đại and got out, as was sometimes suggested, a communist regime would rule in Sài Gòn two weeks after the French had left. The other suggestion, that the United States concentrate on reinforcing French power to crush the communists while leaving Vietnamese politics in abeyance, would not work. Neither Europe nor Asia could be permanently defended by outside force. The war was partly an Indochinese civil war and could be won completely only by a majority of a free people inspired by a national ideal. There was a third solution that could bring the people of Vietnam solidly to the Western side: give them the self-respect of free men. Let the French build up a Vietnamese National Army that could eventually replace the French; let the French give arms to villagers whose desire to defend themselves was beyond reasonable doubt. The United States was committed to $23.5 million of civilian aid to the Vietnamese Government. Sài Gòn also expected to get $200 million out of $300 million earmarked for Southeast Asia. As that aid was given, the United States would have to put tactful pressure on Vietnam and the French to correct their mistakes. It would have to help energetic administrators, tell others to use what they had before asking for more, get a social policy initiated, and teach Indochinese intellectuals that self-rule is not merely something presented with a charter and pink ribbon, but a status to be earned and a responsibility to be accepted. Excellent advice, all of this, but easier given than executed, easier said than done.

Critics of the decision to grant military and economic assistance to France and the Associated States maintained it neither edged the French out of their hopeless attempt to reestablish their colonial role, nor helped them hard enough to do it, or helped them to beat Hồ Chí Minh and then leave gracefully. Acheson thought this criticism was unsound on several accounts: it failed to consider the limits of the extent to which you can coerce an ally; it failed to consider that withholding help and exhorting an ally will only work when the ally can do nothing without help, like the Dutch in Indonesia; and it failed to consider that withholding help from the French could have removed them from the scene but could not have produced a "beneficial" situation in Indochina or in Southeast Asia. Neither could such action have furthered the stability and the defense of Europe.[81]

The outbreak of the Korean War inevitably affected the course of developments in Indochina. By September 1950, the French had agreed to create indigenous armies with United States financial and material aid. Minister Heath in Sài Gòn concurred with this decision but pointed out that only a real role for the Associated States could produce the desired political and psychological effects.[82]

The United States military assistance effort continued to develop throughout 1950 and a glance at a few key dates during that year illustrates the growing linkage of this effort with developments in Europe and in Korea.

May 8, 1950	U.S. announces military and economic aid to Associated States
June 4	First shipload of arms aid leaves U.S.
June 25	North Korea invades South Korea
June 26	President Truman orders (among other things) increase in aid to Indochina
July 8	General MacArthur assumes United Nations Command

July 16	U.S. MAP Mission arrives in Sài Gòn
	Hồ Chí Minh attacks U.S. interventionists on radio
August 3	Permanent MAAG set up in Sài Gòn under General Francis Brink
August 11	First arms shipment arrives
August 23	French decide to send battalion to Korea, September 22; Pleven Plan on European Force[83]
October 1	General Graves B. Erskine and John Fremont Melby arrive in Sài Gòn to reassess arms need, Pentalateral Agreement of 1950
December 6	French, under U.S. pressure, accept compromise on German rearmament

The year 1951 saw a great debate in the United States in which the Republican right unsuccessfully challenged the president's authority to commit U.S. armed forces overseas. Former President Herbert Hoover and Senator Taft opposed sending troops to Europe. Taft accused the administration of having made policy since 1945 without consulting the Congress or the people. However, Republicans Dwight Eisenhower, Thomas Dewey, and Harold Stassen supported the administration's position on military support for Europe. On April 4, 1950, the Senate had approved a fair-share contribution of American troops for European defense but asked the president to consult before actually sending troops, and tried to limit the number that could be sent. The outcome of the great debate confirmed not only the U.S. decision to defend Europe on the ground but also the president's power to commit armed forces abroad.[84]

By 1951, the Indochina War had begun to change in character from a more or less traditional colonial war to a war of liberation on communist lines. The Chinese Communist takeover of the Chinese mainland had completely altered the military situation. South China had become much more important as a secure sanctuary base area for the Vietnamese Communists, similar to Manchuria in the Korean situation. In the same period, Việt Minh tactics and strategy took on the characteristics of a communist war of liberation as they developed political and social structures.[85] General Jean de Lattre de Tassigny, who appeared on the scene at the end of 1950 and served as high commissioner and commander in chief until his death in Paris on January 12, 1952, appeared to understand the importance of the change in the nature of the struggle. His famous speech to the students of the Chasseloup–Laubat Lycée in Sài Gòn on July 11, 1951, reflected this understanding.[86] He told them, "Be men ... If you are Communists, join the Việt Minh; there are some individuals who fight well for a bad cause. But if you are patriots, fight for your country, for this war is yours."

As it was, the terms in which the general appealed to the young Vietnamese to choose sides in the struggle against the communists, terms which sounded inspired and inspiring to Western ears, sounded empty to the young Vietnamese because in their view the vexed question of real independence độc lập remained as unsettled as ever.

De Lattre's main accomplishment was to arrest an incipient panic among the French in Indochina by the force of his personality and to discourage Giáp from continuing conventional military operations for the time being by defeating him narrowly but decisively in the field at Vĩnh Yên. He had thus gained time for the French Government, but it was unable to take advantage of this breathing space to launch any viable new initiative for a political arrangement.[87] From 1951, the Bảo Đại solution visibly faded and withered, French political will to carry on the struggle with the forces available, and in the absence of any prospect of a real political agreement with the non-communist Vietnamese, evaporated. At the same time, the United States became increasingly but inconclusively involved.[88]

A few dates recalled from the 1951–53 period show the parallel development of these two trends.

September 11, 1951	U.S. signs bilateral economic aid agreements with Associated States
December 16	Mendès France urges peace talks
January 12, 1952	De Lattre dies in Paris
May 27	European Defense Community formed
September 29	Daladier urges end to Indochina War
October 12	The 200th ship carrying U.S. military aid arrives in Sài Gòn
February 17, 1953	Reynaud urges buildup of war effort after visit to Sài Gòn and Hà Nội
February 26	Peking Radio outlines Việt Minh 1953 Program
March 30	French entrench camp in Plain of Jars, Laos, to cover Luang Prabang against Việt Minh threat
April 16	Laos appeals to United Nations over Việt Minh threat, bypassing and embarrassing French
April 19	Sihanouk calls for greater autonomy
May 7	Six Civil Air Transport (CIA) Flying Box Cars sent to Hà Nội by U.S. to assist French

May 9	Eisenhower orders special military aid of $60,000,000
May 9	General Navarre assumes command
June 4	Mendès France calls war a crushing blow
June 25	Schumann urges negotiated peace
July 3	American General "Iron Mike" O'Daniel visits Vietnam
July 18	Sixty USAF officers assigned to train French airmen
September 16	Bedell Smith says U.S. will not stand idly by if China moves
October 24	French National Assembly votes debate on war
November 1	Vice President Nixon urges Vietnamese to spur their war effort
November 3	Vice President Nixon says U.S. would oppose negotiated peace
November 21	French forces occupy Điện Biên Phủ
November 30	Stockholm *Expressen* prints Hồ's truce offer
December 17	Nguyễn Văn Tâm (a French protégé put in office as prime minister in place of Trần Văn Hữu) resigns in dispute with Bảo Đại over Tâm's plan to form a Government of National Union to negotiate with Việt Minh)
December 27	Eisenhower says U.S. will maintain forces at appropriate levels to meet Asian commitments

The United States signed the bilateral agreements for economic assistance to the Associated States of Indochina at a time when the Cold War, characterized by "Stalinism abroad" and "McCarthyism at home," inevitably affected United States policy decisions.[89] The NSC-68 paper (April 1950) had anticipated an attack by communist forces in some part of the world and had recommended "the United States should be fully prepared to resist the thrust of any such attack, in cooperation with its allies if possible, but if necessary by its own force of arms."[90] When the North Koreans attacked across the 38th Parallel on June 25, 1950, their action was generally accepted in the United States as an act of war "precipitated and directed by Moscow in support of the world strategy of international Communism."[91] The Korean attack was a challenge to the free world, and to the whole postwar system of collective security, and had to be met. Although there had been no very strong feeling about the strategic importance of Korea as such, the North Korean action changed all this. The Truman Administration considered the North Korean action "endangered the fundamental principles of our global policy and potentially threatened our national security."[92]

President Truman took strong action and public opinion polls showed that 73 percent of the people supported him.[93] He called a special session of the United Nations Security Council which, in the absence of the Soviets, who were boycotting it, gave approval, 9–0, with Yugoslavia abstaining, to a resolution terming the action of the North Koreans a breach of the peace and calling for their immediate withdrawal behind the 38th Parallel. He authorized General MacArthur, as commander in chief of the United States Forces in the Far East, to provide arms and ammunition to the South Koreans and to protect the evacuation of all Americans. The next day, he ordered MacArthur to send air and naval forces to South Korea's aid. The American representative introduced a new resolution to the United Nations Security Council recommending all members of the United Nations furnish such assistance to South Korea as might prove necessary in repelling the aggression and restoring the peace. This resolution was adopted by 7–1, with India and Egypt abstaining and Yugoslavia voting against it. It is important to recall the atmosphere of those days. Although it took the initiative, the United States moved into the Korean War under the "flag" of the United Nations and, initially at least, with wide support.[94]

At the same time, President Truman, on his own responsibility and acting independently of the United Nations, ordered the Seventh Fleet into the Formosan Straits to prevent the Chinese Communists from using the occasion to attack the Nationalists on the island. This decision of June 1950 in effect reversed the policy enunciated in January 1950 that Formosa (now Taiwan) lay outside the American strategic line of defense in the western Pacific.[95]

With these policy decisions reached as a consequence of the North Korean attack, the United States entered a new phase in its overall containment policy in the Far East. In Korea, it was acting to halt armed aggression and to block the spread of Communism. In regard to Formosa, steps were taken to prevent the loss of that island remnant of free China to the communists. On the advice of Secretary Acheson, Truman took the further step or ordering "an acceleration in the furnishing of military assistance to the forces of France and the Associated States in Indochina."[96]

In May 1951, China invaded and quickly occupied Tibet, raising the question of how much further China might go and where. Indochina seemed most likely as the next objective.[97] Peking was giving the Việt Minh increasing military aid and assistance in its struggle against the French. (It is interesting to read the Chinese propaganda output preceding and following their military operations across the borders of the Democratic Republic of Vietnam at the beginning of 1979. They describe the broad scope and the key importance of the aid rendered the Vietnamese Communists in the early days and excoriated the recipients for their base ingratitude.) Concentrations of People's Liberation Army troops along the frontier also raised the possibility the Chinese might intervene as they had done in Korea.

In becoming so much more closely associated with the French military effort, despite the lack of progress towards real independence for the Associated States, the United States was responding to pressure arising from the situation in Europe. Since the end of World War II, its policy had been greatly influenced by the importance of maintaining the full cooperation of France in the allied program for resisting possible Soviet aggression in Europe. It was especially concerned at this time in getting the rather unenthusiastic French Government to join the proposed European Defense Community.[98]

There was some opposition in the department to the development of this closer association with the French. One scholar noted that "Within the State Department there had been for some time doubts about the wisdom of our involvement in Vietnam and some apprehension over where our program of military assistance might eventually carry us. But the momentum of events was already forcing the pace."[99] Secretary Acheson later wrote:

> We agreed to a large increase in military aid. Although the French complained that our aid was not enough, it was more than Indochina was able to absorb. The French complained, too, that their allies did not appreciate their efforts in Indochina and that the Vietnamese did not cooperate. Bao Dai answered that Paris was hesitant and niggardly in letting him create the essentials of an independent state. While this bickering was going on, General MacArthur had begun his ill-fated march to the Yalu and by early November had captured his first Chinese prisoners. At Thanksgiving disaster burst upon him ... Even before the disaster, however, a perceptive warning came from an able colleague in the Department, John Ohly, urging that the appearance of the Chinese in Korea required us to take a second look at where we were going in Indochina. Not only was there real danger that our efforts would fail in their immediate purpose but we were moving into a position in Indochina in which "our responsibilities tend to supplant rather than complement those of the French. We could, he added, become a scapegoat for the French and be sucked into direct intervention. These situations have a way of snowballing," he concluded. The dangers to which he pointed took more than a decade to materialize in full, but materialize they did.
>
> I decided, however, that having put our hand to the plow, we would not look back....[100]

Although, in November 1950, the French National Assembly voted to strengthen French forces in Indochina and create national forces in the Associated States, and although local administration was to be turned over early in 1951, Acheson noted the transfer date kept being postponed.[101] The French signed the basic agreements on independence within the French Union with the Vietnamese on March 8, 1949, with the Lao on July 19, and with the Cambodians on November 8. It was not until December 1950, however, that a series of detailed interstate conventions were signed covering Posts and Telecommunications, Immigration, Reconstruction, Modernization and Equipment, use of the Port of Sài Gòn, Customs, Foreign Commerce, Foreign Exchange, Currency Issue, and Treasury Operations.[102]

In 1951, United States military aid rose to over half a billion dollars. Acheson found that, despite de Lattre's two visits to Washington that year to ask for more and faster aid, he resented inquiries about his military plans and about intentions for transferring authority to the three states. Also, too little, in Acheson's view, seemed to be happening on the ground in Vietnam in regard to developing military power as well as in developing local government and popular support. The Vietnamese forces did rise to four divisions in 1951 but they only had 700 of the 2,000 Vietnamese officers they needed and the military academy at Đà Lạt was only turning out 200 officers per year.[103] An American offer of instructors from the military mission in Korea turning out Korean officers en masse was refused by the French.[104] The rest of the year saw little progress in developing military power in Indochina and the Americans, bogged down in negotiations at P'anmunjŏm, became more and more frustrated. The Joint Chiefs of Staff warned against any statement that might commit or give the French the impression of a future commitment of United States forces in Indochina. The department hewed to this line in further discussions with the French in the autumn.[105]

In January 1952, the French, at a meeting of British, French, and American chiefs of staff in Washington, once again raised the question of what would be done if the Chinese intervened directly in Indochina. The American chiefs took the position only that such a development would be a matter of concern for the United Nations.[106] Two weeks later, the American, British, and French delegates to the General Assembly meeting in Paris were instructed to take the same position. No determination was made of what any or all of the three allies would do if the Chinese intervened even though such action was feared throughout the spring of 1952.[107]

As a result of a White House meeting on May 19, 1952, including Secretary of Defense Lovett and General Bradley, Acheson was instructed to discuss four points with Eden and Schuman:[108]

- further development of indigenous forces and our willingness to give additional help to their effort;
- a possible tripartite warning to Peking against aggression in Indochina, including preparatory diplomatic and military discussions;
- the anticipated reaction of Peking;

- course of action open and acceptable to the three powers should the warning be ignored.

Acheson was to avoid mentioning any specific amount of further aid and internal changes in Indochina beyond the development of the forces. It was hoped, by limiting the agenda, to avoid irritating the French on secondary matters. The Paris talks led to a decision to meet again with Letourneau, Minister for the Associated States, after he completed a visit to Indochina.

Meanwhile, reports from the embassies in Paris and Sài Gòn illustrated the difficulty of the position in which the United States Government found itself. Acheson summarized these reports:

> Paris told us that the French connected Indochina with the Tunisian–Moroccan problem and resented what they considered "United States intervention." Both Paris and Saigon [sic] agreed that Indochina needed to be "revitalized" or the drain on French resources might cause a decision to cut losses and withdraw. Bao Dai [sic] was not the man to pull Vietnam together, yet the French must go further to speed the evolution of the Associated States, just when De Lattre's [sic] death had removed effective French leadership. Saigon, while recognizing French sensitivities, believed that we should insist on information and action at the same time that the French asked us for aid. This of course is what we had been doing for two years.[109]

When, in mid-June, Jean Letourneau, who had also become high commissioner after de Lattre's death, asked for more aid, Acheson told him that, as the United States was paying for more than one-third of the cost of the campaign in Indochina, it did not seem unreasonable to expect more information from the French. The information was needed so that government could explain to its people why it was contributing and what progress was being made. Neither did we think that friendly suggestions from such an active ally should be considered meddling. Letourneau did not disagree with this formulation but nothing much happened. It should be borne in mind that, at this time, the Bonn Agreements were awaiting ratification by the Senate and by the French National Assembly and the situation in Indochina was, as usual, critical. Therefore, no one thought it would be a good idea to end or threaten to end aid to Indochina unless the French did what the United States wanted in the way of military and political reform.[110]

Instead, the U.S. put out a communiqué[111] noting the struggle in Indochina was part of the worldwide resistance to "Communist attempts at conquest and subversion," and that France had a "primary role in Indochina," such the U.S. had undertaken in Korea. It added that, within Congressional authorization, it would increase its aid to building the national armies.[112] Letourneau, for his purposes, spoke of military and political progress in Indochina when he returned home and predicted United States aid would increase during the next six months to 40 percent of total French expenditures in Indochina.

At the end of June, Acheson met with Schuman and Eden in London and discussed the advisability of issuing a warning to Peking against military intervention in Vietnam. Pointing out that it would be "calamitous" to issue a warning and then take no action should it be disregarded, Acheson urged a determination should be made of the steps each of the allies would take to meet an intervention. He made it clear that United States commitments in Korea and Europe would limit any further American participation in Indochina to air and naval action. The idea of a warning was not taken any further by the three allies.[113]

In December, the department became aware of both increasing uneasiness among the French about Indochina and a large gap in its information about the current situation there and French plans to cope with it. Obviously, the earlier French intention to so weaken the enemy before reducing French forces in Indochina that the Associated States' forces could handle the situation had been overtaken by events. Schuman, at a meeting in Paris, asked for more financial help, although, by this time, the United States was bearing 40 percent of the load. Just before Acheson's departure to return to the United States, Letourneau, in the presence of Schuman, made a new pitch for help in raising more troops to meet expected enemy offensives in Laos and Vietnam. Acheson reacted by insisting the United States would have to have full and detailed information on all aspects of the situation in Indochina. The information received was not satisfactory. "This had to be remedied. We must know what the situation was and what we were doing if, as, and when we were to take any further step."[114]

The French inability to win the war militarily in existing circumstances was becoming increasingly clear. Political considerations limited the size of the forces deployed to Indochina. Vietnamese (and Cambodian) dissatisfaction with the degree of independence the French seemed ready to accord thwarted efforts to rally genuine local support of the war effort. Absence of such support caused the French to be concerned about the security of the Expeditionary Corps and made them reluctant to relinquish certain internal security responsibilities. French reluctance to give up such responsibilities further dissatisfied the Vietnamese and the Cambodians and so on. Americans were discouraged by both French and Indochinese attitudes.

Minor difficulties caused disproportionate frustrations.[115] The Americans wanted, for example, to mark the initial delivery of modern American infantry weapons to the Lao National Army (Garand rifles). They sent a delegation from the Legation and the Military Assistance Advisory Group in Sài Gòn by plane to Vientiane, carrying a number of the rifles. They presented the rifles to representatives of the Lao National Army at a ceremony attended by French, Lao, and American officials, during which the Lao prime minister and the American chargé d'affaires made appropriate speeches in the presence of a representative of *The New York Times*. Once the ceremony was over, the rifles were flown back to Sài Gòn for eventual distribution through French military channels. On October 12, 1952, the 200th American ship carrying American military aid arrived off Sài Gòn and the Americans also planned to commemorate this significant occasion. On arriving at the mouth of the Sài Gòn River, the ship's captain in accordance with the ancient laws and customs of the sea, broke from the mast head what he thought was the flag of Vietnam. It turned out to be the Việt Minh flag of Hồ Chí Minh, erroneously supplied by a ship chandler in Manila. The French Navy was not amused.

In 1953, a French general came up with an imaginative plan for the quick development of Vietnamese military power. General Marcel Alessandri, who had distinguished himself by avoiding capture by the Japanese in 1945 and leading his troops on a difficult retreat through the mountains to China, had been named military advisor to Bảo Đại. Alessandri had also served as French commissioner in Cambodia and had led the troops which replaced the Chinese forces in Laos after the Japanese surrender.[116] Alessandri envisaged large a Vietnamese National Army with a *masse de manoeuvre* of up to a million Vietnamese infantry. To save the time needed for training ether arms, he suggested assigning French artillery, engineer, and aviation units to serve as part of the Vietnamese National Army under the overall personal command of Bảo Đại. This army would move into the high country of Tonkin and root out the Việt Minh structure. Its very existence would be a guarantee of real independence understandable by everyone, in Alessandri's view. However, a grand initiative on this scale was simply not on the cards so far as the French Government was concerned. The increasing cost of the war in terms of lives, money, and political complications at home had pretty thoroughly disillusioned French public and parliamentary opinion.[117] All these factors were combining to cause stagnation of the French military effort on the ground and increased pressure in Paris for a negotiation. The disastrous consequences of the decision to fight at Điện Biên Phủ accelerated the approach to negotiation.

In *Mandate for Change*, President Eisenhower recalled that a NATO resolution adopted unanimously on December 17, 1952, at the meeting Acheson attended in Paris, "recognized that the French resistance to the

Chinese-supported rebels was essential to the defense of liberty, acknowledged that the resistance was in harmony with the aims and ideals of NATO, and therefore agreed 'that the campaign waged by the French Union forces in Indochina deserved continued support from the NATO governments.'"[118] He also recalled President Truman had approved a $30.5 million defense-support program for Laos, Cambodia, and Vietnam and that the United States had simultaneously earmarked about the same amount for economic aid and resettlement of refugees from the war in Vietnam. The United States, also on December 21, endorsed the three states for membership in the United Nations.

Eisenhower noted that, despite French sacrifices in blood and money during the Indochina War, the French Government had not yet unequivocally promised to the Associated States the right of "self-determination." In his State of the Union message in February 1953, Eisenhower pointed out that there was a "definite relationship between the fighting in Indochina and that in Korea." When French Foreign Minister Georges Bidault visited Washington in March, Eisenhower hoped to get some agreement on both the European Defense Community and Indochina, but Bidault proved evasive.[119] The final communiqués of this meeting expressed concern a ceasefire in Korea would enable the Chinese to become more active in support of the Việt Minh in Indochina. Eisenhower thought the loss of Indochina to the communists would have been disastrous in its effect on the other free nations in the area. He saw his country's main task as convincing the world the Southeast Asian war was an aggressive move by the communists against the whole area.[120]

The department reported to the president in mid-1953 that one of the chief negative factors in the Indochinese situation was the failure of important elements of the local population to fully support the war effort. Symbols of the colonial era remained despite the 1949 grant of "independence within the French Union."[121] The French still controlled foreign and military affairs, foreign trade and exchange, and internal security. The French monopoly over economic life in the three states was nearly complete. Justified or not by the French defense and financial contribution, this paramount French role was disliked by large elements of the Indochinese populations. Such discontent impeded the development of fighting spirit in the indigenous forces and adversely affected the rate of formation of the Vietnamese Army. The disaffection of King Norodom Sihanouk of Cambodia, who demanded full and real independence within the French Union, had caused a crisis in June; he had removed himself first to Bangkok and later to the region of Angkor

Wat to dramatize his démarche.[122] Near the end of the period covered by this review, the new French cabinet was preparing a declaration of France's readiness to open negotiations for completing the sovereignty and independence of the three states. The department report concluded, "It remained to be seen whether this would produce the necessary response among the native peoples and provide the stimulus for a new turn in the war."[123]

Eisenhower felt that, despite French slowness in making their intentions known, aid should not be delayed. He sent a message to Congress on May 5, 1953, in which he pointed out the need in our own interests to provide greater resources to the French and to the three states of Indochina. A few days later, Under Secretary of State Bedell Smith stated the Indochina affair had become a global problem and that real help for the French had become a necessity for the United States.[124]

In June, Eisenhower sent Lieutenant General John W. "Iron Mike" O'Daniel to Sài Gòn to confer with the French Army. In September, the administration announced a commitment of $385 million up to the end of 1954 in addition to other funds already earmarked for prosecution of the war. On September 17, Secretary Dulles said in a speech before the United Nations General Assembly:[125]

> ... The French Government by its declaration of July 3, 1953, has announced its intention of completing the process of transferring to the Governments of the three Associated States all remaining powers as are needed to perfect their independence to their own satisfaction.
>
> The Communist-dominated armies in Indochina have no shadow of a claim to be regarded as the champions of an independence movement.

Eisenhower hoped the Dulles statement would demonstrate once and for all that the fighting in Indochina was not for the purpose of reimposing French domination. He understood, however, that such a statement would not mean much unless individual Vietnamese could be convinced they were now fighting for their own independence and freedom. He also realized that, while he had gotten through the immediate 1953 Vietnam crisis, more such crises were to come.

The year 1954 marked the end of the beginning of United States involvement in Indochina. The United States, while being drawn in to assume a greater financial and equipment burden, could not do much more in view of the unresolved basic political problem between France and the Associated States over the reality of independence. Hồ Chí Minh's offer of a truce via a November 30, 1953, article in the Swedish newspaper *Stockholm Expressen*, although it appeared nine days after the French occupation of Điện Biên Phủ, had probably been intended to exploit the situation resulting from the French and Vietnamese states of mind politically while a return to guerilla warfare exploited it on the ground. When the Việt Minh grasped General Navarre's intentions, they moved quickly to exploit the excellent military opportunity afforded them by the strange French decision to fight on so disadvantageous a battlefield as Điện Biên Phủ.[126]

Eisenhower found it difficult to understand why, a year before the buildup contemplated in the Navarre Plan could be completed, the French should decide to send ten thousand crack troops into such a position. He instructed both State and Defense to inform their French counterparts of his concern about this move. The Navarre Plan had envisaged sending nine more battalions of troops and support units to Indochina, increasing the size of the French Expeditionary Force to 250,000. It also envisaged raising the Vietnamese Army to 300,000 men during the next year. The French Union Forces would then have 550,000 men against an estimated 400,000 for the Việt Minh. They could then hope to lure the Việt Minh into open combat and beat them by the end of the 1955 fighting season. The resulting military situation would then presumably be manageable by the Associated States forces. The United States would help finance this plan with the $385 million mentioned above.[127] As it was, General Navarre had started "luring" the Việt Minh without having first completed his buildup.

The United States was already providing the French with all the material assistance it could usefully provide without sending American technical personnel to train the French and the Vietnamese in the maintenance and operation of advanced equipment.

Looking at the prospects for American military intervention early in the year, Eisenhower thought, "If three basic requirements were fulfilled the United States could properly and effectively render real help in winning the war."[128] These requirements were a legal right to act under international law, favorable climate of opinion in the Free World, and favorable congressional action. An urgent request from the French clearly reflecting the desire of the three Associated States would meet the first requirement. An appeal by the Associated States to the United Nations for United States intervention as part of a coalition (including the British, ANZUS, and some of the Southeast Asian Nations) might, he thought, develop a favorable climate of Free World opinion and provide at least token forces to assist the United States which would bear the main burden as in Korea. "This need was particularly acute," wrote the president, "because there was no incontrovertible evidence of Chinese participation in the Indochina conflict."[129]

Considering the type of forces which might be employed in any intervention, Eisenhower believed, as of January 1954, there was no need to put United States ground forces in Southeast Asia. There was a possibility of supporting the French with air strikes, perhaps from carriers, on communist installations around Điện Biên Phủ but Eisenhower had grave doubts about the effectiveness of air strikes "on deployed troops where cover was plentiful."[130] He also judged there was a risk of intervening with air strikes and failing to accomplish the desired purpose. He did not want to use American forces if their use would not be decisively effective. Consequently, he preferred to concentrate on trying to convince the French and the British that a coalition was needed to give moral meaning to an intervention. He also saw the need for further measures to convince the Vietnamese and the world the French sincerely intended to grant complete independence as soon as possible and for an increase in every form of material assistance.[131]

The provision of more material aid was complicated. Aircraft were sent to help the French, but the United States could not, by law send, Air Force personnel. After consultation with leaders of both houses of Congress, 200 technicians were sent to stay only until mid-June. The president also set up an ad hoc committee consisting of Under Secretary of State Bedell Smith, Deputy Secretary of Defense Roger Kyes, the Joint Chiefs of Staff and CIA Director Allen Dulles. He designated General O'Daniel, who was then in Indochina on temporary duty, to be chief of the Military Assistance Advisory Group. This was the general situation when the Berlin Conference of Foreign Ministers convened on January 25. Bidault believed if the Laniel Government was to survive he would have to return to Paris with some sign of agreement to discuss Indochina at a Geneva Conference. The life of the Laniel Government was important to the United States because the latter believed no succeeding government could be stronger on the questions of Indochina and the European Defense Community. We had, therefore, to be sympathetic to the French desire for a conference but we believed the Western allies were beginning to put too much faith in the validity of negotiations with the Soviet Union and the Chinese Communists.[132] Dulles pointed out to Bidault that over anxiety to negotiate could cause further deterioration of morale in Indochina and even in France. On February 9, Dulles reported to the president that French pressure for an Indochina conference was building and that if the United States was held responsible for blocking a conference the moral obligation to carry on the war might be shifted from the French to the Americans.[133]

Eventually, Dulles was obliged to propose a restricted four power conference on the Far East. Three considerations influenced him in this direction. The French were in desperate straits. The British and French desire for a conference would appear as less of a sign of disunity among the allies if the United States proposed the conference formally and limited its scope. If a conference was inevitable, as it appeared to be, it would be desirable to initiate it before unfavorable developments occurred in the fighting in Indochina. Dulles warned Bidault, however, that prospects for a conference would increase communist efforts toward a military knockout during the current fighting season. He reported it would also be necessary to assure the French that America's agreements to continue military aid would be carried out. In response, Eisenhower cabled Dulles on February 10: "Administration has no intention of evading its pledges in the area providing the French performance measures up to the promises made by them as basis for requesting our increased help."[134] On February 18, the Berlin Conference ended with an agreement to meet at Geneva on April 26 to discuss problems of Korea and Indochina.

On March 13, the Việt Minh units before Điện Biên Phủ, having been heavily reinforced, made their first large-scale assault against the French positions. Two days later, Việt Minh artillery knocked out the French airstrips, at least temporarily. The Việt Minh suffered heavy losses but intelligence reports on French prospects started to become very pessimistic. Eisenhower found it difficult to understand why, in view of Navarre's earlier statements that he hoped his forces would be attacked at Điện Biên Phủ, the French were reacting so pessimistically to the actual attacks. The military operations at Điện Biên Phủ are a story in themselves but the big decision on Indochina facing the United States Government at this time was whether or not to intervene militarily.

The decision, the fourth one on Indochina, was not to intervene. There has been much speculation the United States came close to direct intervention and even to the use of nuclear weapons. None of this speculation bears much scrutiny. President Eisenhower had pretty clearly in mind what he considered the basic requirements for proper and effective intervention. He had also:

> ... let it be known that I would never agree to send our ground troops as mere reinforcements for French units, to be used only as they saw fit. Part of my fundamental concept of the Presidency is that we have a constitutional government and only when there is a sudden, unforeseen emergency should the president put us into war without congressional action.[135]

When asked by Admiral Radford and French Generals Ely and Valluy what would be the American reaction if the Chinese Communists themselves attacked French positions in Vietnam with their MiG aircraft, Dulles had replied:

> I said that I would not, of course, attempt to answer that question. I did, however, think it appropriate to remind our French friends that if the United States sent its flag and its own military establishment—land, sea or air—into the Indochina war, then the prestige of the United States would be engaged to a point where we would want to have a success. We could not afford thus to engage the prestige of the United States and suffer a defeat which would have world-wide repercussions.[136]

General Ely has written that despite the fact the use of nuclear weapons may have been discussed from time to time, their use at Điện Biên Phủ was not seriously considered.[137] René Pleven told the BBC in 1975 that the French had never asked for the use of an atomic weapon.[138] Admiral Radford recalled in a letter to the author of *The Meaning of Limited War* that: "... as far as I recall such plans as were probably made were contingent plans and they were probably made by the services individually as a precautionary measure. As far as the President, the Secretary of Defense and the JCS [Joint Chiefs of Staff] were concerned, no orders were ever issued to make detailed plans—this is as I recall it."[139]

It appears that, in the absence of the fulfillment of Eisenhower's basic requirements for military intervention, and in view of the inevitability a French military defeat at Điện Biên Phủ, Eisenhower and Dulles turned their attention to working out the Manila Pact in lieu of a plan for military intervention. The impression Dulles had received from Eden, that the British had taken a definite stand against any collective conversations looking towards the development of an anti-communist coalition in Southeast Asia, and that Eden had come into the conference under instructions to press earnestly for a cease-fire in Indochina, clearly wiped out any chance of developing a climate of opinion in the Free World favorable to any American intervention.

As time marched on toward the loss of Điện Biên Phủ and the conclusions of a cease-fire in Indochina, the president received word from General Alfred Gruenther at NATO of French "gloom and shakiness." In reply, Eisenhower recalled that he and Gruenther had been warning the French for three years they could not win the Indochina war and in particular could not get real American support in the region unless they would unequivocally pledge independence to the Associated States once military victory had been achieved. He also noted his administration had been arguing that: "No Western power can go to Asia militarily; except as one of a concert of powers, which concert must include local Asiatic peoples." Eisenhower went on to express the opinion that the loss of Điện Biên Phủ did not necessarily mean the loss of the Indochina War, that the exploits of the garrison should be extolled as indicative of French character and determination, and that the United States, France, Thailand, the United Kingdom, Australia, New Zealand, and others "should begin conferring at once on means of successfully stopping the Communist advances in Southeast Asia." He thought a plan should be developed including the use of the bulk of the French Army in Indochina, that it should assure freedom of political action to Indochina promptly when victory was achieved, that additional ground forces should come from Asiatic and European troops already in the region, and that the general aims and purposes of such a concert of nations should be announced publicly as in NATO.[140]

On April 29, three days after the Geneva Conference opened, Eisenhower told a press conference in Washington that, under existing conditions, the United States would probably not get what it would like by way of a settlement at Geneva, but rather a *modus vivendi*. He saw no reason for the United States to intervene militarily and was not even sure the Vietnamese population would want such intervention. Vice President Nixon had told the American Society of Newspaper Editors on April 16 that America might one day have to send troops. In reply to a question at his news conference about a rider to a House Appropriations bill limiting the president's authority to dispatch troops anywhere in the world without Congressional authority, Eisenhower said, "an appropriations bill was not the place to legislate Executive responsibility" and "such an artificial restriction would damage the flexibility of the President in moving to sustain United States interests." He made it known he would veto the bill if it were passed with the rider; the rider did not survive.[141]

Meanwhile it became clear the British would support and back the enforcement of any peace agreement the French could make but were not interested in entering any defense agreement until after the Geneva Conference. The Australians and New Zealanders indicated they were no longer favorable to united action in this sense. The French still had some hopes for American military intervention at Điện Biên Phủ but Eisenhower considered the situation there had become impossible. During a meeting called to again discuss the possibility of an American air strike in Indochina, Eisenhower remarked that if the United States were unilaterally to let itself be drawn into conflict in Indochina, and elsewhere in a succession of Asian wars, the drain on resources could weaken its overall defensive position. From this it followed that if we were fighting all over and "if Red Chinese aggressive participation were clearly identified, then we could scarcely avoid ... considering the necessity of striking directly at the head instead of the tail of the snake, Red China itself."[142]

At the end of April, Secretary Dulles had a frank conversation with Foreign Secretary Anthony Eden in which he expressed disappointment that the British delegation had remained silent when the communists, during the first week of the conference, had attacked the United States for "imperialistic actions." He also complained that the British, as he understood it, had agreed he could start up consultations in Washington to discuss an alliance with the nations involved and that the British had repudiated this understanding, offering no alternative. He reassured Eden that the United States was not seeking war with China or large-scale intervention in Indochina. He believed, rather, that any such developments could best be avoided by a show of Western firmness.[143]

On May 1, the Việt Minh began their final assault on Điện Biên Phủ, which they overran and captured on May 7.

On May 8, the French Government presented to the Geneva Conference a proposal for ending the hostilities in Laos, Cambodia, and Vietnam, the latter, of course, presenting the most complicated situation. Eisenhower approved instructions to the U.S. delegation that the United States would not associate itself with any proposal for a cease-fire which would take effect "in advance of an acceptable armistice including international mechanisms for enforcement."[144] It would, however, "concur in initiation of negotiations" for the armistice. It would also encourage the French Union forces to continue the fight in Indochina as the conference went on, would furnish more aid, and would continue to try "to organize and promptly activate a Southeast Asia regional grouping." The communists, for their part, aware there was no likelihood of united action by the Western powers until after the conference, were able to prolong the conference while using their military advantage in the Red River Delta to apply pressure to the French Union side. Eisenhower thought the French side still had sufficient forces to win if they could convince the Vietnamese regulars to fight alongside the other French Union forces and persuade the populace to support them. He observed, however, "But guerrilla warfare cannot work two ways; normally only one side can enjoy reliable citizen help."[145] Eisenhower still thought it necessary for the French to give up their claim to exclusive direction of the fight against Communism in the area to a coalition. Eisenhower and Dulles therefore decided to have Ambassador Dillon spell out their views to the French again as follows:[146]

- France and the Associated States should formally request United States participation and invite the ANZUS powers to also help;

- The United Nations should be brought in to form a peace observation commission;
- France should guarantee complete independence to the Associated States, including an "unqualified option to withdraw from the French Union at any time";
- France should keep its forces in action, with United States assistance—"primarily air and sea" as supplementing, not substituting, French forces;
- Agreement should be reached on American participation in training of native troops and working out a command structure for united action;
- All these decisions should be accepted by the French cabinet and authorized or endorsed by the French National Assembly;

Eisenhower found that, although they completely understood most of these points, Laniel and Maurice Schumann (France's deputy foreign minister) boggled at the right of withdrawal from the French Union. Soon afterwards, the French also expressed concern about the retention of their forces intact during the period of united action. Schumann noted the French could not approve the European Defense Community if they had to keep full forces in Indochina indefinitely. They were also concerned about the popular reaction in France should the Expeditionary Force suffer a serious defeat "because the United States had not come to their rescue."

Remarking that a lot of people seemed to be assuming the United States was primarily responsible for the defense of Indochina, as it had been in the case of South Korea, Eisenhower clarified his own attitude on June 3:[147]

- Unilateral action by the United States without the clear invitation of the Vietnamese people and satisfactory arrangements with the French would mean the collapse of the American policy of united action.
- If the nations of Southeast Asia were completely indifferent to the fate of Indochina, that would suggest the United States ought to reappraise its basic security policy.
- It was in the United States' interest to commit forces in the event of overt Chinese aggression, but the Southeast Asian nations could not disclaim responsibility for their own safety, leaving the whole burden of Free World security to the United States.
- If the president had to go to the Congress for authority to intervene in Indochina, he wanted to be able to say that we had allies—Thailand, Australia, New Zealand, the Philippines—and above all, the bulk of the Vietnamese people, ready to join with us.

On June 3, the French Government named General Ely as commissioner general in Indochina and commander in chief of the French Union forces in the area. Eisenhower thought Ely was taking over a disintegrating situation. He saw the communists stalling at Geneva, the fighting intensifying, and the possibility of partition in Vietnam, and possibly even in Laos and Cambodia, becoming generally accepted.

There were indications by June 9 that, although the French had taken no position on our preconditions for united action, the British might be getting ready to break from the conference while recommending Laos and Cambodia put their cases to the United Nations. Such tactics appealed to the United States Government, but Eisenhower judged it had been overtaken by events. On June 8, Vyacheslav Molotov, Soviet Minister of Foreign Affairs, strongly attacked the United States, Bidault left for Paris the same day, and, on June 12, the Laniel Government fell. As Eisenhower put it, "We decided that it was best for the United States to break off major participation in the Geneva Conference. The days of keeping the western powers bound to inaction by creating divisions of policy among them in a dragged-out conference were coming to an end."[148]

Pierre Mendès France became premier and foreign minister on June 18, winning a vote of confidence of 419 to 47 and pledging he would obtain a peace in Indochina by July 20. Churchill wrote Eisenhower that, as a result of mistakes the French had made in Indochina, Mendès France had decided to get out on the best terms he could secure and that he, Churchill, was inclined to agree he was right. Churchill, to Eisenhower's delight, thought this all the more reason for setting up a Southeast Asia Treaty Organization (SEATO), corresponding to the North Atlantic Treaty Organization.

Eisenhower and Churchill met in Washington on June 25 and drew up a seven-point joint position on what the two nations would find acceptable in any settlement the French might note. However, the British saw the seven points as "a hope," whereas the Americans wanted them as "a minimum." On July 10, Dulles sent a message to Mendès France explaining the United States' reasons for preferring to avoid full diplomatic participation in a conference, the results of which it could not approve. On July 12, he flew to Paris where, between July 13 and 15, he met with Mendès France and Eden, securing agreement to a position paper essentially the same as the one agreed to between the Americans and the British during the Churchill visit. Bedell Smith, who had been recalled to Washington, returned to Geneva. On July 20, Mendès France's deadline date, the three cease-fire agreements were signed, to be followed on July 21 by a Final Declaration of the Conference and by a unilateral United States Declaration.[149]

In his press conference on July 21, Eisenhower said he was satisfied the bloodshed was over, that the United States had not been a belligerent in the war, and that the primary responsibility for the settlement in Indochina had rested with the countries doing the fighting. He said that, though the U.S. had tried to be helpful, it was not a party to nor bound by the decisions taken at the conference, but hoped they would lead to establishment of peace.[150] He added it had made a unilateral declaration to the effect it would not use force to disturb the settlement and that it would view any renewal of communist aggression as a matter of grave concern. "We would actively pursue discussions with other free nations to establish an organization of collective defense of Southeast Asia to prevent further Communist aggression."

Robert M. McClintock noted in *The Meaning of Limited War* that the United States had realized during the preceding years that France needed assistance if it were to stem the tide in Indochina after the communist victory on the Chinese mainland. At the same time, the United States was seeking to sustain France in Europe by budgetary support and by economic aid under the Marshall Plan and the NATO alliance. "Thus, American policy both in the Atlantic and the Pacific was linked with the destinies of France, and concerns for the defense of Europe swayed Washington's decisions on the defense of Southeast Asia."[151] Under the Truman Administration, and in the first part of the Eisenhower Administration, it was United States policy to conduct the holding action through surrogate forces—the French Expeditionary Corps and the South Vietnamese Army. This, as McClintock pointed out, had involved the United States constantly with the extremely difficult problem of French sensitivities. These sensitivities had limited and even frustrated the application of American material assistance and advice on modern training methods. In any event, after Điện Biên Phủ and Geneva, there was no doubt American policy in regard to Indochina had to be changed. McClintock wrote that while he was serving as chairman of an Interdepartmental Working Group to formulate such a new policy he had written, "Fundamentally U.S. policy toward Indochina should be determined by what is in our national interest in Southeast Asia. U.S. policy toward France should be determined by what is in our national interest in Europe. Our policies thus far have failed because we tried to hit two birds with one stone and missed both."[152]

The task force in question, assembled in August 1954, recommended, to the secretary of state and the president, "A U.S. policy toward Indochina following the Geneva cease-fire agreements which will preserve the integrity and independence of Laos, Cambodia and Vietnam in order that they might form a barrier to further Communist encroachment in Southeast Asia."

It recommended specifically:[153]

> 1. The U.S. should furnish direct, adequate economic, financial and military assistance to the three countries in Indochina. However, this assistance should be conditioned upon performance by the three countries in instituting needed reforms and carrying them out, if necessary, with U.S. or other assistance. The corollary to the policy of direct aid is the requirement to renegotiate with France the existing instruments which now channel U.S. aid for Indochina, both military and financial, exclusively through French hands.
>
> 2. The three Indochinese states should receive guarantees of their territorial and political integrity from an eventual Southeast Asia Collective Defense System. Initially however the three countries should not adhere to the formal collective defense treaty but should benefit by its provisions as does western Germany under the NATO pact. Cambodia, Laos and Free Vietnam should be informed by the signatories of the new defense treaty that their integrity is guaranteed by the treaty.

The task force recommendation went to Secretary Dulles on August 12, 1954. It was approved by him and by the White House and promulgated as policy in a telegram of August 18 instructing Ambassador Dillon in Paris to "inform Prime Minister Mendes-France [sic] that U.S. aid in Indochina would henceforth go direct to the recipient states and not through the French channel."

The Manila Pact came into existence on September 8, 1954. On October 5, the French military forces left Hà Nội under the terms of the Geneva Agreements (the United States Consulate remained open there until December 12, 1955). By October 11, 1954, the Democratic Republic of Vietnam had assumed control of Hà Nội. President Eisenhower informed President Ngô Đình Diệm of Free Vietnam (south of the 17th Parallel) in letters of October 23 and 24 that American aid would go directly to Vietnam. On October 4, General J. Lawton Collins was named as the president's representative in Indochina.[154] On the 18th, General Collins proclaimed American support for Ngô Đình Diệm. The United States had made its fifth decision on Indochina:

Between the end of World War II in the Pacific in August 1945 and the signing of the Geneva Accords in July 1954, the United States had become increasingly involved in Indochina in support of France and the Associated States against the North Vietnamese Communists supported by China and the Soviet Union. European economic recovery and military security, communist assumption of power in China, and Soviet-sponsored aggression in Korea all served to increase American involvement. The failure of the French to reach fully satisfactory agreement with the Associated States, principally Vietnam, on the reality of independence served to vitiate American efforts to assist in the war and at the same time encourage the arrival of real independence. American involvement during this period took the form of grants of economic and military assistance, provision of military advisors and even the use of American transport aircraft and temporary duty personnel. It excluded direct military intervention by United States armed forces. The Truman Administration held that manpower must come from the national forces of the Associated States.[155] The Eisenhower Administration maintained no Western power could intervene effectively except as part of a coalition including Asians.

After Điện Biên Phủ and Geneva, the United States specifically rejected unilateral American intervention in the existing circumstances. United States involvement was, instead, to take the form of a major economic and military assistance supply role in Indochina and a treaty commitment of Southeast Asian dimensions. The Eisenhower Administration decided to extend direct aid to the Associated States and to organize with other free nations "A Collective defense in Southeast Asia to prevent further direct or indirect Communist aggression in that general area."[156] The SEATO Treaty, signed in September 1954, was ratified in February 1955 by a Senate vote of 82 to 1.

This choice of a direct assistance role, particularly in support of the new Diệm Government in Vietnam, backed by a treaty guarantee represented the fifth United States decision on Indochina.

Both the Truman and Eisenhower Administrations had rejected unilateral United States military intervention in Indochina but both had taken, or were to take measures, that cumulatively were to add up to the beginnings of United States involvement. These measures were prompted by what were seen as the requirements of United States national security interests and by an idealistic view that the countries of Southeast Asia should be permitted to make what political and economic progress they could free from external aggression and subversion. In commenting on the "fifth set of decisions" in a speech on August 15, 1967,[157] Assistant Secretary of State for East Asian and Pacific Affairs William P. Bundy noted they flowed from a judgment that the threat of aggression by North Vietnam and Communist China against Thailand, the Philippines, South Vietnam, Laos, and Cambodia was a real one. It was also judged that a successful North Vietnamese or Chinese Communist takeover of any of these countries would soon make it impossible for the others to maintain their independence. It was further judged that although the United States desired no special position in Southeast Asia, it could only regard transfer of that area, or much of it, to communist control through subversion or aggression as creating a situation of aggressive domination over much of Asia, such as the Japanese militarists had tried to create, which would be "profoundly contrary to our national interests." We also believed the "nations of Southeast Asia were in fact valid national entities and that while their progress might be halting and imperfect both politically and economically, this progress was worth backing." Bundy pointed out this policy undertaking received support at the time that went far beyond those who were emotionally opposed to communism in China and Asia.

PART II

Beginnings of United States Involvement (1955–1963)

President Eisenhower considered the Southeast Asia Collective Defense Treaty or Manila Pact provided a moral, legal, and practical basis for helping our friends in that region. As for the Geneva accords, he wrote:

> By and large the settlement obtained by the French Union at Geneva in 1954 was the best it could get under the circumstances. It ended a bloody war and a serious drain on French resources. More important it saw the beginning of development of better understanding between the western powers and the nations of Southeast Asia. It paved the way for a system of true cooperation between both in the never-ending struggle to stem the tide of Communist expansionism.[1]

Eisenhower also developed the "new look" in regard to the armed forces. He described the "new look" as:

> First a reallocation of resources among the five categories of forces [nuclear retaliatory or strike forces—forces to keep the sea lanes open in the event of emergency, forces to protect the United States from air attack—reserve forces] and second, the placing of greater emphasis than formerly on the deterrent and destructive power of improved nuclear weapons, better means of delivery and effective air-defense units.[2]

Eisenhower wrote he did not intend to employ the same policies and resources used in Korea to fight another war. He disagreed with the concept of greatly reinforcing conventional forces to meet the threat of multiple small wars because he believed that concept implied the United States would never use nuclear weapons. Such a concept, he thought, would give an advantage to a potential enemy who enjoyed superiority in military manpower. Instead, "The Communists would have to be made to realize that should they be guilty of major aggression we would strike with means of our own choosing at the head of the Communist power."[3] In January 1955, Eisenhower obtained a joint resolution of the Congress (House 410 to 3; Senate 83 to 3)[4] authorizing him to use the armed forces to defend Formosa and the Pescadores against armed attack. Two weeks later, he also signed the Mutual Security treaty with Taiwan which had already been approved by the Senate. As Eisenhower saw it, these two documents taken together would eliminate all doubt as to the United States' intentions in regard to Formosa and the Pescadores and would avoid the situation confronted it in the 1950 Korean crisis. This action was accompanied by the evacuation, with United States assistance, of the Tachen Islands (considered neither capable of defense nor vital to the security of Formosa). Subsequently, the crisis, in Eisenhower's words, began to dissolve after Dulles talked to Molotov at Vienna, Zhou Enlai took a moderate tone in his report on the Bandung Conference, and the Chinese (on August 1) released the 11 American fliers they had been holding since early 1953 and began talks about the release of two detained American civilians and other specific problems.[5]

Eisenhower had noted that, "In any delicate international situation there is rarely a shortage of outside advisors who are willing to contribute, at times out of experience, out of naïveté or out of politics, answers that seem to them to be simple, clear and decisive."[6] He also observed that, throughout the nine months of the Formosan crisis, his administration had received varieties of advice from leaders in the free world, ranging across the spectrum from one extreme to the other, and had ignored all of it, preferring to avoid both appeasement on the one hand and global war on the other.[7]

At Geneva, Dulles had followed the same general approach Eisenhower pursued in regard to Formosa. The Geneva Agreements did not end the war in Indochina, nor did they impose political or territorial settlements. They were in fact cease-fire agreements.[8] In Vietnam, the people of the two zones were to decide their future within two years through a general election by secret ballot under international supervision. Meanwhile, they were supposed to be able to choose in which zone they preferred to live. The unilateral American declaration at Geneva and the maneuvering which Dulles did at the conference were intended to restrain the communists by implying the possibility of a United States intervention. The official North Vietnamese history published in 1965 shows: "… that the prospect of American intervention did concern the Communists deeply and gave them pause after Điện Biên Phủ and Geneva."[9] The official history of the Vietnamese Communist Party (Hà Nội, 1970) tends to confirm this as do Soviet Premier Nikita Khrushchev's memoirs.[10] Điện Biên Phủ had discouraged the French and ended their will to carry on the fight. It was by no means a major French military defeat, however, and it would not have been easy for the Việt Minh to have expelled the remaining French military forces if French policy had required them to stay on in a combat role.

As the BBC put it, "There was a non-Communist Vietnam with a future yet to play for and decide. Dulles had won a pause of two years before elections were supposed to decide it."[11] At this point, it appeared indeed Vietnam might be saved with United States and and lost without it.[12]

Saving Vietnam with United States aid was not to be an easy matter and there were some doubts about Diệm's ability to do it even with U.S. assistance. According to Dulles' biographer, "The British had written him [Diệm] off completely. The French were openly sabotaging his attempts to establish native central authority."[13] Dulles concluded, however, that in the absence of any more promising political figure the United States had no choice but to back Diệm. Dulles persisted in this view even when, in the spring of 1955, according to his biographer, "After several months Collins, under the persuasion of General Ely, became convinced that Diem [sic] could not master the situation."[14] Dulles' Deputy Undersecretary Robert Murphy and Assistant Secretary Walter Robertson all stoutly maintained, with logic, that there was no point in abandoning Diệm unless a better, or at least equally good, leader could be found.[15]

The biographer described a NATO Council meeting in Paris in the spring of 1955 at which the divergent French and American views on Diệm were threshed out and, at least on a high level, reconciled. At the first of three sessions on Vietnam, French Prime Minister Faure announced that the French were not going to support Diệm anymore because he could not unite the country and because he was anti-French and stubborn and would not take outside advice. Dulles replied that the United States saw no better alternative to Diệm. Faure took the line that France, unwilling to let Vietnam remain a source of friction between the United States and France, would offer to withdraw from Vietnam. Dulles countered that the United States would withdraw instead if the point between the two countries was so serious but would in any case support an independent government in Vietnam. At the second session, Faure took the position that if either France or the United States gave up their interests in Vietnam it would mean both powers were abandoning Vietnam and that would be bad. Faure added he had not spoken of French withdrawal in terms of a clash with the United States. Dulles agreed with Faure that Diệm did not possess all the qualities the French, Americans, and British would like him to have but he was a nationalist, an anti-communist, and he was needed if Vietnam were to be saved from communist control. The allies would have to put up with his willfulness and the fact that he was anti-French and probably anti-American. At the third session, Faure presented a six-point program for the Americans, British, and French to follow in regard to Vietnam. It included a political enlargement of the Diệm Government, a peaceful resolution of the problem of the sects, cessation of anti-French propaganda, retention of Bảo Đại in his existing role, removal of any French and American officials who disturbed Franco–American "harmony," and assurance that French economic, cultural, and financial relations with Vietnam would be maintained. Dulles pointed out that some of these points "… are based on the assumption that Diem [sic] will take orders from us."[16] He went on to say the United States could accept the objectives the French had in mind but could not achieve them by dictating to Diệm.[17]

Meanwhile, on the ground in Vietnam, it was apparent the task before Diệm was an enormous one and there was less than a meeting of the minds between those French and Americans who were supposed to be helping him achieve it on the operational level. There were Vietnamese elements, all of them enjoying French connections, Bảo Đại, General Nguyễn Văn Hinh (chief of staff and also a French Air Force officer), and the leaders of the armed sects who were ready and willing to contest Diệm's authority in defense of their own particular interests. At the same time, Diệm had to prepare to absorb the flow of refugees from the North which eventually amounted to between 850,000 and 900,000, or almost seven percent of the population of the North.[18]

American Colonel (later Major General) Edward Lansdale had been conspicuously successful in assisting Ramon Magsaysay of the Philippines develop the tactics which defeated communist guerrilla attempts to overthrow the newly independent government and ensure a truly free popular election (which made Magsaysay president). As Lansdale recalled it for the BBC, Secretary Dulles sent him to Vietnam after Điện Biên Phủ but before the signature of the Geneva Accords to help the Vietnamese people; that is, to "Do what you did in the Philippines."[19] Lansdale saw his role as helping the Vietnamese Army to do battle with the guerrillas and helping the Vietnamese administration to work for the Vietnamese people. He estimated at the time that the true Vietnamese nationalists were standing aloof from both the French on the one hand and the communists on the other. He became allied with what he saw as a "nationalist affair."[20] The Final Declaration of the Geneva Conference called for consultations to begin on July 20, 1955, for the preparation of free general elections by secret ballot by July 1956. The elections were to be held under the supervision of representatives of the governments of India, Canada, and Poland. Neither the United States nor the Government of Vietnam had been a signatory of the Agreement on the Cessation of Hostilities in Vietnam and both dissociated themselves from the Final Declaration.[21] That agreement had been signed by representatives of the commander in chief of the People's Army of Vietnam on the one hand and the commander in chief of the French Union Forces in Indochina on the other. The idea of "free general elections by secret ballot" under the kind of regime the communists installed in North Vietnam after the signature of the Geneva Agreement, and the prospects for supervision under the limitations within which the International Commission for Supervision and Control operated in North Vietnam, or for that matter in South Vietnam, seemed quite unreal to many observers, including British Co-chairman of the Conference and Chief Sponsor of the Final Declaration Anthony Eden. In any event, Lansdale saw the timetable for elections as far too short to permit the State of Vietnam, which was disorganized and lacked cadres, to just go slow and let the communist guerrillas come in, organize politically, and rig the elections. He believed Secretary Dulles saw a void coming up with various French advisors pulling out and hoped the Vietnamese could form a viable entity to replace the old colonially administered one and prevent the communists from just taking over through a rigged election.[22]

Former Secretary of State Dean Rusk told the BBC an argument could be made that the elections should have been held, "... but I think those who would make that argument ought to blush just a little bit if they talk about free elections because there was no possibility of free elections either in North Vietnam or in South Vietnam in 1955 or 1956."[23] In response to the suggestion the United States, in opposing or encouraging Diệm to oppose the elections, was deliberately stepping around the provisions of the agreement, Rusk observed:

> Well you know, remember the same time the Soviets were utterly opposed to free elections in Germany, utterly opposed to free elections in Korea. So, the question must have arisen that why should we accommodate them in one spot if they wouldn't accommodate us in these other places. In other words, did we give them what they wanted, and just say "too bad chaps" if they refused to give us what we wanted in areas of equal or more importance to us?

Rusk agreed this observation indicated that, up to that time, Vietnam had still been considered in the general world design and strategy of the United States rather than as a particular problem itself.[24]

Asked by the BBC how the Americans had drawn parallels between Vietnam and Korea, Rusk replied:

> Not a close parallel between the two geographic positions but clearly a sense that how we reacted under our security treaty in Southeast Asia [SEATO] would have some bearing on how we would be expected to react in other security treaties, particularly in NATO. The issue to many of us was to do with the fidelity of the United States to its mutual security treaties. Now if that should evaporate or seriously erode then I think we can anticipate very great dangers appearing again.[25]

Senator William Fulbright told the BBC that people in Congress were not particularly concerned about the Vietnam elections issue at the time partly because there had been no previous engagement in Southeast Asia and partly because the Geneva Accords came at a time when they were preoccupied with Senator Joe McCarthy who "was attacking senators along with everybody else." Fulbright expressed the opinion, however, that the United States' positions on the Geneva Accords and on the creation of the Southeast Asia Treaty Organization were mistaken and that they had flowed from "this highly emotional attitude that developed with regard to Communism and in accord with the Truman Doctrine that everywhere we would meet any challenge from the Communists."[26]

William Colby, who was to be CIA Station Chief in Sài Gòn and eventually Director of Central Intelligence, recollected that the United States military did think of Vietnam in terms of Korea and aimed at strengthening the South Vietnamese Army to meet an attack by the North Vietnamese Army. He believed political people in the Embassy thought more in terms of a political solution in which a good, non-authoritarian government open to all opposition currents would produce a consensus which would "freeze the Communists out." He thought the Vietnamese problem was more analogous to the Malaysian one and that the real answer was to build up self-defense at the local level and move on to building up a new social structure as a new political base.[27]

At any rate, American efforts to save Vietnam as an independent non-communist state would center on the man whom Secretary Dulles had identified as a nationalist and an anti-communist who could not be dictated to.

Senator Michael Mansfield recalled that when Diệm visited the United States in 1951 or 1952, he had met him, along with Senator John F. Kennedy, at a reception. Mansfield was impressed with Diệm then and throughout the time he was in power in Vietnam. He thought Diệm had been undercut by some of his own people and not been given the support he should have been given by the United States Government. He was personally aware of what Diệm was trying to achieve and felt he was on the right track. He found Diệm a man of independence and integrity whose only goal was the independence of his country. He was willing to accept American help but only under certain conditions. Mansfield thought Diệm trusted some Americans too much and that they took advantage of him. He believed the French had never liked Diệm, never trusted him, and worked with him only because they had no other choice.[28]

Sir Robert Thompson, former secretary of defence of Malaya and, later, head of the British Advisory Mission in Vietnam, told the BBC Diệm was a great nationalist, "absolutely untainted by any working with the French" and, in his early days, a hero to the Vietnamese. Thompson also thought the Americans had failed to appreciate not only the protracted nature of the Indochina conflict but also its political nature. He saw the communist followers of Hồ Chí Minh in competition with the anti-communist forces built up by the French to determine the succession to the French throughout Indochina as a whole and not simply in Vietnam. He thought the communists had an advantage because of their declaration of independence in 1945 but especially in the way they had destroyed leaders of the Vietnamese anti-communist nationalist elements. The Americans, according to Thompson, thought colonialism was the reason for communist success but it was really a question of who was going to succeed the colonialists in accordance with Lenin's principles. The Việt Minh intended to do this and, with the collapse of the French effort and the preoccupation of the British elsewhere, only the Americans were left to try to prevent this succession. Thompson also thought the extreme lack of resources in Indochina, after the succession of World War II, Japanese occupation, and the first (French) Indochina war, required the Americans to provide large quantities of resources from the outside merely to keep the government afloat. This served to cast the Americans in the undesired role of political and economic substitute for the French colonial power.[29]

Opinions were to vary over the next nine years as to whether the creation of a state in South Vietnam was a viable alternative to a communist absorption of the area, and over the effectiveness of United States efforts in pursuit of such an objective.

Colby told the BBC that, at the end of the 1950s, the Diệm Government was succeeding in its development program and in its educational and health programs, and that its economy was moving ahead in leaps and bounds. He thought that in another five years the appeal of the communists in the South would have been nil. The communists did have some assets in the South, particularly in the form of some 50,000 young cadres, moved north in 1954 when the refugees from the North were moving south, and reinfiltrated, starting in about 1960, to rejoin those who had stayed behind. The appearance of these cadres, well trained and disciplined, indicated the commencement of a serious political and guerrilla effort. Colby thought at the time that the threat was manageable and that the government in the South could deal with it through a vigorous political development effort. The CIA began a few programs of arming villagers for self-defense as incidents increased. These experiments and discussions with the Vietnamese led to the strategic hamlet program which reflected Diệm's view that an independent non-communist Vietnam would require a new social base. It could not, in his view, operate through the old administrative structure; "… the process then was to start at the village-hamlet microcosm, develop the new leadership and the new philosophy and sense of unity out of that base rather than operating through the French-trained bureaucracy."[30] The CIA was given the mission of helping Diệm develop a government that would be able to compete with and, if necessary, stand up to the Hồ Chí Minh regime.[31] For his part, Diệm had arrived in Sài Gòn on June 25, 1954, determined to establish a strong anti-communist government, eliminate the power of the religious sects and the other armed pressure groups, eliminate French influence, and reduce Bảo Đại to no more than a figurehead.[32] Lansdale, who had been sent to Vietnam shortly before Diệm's arrival, did in fact provide moral support and guidance to Diệm in the early months but neither the Embassy in Sài Gòn nor the administration was completely sold on Diệm in the very beginning.[33]

In August 1954, Leo Cherne of the International Rescue Committee (IRC) found the American Embassy in Sài Gòn held the view that Diệm's regime was only a temporary and transitional one to which the United States should make no commitments either officially or unofficially since the French still retained responsibility in that regard. After meeting Diệm, Cherne formed the opinion that if Diệm could survive the first several months of "French obstructionism," "internecine Vietnamese opposition," and "apparent American indifference," he would be an effective leader. Despite the advantages which the communists drew from their military victory at Điện Biên Phủ and from Indochinese resentment of the former colonial status, Cherne thought it would be possible to give the people of South Vietnam something to fight for and to unite them to resist Communism. This could be done by organizing resources to settle refugees from the North and by sustaining the government which was close to bankruptcy. He believed the IRC should launch a major program to assist in handling the refugees and that the United States should disassociate itself from the French and commit itself fully to support of the new Vietnamese Government. The IRC sent Joseph Buttinger out to work on the refugee problem; his disappointment at what he regarded as the lukewarm official American attitude toward Diệm led to the formation of the "American Friends of Vietnam." Meanwhile, however, U.S. policy towards Diệm had begun to change as it became clear he had outlasted the pessimistic predictions of American as well as French observers.[34]

Senator Mansfield had returned from a visit to Vietnam in the late summer of 1954 convinced Diệm deserved support and that the alternatives to him in sight were not promising. These alternatives, as he saw them, were either a communist takeover or a return to the weak type of government dependent on foreign support that had existed before the events of 1954. Mansfield recommended immediate suspension of United States aid to Vietnam and to the French Union Forces there should the Diệm Government fall.[35] This recommendation influenced the Eisenhower Administration to dispatch the message of October 23, 1954, which offered direct American aid to Vietnam but clearly made such aid conditional on Diệm's readiness to take American advice and on his willingness and ability to undertake "needed reforms."[36] As one observer noted, "This was to be only the beginning of the American dilemma with respect to Vietnam. Washington's attempt to balance off aid against performance was inherited by Kennedy, later by Johnson, and then by Nixon."[37] The success or lack of success of this balancing act varied in the eyes of various beholders throughout the remainder of Diệm's time in office and under his various successors until 1975. At times it produced a sort of adversary relationship between the United States and the government it was supporting in Vietnam at any particular time. However, according to one well-placed Vietnamese observer[38] the Americans solidly bolstered Ngô Đình Diệm until 1963 when they "decided that Diem [sic] must go."

By November 1954, Diệm, with American backing, had defeated the challenge to his authority presented by General Nguyễn Văn Hinh, a Bảo Đại protégé with French connections.[39] Early in the same month, Ambassador Donald Heath left after some four years in Vietnam and was replaced by General J. Lawton Collins who was designated as Special United States Representative in Vietnam. Collins was "... to consider with the Vietnamese authorities how a program of American aid given directly to Vietnam can best assist that country." Collins was to explore this matter with Diệm and his government, "... in order to help them resolve their present critical problems and to supplement measures adopted by the Vietnamese themselves." Collins was also to "... maintain close liaison with the French Commissioner General, General Paul Ely, for the purpose of exchanging views on how best, under existing circumstances, the freedom and welfare of Vietnam can be safeguarded."[40] One historian of the period thought that "The emphasis on the supplementary nature of American Aid was an attempt to convey to Diem [sic] the tentative nature of the American commitment."[41]

Collins moved ahead, working out with General Ely a plan for the withdrawal of French troops and developing with both French and Vietnamese a program for training a new Vietnamese Army.[42] General O'Daniel soon had an American–French planning group working on training plans, including one which the Lansdale Group helped prepare for pacification of Việt Minh and dissident areas. The Lansdale Group changed the concept of the plan "... from the old rigid police controls of all areas to some of our concepts of winning over the population and instituting a classification of areas by the amount of trouble in each, the amount of control required, and fixing responsibilities between civil and military authorities. With a few changes, Security Action (Pacification) Directive ..."

Anticipating the outcome of the negotiations begun by Generals Collins and Ely, General O'Daniel informally organized the combined American–French Training Mission which became TRIM (Training Relations and Instruction Mission). This was commanded by O'Daniel under the overall command of General Ely; Colonel Lansdale was transferred from the Embassy to take charge of TRIM's National Security Division. In January 1955, Collins gave Lansdale authority to coordinate "this National Security work" among all American agencies in Vietnam.[43]

Collins found himself in disagreement with Diệm on "some key staff appointments to the Vietnamese Army." He also found it more and more necessary to remind Diệm of the reforms on which continued American aid was conditioned. If Ambassador Heath's relations with Diệm during his last few months "did not augur well," Collins' relations with Diệm remained "correct and cool."[44] Nevertheless, when Collins went back to Washington to report in February, he argued successfully for continued support of Diệm's government and President Eisenhower made it clear in a message to Bảo Đại that the United States intended to continue such support.[45]

Diệm was now moving towards his major crisis with the private armies of South Vietnam, the crisis which led to the confrontation between Secretary Dulles and French Premier Faure described a few pages back. There were three major armed "sects," although only two of them enjoyed a religious character. The first of the latter two was the Cao Đài whose pope, Phạm Công Tắc at the time, presided at the Holy See of Tây Ninh, northwest of Sài Gòn, near the Cambodian border, and whose religion drew on Confucianism, Taoism, Buddhism, spiritualism, and Catholicism and taught veneration of Sun Yat-sen and Victor Hugo. The second was the Hòa Hảo of Buddhist persuasion. Both sects had military forces, paid for and supplied by the French authorities, to defend the areas they controlled. The Cao Đài, which considered itself a religious organization rather than a "religion," had not only a hierarchy but a regular administrative and financial apparatus. The Hòa Hảo could also be described as a politico-religious organization.[46] Both sects were trying to strengthen their bargaining positions with the government by extending the areas under their control, collecting taxes, drafting troops, and holding posts in Diệm's Cabinet.⁴⁷ The third group, the Bình Xuyên, had more in common with the Capone gang of Chicago, being composed essentially of racketeers and pirates. The Bình Xuyên's position had been improved when Bảo Đại, before his last departure for France, sold it the concession for the Sài Gòn–Chợ Lớn police forces for a bribe.⁴⁸

The French discontinued their customary subsidies to the Cao Đài and Hòa Hảo armies early in 1955 and the armies looked to Diệm's government to fill the gap. The government apparently did so until about March 5 when, meeting under the chairmanship of the Bình Xuyên leader, Bảy Viễn, the sects decided to form a United National Front under the leadership of Cao Đài leader Phạm Công Tắc. His leadership was conditional on his making all his forces over to the Front rather than integrating them into the National Army. Hòa Hảo leader Ba Cụt would command all the forces in an emergency. The Front would also get control of "the fiscal and manpower resources of the country" if they could act together.⁴⁹ Lansdale described this Front initiative as "a sudden madness that nearly tore Vietnam apart at the seams."⁵⁰ As he saw it, Diệm was learning his job, the refugees from the North were being resettled, and the Army was profiting from TRIM instruction. Furthermore, the pacification campaign in Cà Mau had gone well and the one planned for Central Vietnam (Operation *Giai-Phong*) was expected to go better. Land that had lain idle during the war was being farmed and integration of several sect forces into the National Army was proceeding—"… the Lien Minh guerrillas of Trinh Minh The, the 10,000 Cao Dai [sic] troops of General Nguyen Thanh Phuong [sic], the remaining Hoa Hao [sic] regiment under General Nguyen Giac Ngo (whose other regiment had been integrated previously), and four Hoa Hao battalions under Lieutenant Colonel Nguyen van Hue."⁵¹

"Bao Dai [sic] and the French, each for different reasons, were not at all displeased by Diem's [sic] desperate situation." Bảo Đại ordered Diệm and his chief of staff to France, for consultations. The French Government went public about its lack of confidence in Diệm and he appeared to be heading for a military clash with the Bình Xuyên. General Collins opposed Diệm's intention to seek such a showdown and arranged a truce early in April after there had been some skirmishing. The French, for their part, deployed their forces in Sài Gòn in a manner disadvantageous to Diệm and withheld from him ammunition and other supplies. Most observers thought Diệm's position was hopeless.

Collins went back to Washington again on consultation on April 20. President Eisenhower's remarks to the press after a talk with Collins made it clear there was a question of a change in policy in regard to support of Diệm. However, Dulles and his principal colleagues won their point, as noted a few pages back, that there was no real alternative to Diệm at the time. The Department of State made it clear in an announcement on April 29 that "the present head of the legal government of Free Vietnam which we are supporting is Diem [*sic*]." Fighting had begun in Sài Gòn on April 28 between the Bình Xuyên and Diệm's Vietnamese Army forces and, by the time General Collins had returned on May 2, it was clear Diệm had won.[52]

On May 6, the United States Government again publicly restated its support for Diệm's government. On May 10, the White House announced the United States had, at Vietnamese request and with French agreement, taken over responsibility for the training of the Vietnamese Armed Forces.[53] Ambassador Frederick Reinhardt, who arrived to replace General Collins in Sài Gòn, made it clear that "I came here under instructions to carry out United States policy in support of the legal government of Vietnam under Premier Ngo Dinh Diem [*sic*]."[54]

Having won out over his various opponents, including Bảo Đại, it is not surprising that Diệm soon moved openly to remove the ex-emperor from the political scene. After absorbing the Imperial Guard into the Army, expropriating the crown lands for eventual use in resettling refugees, and carrying out the land-reform program, he announced a referendum for October 23 in which the people would choose between him and Bảo Đại.[55] A little later, Diệm announced that the election to decide the question of unification with North Vietnam provided for in Paragraph 7 of the Final Declaration of the Geneva Conference and anticipated for July 1956, would not take place. He pointed out that South Vietnam had not signed the Geneva Agreements, claimed they had been signed against the will of the Vietnamese people, and declared South Vietnam would not consider any proposal from the "Viet Minh" in the absence of proof that the latter "put the superior interest of the national community above those of Communism."[56]

Secretary Dulles had anticipated Diệm's position in a news conference on June 28, recalling that neither the Government of Vietnam nor the United States had signed the Geneva Accords and stating that the latter would not be afraid to see genuinely free elections such as the Accords called for. In October, Assistant Secretary of State Walter S. Robertson noted that refugees from North Vietnam, and many of their countrymen in the South, doubted elections could be held under genuinely free conditions in Việt Minh-held territory (in the South), while communist-run elections in the more populous North would certainly produce a communist victory there. In short, the elections would cause the South to be taken over by the communists through "seemingly legal means." Senator Mansfield was equally skeptical:

> Elections should and must play a major part in the unification of Vietnam if unification is to be achieved by peaceful means. Unless they are to constitute more than mere ritual, however, elections must have as their purpose providing the people of Vietnam with an opportunity to make a free choice ... the conditions for such a choice hardly yet prevail even in the south. Much less do they exist under the ironclad dictatorship of the North.[57]

Diệm moved towards the eventual unhappy climax of his rule; afterwards, many opinions surfaced on the significance of the issue of free elections and the relation of this question to the origins of the insurgency in Diệm's Vietnam. Assistant Secretary of State William P. Bundy addressed the free elections issue in his speech on August 15, 1967, at College Park, Maryland. Bundy described United States support of Vietnam through economic and military assistance and through the SEATO Treaty Protocol between 1954 and 1961 as a "tangled and difficult story." He thought mistakes had been made in economic and particularly in military assistance policies and believed the United States should have tried harder to "counter the growing authoritarian trends of the Diem [sic] regime in the political sphere." He thought, however, that the handling of the elections issue had not been a mistake. Our interpretation was that the elections were certainly to be free and were to be in effect a plebiscite as to whether reunification was desired.[58]

Bundy thought that much "hindsight nonsense" had been written about what had happened in 1956 on the issue. He believed examination of contemporary sources and discussion would show that:

> ... by 1956 two propositions were accepted: first, that South Viet-Nam, contrary to most expectations in 1954, was standing on its own feet and had demonstrated that the makings of a valid non-Communist nationalism existed there; and, second, that North Viet-Nam—which had gone through a period of harsh repression in 1955 and 1956 in which Bernard Fall estimates that nearly 50,000 political opponents were killed outright—would not conceivably have permitted any supervision or any determination that could remotely have been called free.[59]

He noted that Diệm, in the face of these facts, had refused to go ahead with the elections and that the United States had supported him. He quoted contemporary statements by the then junior senator from Massachusetts and by Professor Hans Morgenthau:

> Kennedy categorically rejected "an election obviously stacked and subverted in advance, urged upon us by those who have already broken their own pledge under the agreement they now seek to enforce."

Morgenthau, after referring to the tremendous change between 1954 and 1956, and saying that the conditions for free elections existed neither in North or South Vietnam had concluded: "Actually, the provision for free elections which would solve ultimately the problem of Viet-Nam was a device to hide the incompatibility of the Communist and Western positions, neither of which can admit the domination of all of Viet-Nam by the other side. It was a device to disguise the fact that the line of military demarcation was bound to be a line of political division as well."

Guenter Lewy, in *America in Vietnam*, carried this analysis further. He pointed out there had been a lot of misunderstanding about the final outcome of the 1954 Geneva Conference. He recalled the "accords" added up to six unilateral declarations, three cease-fire agreements, an unsigned final declaration, and the minutes of the last plenary session on July 21. He believed that "Only the cease-fire agreements, signed by the respective military commands, can be considered formally binding accords. The language of most of the documents was ambiguous and reflected the absence of consensus at the conference. Calls to 'observe the Geneva accords,' often heard in later years, thus were necessarily devoid of concrete meaning."[60]

Lewy noted it had been held that Diệm's failure to accept elections in 1956 under the Final Declaration of the Geneva Conference justified North Vietnam's support for the insurgency in the South. He recalled two other students of the subject had argued that "when a military struggle for power ends on the agreed condition that the competition will be transferred to the political plane, the side that violates the agreed condition cannot legitimately expect that the military struggle will not be resumed." Lewy asked if there was such an "agreed condition"; he replied, in effect, that there was not. Lewy cited the Final Declaration of the conference to the effect that the Agreement on Vietnam was essentially a cease-fire agreement setting up a provisional demarcation line which was not in any way a political or territorial boundary:

> Free general elections by secret ballot, supervised by an international commission were to be held in July 1956 in order to bring about a final political settlement. Meanwhile everyone was to be allowed to decide freely in which zone he wished to live. And yet there are strong indications that nobody at the conference took the idea of an early unification through free elections seriously. Why have a massive exchange of population if the two zones were to be unified within 700 days or so?[61]

Lewy observed that the Final Declaration remained unsigned, was not adopted by a formal vote, and was not unreservedly accepted by five of the nine delegations present at the final session. He wrote that:

> In the absence of either written or verbal consent by all of the nine participants, the most judicious study of the Geneva Conference of 1954 concludes, the final declaration created

no collective conference obligation, and unless all the participating states consented to its terms and bound themselves thereto according to the procedures required by their respective constitutions, "the operative terms of the declaration were not binding upon all of the participants of the Geneva Conference."

Under certain circumstances, Lewy noted, oral agreements may be binding under international law, but both South Vietnam and the United States had stated their opposition clearly. "Neither of them, therefore, could be considered bound by the provisions for elections in 1956."[62]

In any event, neither the atmosphere imposed by the communist regime in North Vietnam nor the modus operandi pursued by the International Commission for Supervision and Control of the Armistice would have contributed anything towards the freedom of any elections held in the north. Bernard Fall described the "Nghé An incident" of November 2, 1956, in his *The Two Viet-Nams*:

> Since, by sheer accident, Canadian members of the International Control Commission were present when the outbreak took place, its completely fortuitous and popular origin can be well substantiated. It apparently started when villagers surrounded a Communist jeep with petitions asking that they be allowed to go south of the 17th parallel. A Viet Minh soldier or militia member tried to disperse the villagers with his rifle butt, but the enraged farmers beat him and took his rifle. Thereupon the VPA [Vietnam People's Army] soldier found it expedient to withdraw, only to return with a squad of troops; they met a fate similar to his, and shots were exchanged. By nightfall, the movement had swept over the whole *huyen* (district), and danger mounted that the farmers, like those of the first Nghé-An Soviet of 1939 would march on the provincial capital of Vinh, just as they had marched twenty-six years earlier in protest against the colonial power. Hanoi [sic] no longer had any choice; it responded in exactly the same way as the colonial power had, sending the whole 325th Division to crush the rebels. It did so with typical VPA thoroughness; allegedly, close to 6,000 farmers were deported or executed. With headlines pre-empted by the news from Suez and Hungary, the world press had little space left for the farmers of Nghé-An. And no U. N. [sic] member—neither of the always touchy Bandung bloc so concerned about the fate of its brothers in colonial shackles, nor of the habitually anti-Communist nations— mustered sufficient courage (or marshaled sufficient facts) to present the Nghé-An case to the conscience of the world.[63]

American observer Anita Lauve reported in August 1970 that the Government of South Vietnam had protested vigorously to the International Commission (ICC) over Nghé-An, charging North Vietnam with violating Article 15d (injury to life and property of civilians) and 14d (denial of freedom of movement). She noted the ICC team in Nghé-An Province received 1,684 petitions from local residents but, since the ICC had earlier ruled that 15d was inoperative after the 300-day regroupment period, it ignored the complaints under this heading. The 985 petitions charging a denial of freedom of movement were referred to the communist government in North Vietnam for comment. Lauve noted that, about four years later, the ICC reported the North Vietnamese comments were still under consideration and that in its eleventh and final interim report the commission stated it had not "been in a position to consider the 985 petitions received from Quynh Luu District."[64]

Miss Lauve also noted that communist massacres had been going on for some time before the Nghé-An affair, going back to the issuance of a Population Classification Decree which divided the rural population into categories to separate "our friends from our enemies."[65]

The decree made it clear that the "wicked landowners" who had to be eliminated were also "traitors" who had collaborated with the French. The party cadres trained for participation in the land-reform program were taught that '"feudalism" (landownership) and "imperialism" (colonialism) were inseparable and had to be jointly overthrown.[66] The terror campaign that continued for a while thus dealt with political opponents as well as with land reform. It was eased after the cease-fire because the communists wanted to check the refugee movement to the South and avoid charges of reprisals against those who had been on the other side during the fight. To take care of people in the latter category, the communist regime altered some of its land-reform regulations and reclassified the population in a way that would provide a cover for reprisals while appearing to respect the Geneva Agreement prohibition of reprisals. "The government decree established four categories of landowners: democratic people and patriotic scholars; landowners who participated in the resistance; ordinary landowners; and powerful, dishonest and wicked landowners, for whom special treatment was reserved."[67]

After the departure of the last French troops in May 1955, the terror recommenced and "The fourth category of landowners became the catch-all for those who had been associated with the French or the National Government during the hostilities."[68] Estimating the number of victims during the combined land-reform reprisals operations, Bernard Fall wrote, "While it is obviously impossible to give precise figures, the best-educated guesses on the subject are that probably close to 50,000 North Vietnamese were executed in connection with the land reform and that at least twice as many were arrested and sent to forced labor camps."[69]

French Professor Gerard Tongas, who stayed on in Hà Nội after the 1954 cease-fire until 1959, and who was initially favorably disposed towards the Việt Minh regime, had a police permit which permitted him to travel freely—the only foreigner, it appears, who had such freedom of movement. He wrote that the land-reform program was "the pretext for an indescribable slaughter that produced—I have been able to get information since—one hundred thousand dead."[70]

A legalistic position adopted by the Government of South Vietnam, practical limitations on the ability of the French Liaison Mission to act for the Government of South Vietnam, the viewpoint of certain members of the Indian Delegation, and the agility of the North Vietnamese in bringing their legislation technically into accord with the Geneva Agreement produced a false image of much more widespread violations in the South than in the North. In 1954, the Government of South Vietnam started sending its complaints to the French Liaison Mission for anticipated French action with the ICC. South Vietnam took the position that, not having signed the Agreement, it was not legally bound by it and should therefore neither cite the Agreement nor ask for investigations or accompany its complaints with the required type of substantiating evidence. The French did not believe they were in a position to revise the Vietnamese complaints and accept full responsibility for them. The French did believe it was impossible to obtain the type of information required by the ICC under the conditions prevailing in North Vietnam. For this reason, the French thought it better to concentrate on evacuating as many potential victims of communist reprisals as possible. When the South got around to agreeing early in 1955 to cite the Agreement and request investigations, "Hanoi had already cleverly revised its legislation to provide the legal camouflage needed to undertake reprisals under the guise of 'land reform.'"

Miss Lauve thought this legal camouflage might not have resisted determined investigation and wrote:

> Because, however, there were no subsequent ICC citations against the DRV [Democratic Republic of Vietnam] for either reprisals or denial of democratic freedoms during the land reform program, the DRV legislation apparently met the ICC's criteria, and the trials by People's Tribunals were accepted as a part of the civil administration with which the ICC could not interfere. If so, it may well be because the Hanoi [sic] regime was familiar with the viewpoint of certain key members of the all-important Indian Delegation to the ICC, and drafted its legislation accordingly.

She cited as illustrative of this viewpoint the writings of the Public Relations Officer and Deputy Secretary General Dr. B. S. N. Murti (*Vietnam Divided* (New York: Asia Publishing House), 1964, 61–2).[71] In short, Murti wrote that although Article 14 of the Agreement implied there must be a regime of democratic liberties for the whole population in the two zones, there was no implication the same standard should be maintained both in the North and in the South. He held, rather, that the standard of democratic liberties depended on the standard prevailing in the area concerned.[72]

Professor Tongas described the result as he saw it:

> The most bloody, the most vile reprisals were undertaken, especially against Vietnamese who had worked for the French. These, carried out in a more or less camouflaged manner on numerous occasions, were undertaken in a spectacular manner during the monstrous agrarian reform.
>
> Faced with these terrifying violations of the Geneva Agreement, what was the attitude of the ICC? It saw nothing, knew nothing, denounced nothing. Why? Because it was not officially informed with substantiating proof ... Who then, under such a regime of terror would dare to brave the official wrath? Determined men ready for any sacrifices, death volunteers—in other words, informants left behind or sent by the other party, who would be able to submit to the ICC in South Vietnam well substantiated complaints, thanks to their valuable information. But there are no such informants in the North, whereas they are legion in the South, which explains why it would appear from a reading of ICC reports that the authorities in South Vietnam are responsible for infinitely more violations of the Geneva Agreement than are those in the North. The truth is thus grossly falsified to the advantage of Communism.[73]

Or, as a former member of the Canadian Delegation to the ICC was to put it:

> The International Commission, beginning in 1955, was kept informed of these developments by the South Vietnamese authorities through an increasing number of complaints submitted to it [of communist subversion directed from Hà Nội]. However, it took years before the Commission took any action. In the meantime, however, it diligently dealt with complaints from the Hanoi [sic] authorities that the South Vietnamese Government was violating the rights guaranteed by Article 14(c) of the Cease-Fire Agreement to what Hanoi and the Commission called "former resistance members."
>
> ...
>
> It also seems evident that North Vietnam was using the International Commission and complaints concerning Article 14(c) [prohibition against reprisals] to impose restraints on the limited efforts of Saigon to counter the terrorist activities of Hanoi's agents.[74]

In 1962, a member of the British House of Commons used the ICC record of complaints to support a charge that the Governments of South Vietnam and the United States were responsible for the deteriorating situation in Vietnam. A representative of the British Government (one of the Geneva co-chairmen) replied:

> The rebellion in South Vietnam is by no means just a spontaneous, popular uprising against an unpopular Government, as the hon. Gentleman and others of his hon. Friends have tried to suggest. It is, in fact, a carefully engineered Communist take-over bid. Over a long period, there has been a steady infiltration of trained military and political organizers from North Vietnam into the South ... There is abundant evidence that the rebellion has been fomented, organized, in part supplied and wholly directed from the North. The principal weapons of this movement are terror and intimidation.

...

> The hon. Gentleman also mentioned the number of complaints against the South Vietnamese contained in the reports of the Commission. We should not be misled into drawing wrong conclusions because of the number of these complaints from the North against the South. It was only in July, 1961, that the Commission decided that it was competent to deal with complaints about North Vietnamese subversion. This is the nub of the problem.[75]

In discussing the origins of the insurgency in South Vietnam, some writers in the 1960s cited Diệm's campaign of forceful suppression of the Việt Minh as the real cause of the insurgency. William Bundy in his "Path to Viet-Nam" speech rejected this "romantic" view, pointing out that although growing discontent with Diệm's policies might have led to an internal revolution eventually, this was not what had actually happened; "... what happened was that Hanoi [sic] moved in, from at least 1959 onward (Bernard Fall would say from 1957), and provided a cutting edge of direction, trained men from the north, and supplies that transformed internal discontent into a massive subversive effort guided and supported from the outside in crucial ways."[76] In elaboration, he cited his predecessor Roger Hilsman:

> Vietnam, in truth, was in the midst of two struggles, not one. The guerrilla warfare was not a spontaneous revolution, as Communist propaganda would have it, but a contrived, deliberate campaign directed and managed from Hanoi. But Vietnam was also in the throes of a true revolution, a social and nationalistic revolution very much akin to the "new nationalisms" that pervaded both the Congo crisis and Indonesia's confrontation with Malaysia. Even while the struggle went on against the Viet Cong [sic], power was in the process of passing from the French-educated mandarin class to representatives of the new nationalism, the Buddhists, the students, and the "young Turks," in the military.[77]

Writing in 1978, Guenter Lewy stated that evidence then available from captured documents and the testimony of knowledgeable defectors contradicted almost all of the thesis that the insurgency was begun in the South by southerners reacting against Diệm's repression campaign. Lewy agreed with most other observers that Diệm's arbitrary and authoritarian methods had gradually alienated important segments of the urban population and that his replacement of elected village chiefs and councils with his own appointees had caused him to lose ground in the countryside. However, he found that available evidence showed that "The decision to begin the armed struggle in the south was made by the Central Committee of the Vietnamese workers," the Lao Dong Party (VWP, Vietnam Workers Party), the Communist Party of Vietnam, in Hà Nội in 1959. Lewy cited Jeffrey Race, "a critic of the subsequent American intervention," to the effect that the idea "a coordinated policy of armed activity was initiated in the south by a militant group outside the Party, or by a militant southern faction breaking with the national leadership, is not supported by historical evidence—except that planted by the party..." According to Lewy, the evidence clearly showed that the National Liberation Front was formed at the instigation of the party in Hà Nội as a typical communist front organization to conceal the communist direction of the insurgency.[78]

By late 1958, Diệm's campaign of suppression of the communists had inflicted heavy losses on the party apparatus in the South. The party's own assassination campaign against local administrators, teachers, and social workers no doubt goaded the Diệm Government to greater violence, thus increasing the net pressure under which the people lived. This atmosphere was apparently seen by the southern branch of the party as desirable in increasing the revolutionary potential. They asked for a policy change permitting the formation of armed units throughout the South. The Fifteenth Conference of the Central Committee, meeting in Hà Nội in January 1959, made such a decision and issued it in May. As a result, by July, the large-scale infiltration cited by Assistant Secretary Bundy in his speech had begun. It included, from 1959 to 1960, some 4,000 southerners who had gone north in 1954 in the operation referred to by William Colby. These people were armed cadre trained to raise and lead insurgent forces. As General Giáp put it in 1954, "The north has become a large rear echelon of an army. The north is the revolutionary base for the whole country."[79]

The DRV made public its commitment to support the southern insurgency at the Third Congress of the VWP in Hà Nội in September 1960.[80] The party, in the person of Secretary General Lê Duẩn, was to make the North "an even more solid base for the struggle for national reunification" while freeing "the south from the atrocious rule of the U.S. imperialists and their henchmen." The Congress resolved to create a broad National United Front directed against the Americans and Diệm, and based on the workers and peasants.[81] The People's Liberation Armed Forces (PLAF) were established on February 15, 1961, and although this PLAF no doubt contained some non-Communists, most observers generally came to agree that it was not "an independent and indigenous southern political entity with a policy of its own" and accepted the fact it was controlled by Hà Nội. The People's Revolutionary Party (PRP), established in January 1962, was also generally accepted as the southern branch of the VWP.[82]

So, as Assistant Secretary Bundy had remarked, Diệm was faced with two ongoing problems simultaneously—an armed campaign of subversion run against him from the North and an increasing internal dissent aroused by his own policies and their administration.

As William Colby put it, Diệm's approach contained flaws that would become serious as time went on and American aid in a way handicapped him because it could be presented by the Communists as a "shadow" on his nationalism. Awareness of this problem probably inspired some of the orneriness displayed by Diệm and certain colleagues in dealing with the Americans on aid matters. Furthermore, during his very early difficult days, Diệm had learned the importance of keeping control of power and of the means of exercising it. He seemed surprisingly uninterested in either public opinion or the opinion of the "elite" elements of the society. He operated, therefore, as a benevolent dictator, deciding himself what was best for the people and leaving in the cities a political vacuum in which the elite elements formerly tied to the sects or to individual regional particularists tried to operate in their turn. In the countryside, the vacuum was filled by the "Communist stay behind networks."[83]

Another observer thought that although Diệm's policies and programs from 1956 on were leading to disaster, this was not generally apparent at the time because Diệm and his government looked so good in comparison to some of their opposite numbers in other ex-colonial areas. Discontent and impatience with Diệm's modus operandi were counterbalanced for many by this "image" and by his apparent success in meeting economic and political problems. To the same observer, "Diem's [sic] problem was that he was too much of a mandarin to be a democrat, too much of a democrat to be a dictator and too much of a dictator to attract spontaneous popular support. Ho Chi Minh [sic] had no such inner conflicts."[84]

In May 1957, Diệm paid a state visit to the United States, visiting Honolulu and San Francisco en route to Washington where he was received at the airport and entertained at state dinners by President Eisenhower and Secretary Dulles, addressed a Joint Meeting of Members of the Senate and the House of Representatives and a luncheon at the National Press Club, and visited New York, Detroit, Lansing, Knoxville, the Tennessee Valley, and Los Angeles. The visit was a success. Diệm was well received by the Congress and enjoyed a good press.[85]

His reception reflected the appreciation that he had made progress in meeting his economic and social problems. Despite American support and assistance, however, it soon became clear he was not getting the support of important elements of the urban society and that he was not finding the answer to the increasing security problem, both urban and rural.[86] A British writer (Duncanson) described this administrative failing as "uncoordinated and changeable policy accompanied by disregard for the law …," which made planning impossible and muddled thinking in the president's entourage as well as lack of leadership in the control and discipline of government departments.

This problem has often been described in terms of Diệm's suspicion of those outside his immediate family group and in terms of his remote "mandarinal" approach to the people he was supposed to lead. Duncanson takes the philosophical view that America's genuinely altruistic help failed to make South Vietnam viable because of "inability to sever at an early stage the symbiotic relationship between government and revolutionary forces," and from "misunderstanding of the persuasiveness of the Tagorist outlook." By this interpretation, he said he meant that, in the life of the Vietnamese peasant, there were no free choices. He could not hope to determine his own destiny. If "now and again he does not choose to comply with the wishes of the power he estimates will prove the stronger in the end, it is out of fear of some more immediate intimidation." Duncanson held that the two "pillars of support"—financial aid and a powerful army—the United States provided for Diệm were based on the assumption the peasant could make a free choice and that his choice could be influenced by appeals to ideology and to material comforts. To make them more effective, these two "pillars of aid" were closely tied together and "it was that bond that destroyed the leaders it was meant to uphold."[87] Duncanson argued that the chain of events which brought Diệm down:

> ... owed less to his tyranny or religious prejudice than the outside world was led to believe; the decisive factor was more prosaic—his ignorance how to administer the ordinary machinery of government over which he presided and which a more statesmanlike leader might have so disposed as to prevent revolutionary activity from reviving in his territory at all, formidable though the Marxist–Leninist leadership and methods had always been.[88]

On the occasion of the state visit to Washington (May 11, 1957), a joint statement issued by Eisenhower and Diệm recapitulated the "remarkable achievements" of the Republic of Vietnam since July 1954. It took note of the resettlement of nearly one million refugees from the North, the effective establishment of internal security, the promulgation of a constitution and the election of a national assembly. It recorded that plans for agrarian reform had been launched and a program developed to meet long-range economic and social problems to promote higher living standards for the Vietnamese people. It expressed hope for peaceful unification of Vietnam under the terms of the United Nations Charter and noted that only Soviet opposition kept the Republic of Vietnam from United Nations membership although a large majority of the membership had found the Republic qualified for admission. It noted the apparent reduction of communist hostilities in Southeast Asia since

1954, except in Laos, and expressed concern about continuing communist subversive capabilities in Southeast Asia and elsewhere. It agreed on the nature of the continuing threat to the safety of all free nations from the Chinese Communists. Its most substantive paragraph read:

> President Ngo Dinh Diem [sic] reviewed with President Eisenhower the efforts and means of the Vietnamese Government to promote political stability and economic welfare in the Republic of Vietnam. President Eisenhower assured President Ngo Dinh Diem of the willingness of the United States to continue to offer effective assistance within the constitutional processes of the United States to meet these objectives.[89]

Two years later, in a speech at Gettysburg College on "The importance to the United States of the security and progress of Vietnam," President Eisenhower addressed Vietnam's "two great tasks: self-defense and economic growth," its need for capital, and its need to support necessary military forces without crushing its economy:

> Because of the proximity of large Communist military formations in the north, Free Vietnam must maintain substantial numbers of men under arms. Moreover, while the Government has shown real progress in clearing out Communist guerrillas, those remaining continue to be a disruptive influence in the nation's life.
>
> Unassisted, Vietnam cannot at this time produce and support the military formations essential to it or, equally important, the morale—the hope, the confidence, the pride—necessary to meet the dual threat of aggression from without and subversion within its borders.
>
> Still another fact: Strategically South Vietnam's capture by the Communists would bring their power several hundred miles into a hitherto free region. The remaining countries in Southeast Asia would be menaced by a great flanking movement. The freedom of 12 million people would be lost immediately and that of 150 million others in adjacent lands would be seriously endangered. The loss of South Vietnam would set in motion a crumbling process that could as it progressed, have grave consequences for us and for freedom.
>
> Vietnam must have a reasonable degree of safety now—both for her people and for her property. Because of these facts, military as well as economic help is currently needed in Vietnam.
>
> We reach the inescapable conclusion that our own national interests demand some help from us in sustaining in Vietnam the morale, the economic progress and the military strength necessary to its continued existence in freedom.[90]

Opinions have varied on how well or how poorly the United States provided such help to Vietnam and its "difficult" leader over the nine years from 1954 to 1963.

As an Englishman saw it, the Americans were initially over-impressed by the danger of a military invasion from the North, under-impressed by the threat of subversion, and over-optimistic about the likelihood of diminishing the appeal of the communists by raising living standards in the South. He found the Americans too cautious about offending Vietnamese independence and self-determination and too confident in Diệm's ability to govern because of his unimpeachable ideological reliability. He also found the Americans reluctant in the use of financial aid because of fear of future public criticism. He thought that despite the United States' objections to the Geneva Agreement, it honored the limitations imposed by the Agreement in regard to military assistance. He remarked that the number of United States military assistance personnel in Vietnam did not exceed the post-Geneva total of French Military Mission and Military Assistance Advisory Group personnel (888) until 1961, "a full year after the Viet Cong [sic] had taken up arms openly against the Republic." He thought the staffs of the civilian agencies engaged in assistance were, until 1961, "minute—possibly 300 all told—by comparison with their successors in the years after the Communists took up arms again."[91]

This same observer divided the "nine-year association" of the United States with Diệm's government into three phases. The first, 1954–56, was essentially a relief operation. The second, 1957–61, saw the consolidation of Diệm's government, the appearance of its weaknesses, and disappointments over its economic development. This period also saw a general decline in the American public's support for Diệm's government and in the support of many individual Americans working in Vietnam. The anxiety over the increasing success of the Việt Cộng, he thought, reversed this trend in 1962 and 1963 and led to a "renewal of American generosity and resolve to assist a sorely pressed ally in the cold war, even if it was then used to overturn President Diem [sic] personally." He concluded, with regret, that the American aid program failed, chiefly because of a failure to spell out formally the relations between American advisors and Vietnamese officials in a "treaty," leaving instead everything to "mutual goodwill" and "reasonableness." He also thought the Americans counted too much on concentrating support "on a leader as a rallying point for vested interests harnessed to a national endeavor" while disregarding "the impersonal institutions of the state" and "underestimating the value of the civil service." He thought that lack of self-confidence on the part of American advisors, the preconceptions and prejudgments of American public, press, and politicians at home, and, finally, "want of coordination and want of direction in the application of aid and advice all contributed to failure." He concluded that by giving aid and advice in the absence of any formal framework of agreement that might have been criticized as colonialism, the Americans confirmed the defects of the Diệm regime instead of correcting them. At the same time, the Americans constantly told the government it should share power with other politicians or establish representative institutions or allow more freedom of expression. Diệm regarded exhortations of this sort as the very kind of pressure the Americans were trying to avoid.[92]

An experienced American observer, on the other hand, saw the record of this nine-year period as an accumulation of errors and omissions on the part of Diệm which frustrated American efforts to help him. It was a record of alienation of the sects, the intellectuals, the rural population, the Buddhists, the students, and the Army. Diệm, he believed, did not seek reconciliation with the sects, rapprochement with the intellectuals, or correction of abuses regarding land tenure or the execution of the national security law. Mismanagement of the strategic hamlet program and mishandling of the Buddhist hierarchy and laymen made things worse and led up to the mass rioting of 1963. "In horror, Americans helplessly watched Diem [sic] tear apart the fabric of Vietnamese society more effectively than the Communists had ever been able to do. It was the most efficient act of his entire career."[93]

Another American observer on the scene in 1963 wrote that, during the nine-year period, most foreign affairs experts in and out of the press in the United States complained that the American ambassador in Sài Gòn at any given time was going about his job in the wrong way. They offered various prescriptions for the right way to do the job. Some thought the ambassador should be tough; he should make Diệm understand he would do as he was told or lose American aid. Others thought the ambassador should be soft, understanding Diệm and letting him do things in his own way. Still others thought Diệm should be dropped as hopeless. As this observer saw it: The first four ambassadors who tried to deal with Diệm dutifully rotated the "tough" and "soft" approaches.

> General J. Lawton ("Lightning Joe") Collins (1954–1955) tried futilely to run Diem [sic] the way he ran the VII Corps in World War II. G. Frederick Reinhardt (1955–1957), who had it relatively easy because the Communists were quiescent, was soft and repaired relations. Elbridge Durbrow (1957–1961) was so tough that Diem virtually boycotted him. Nolting (1961–1963) was soft and wound up in despair. In the U.S. relationship with Diem, the only constant was Diem—until the fifth Ambassador, Henry Cabot Lodge (1963–1964) applied the "dump him" policy.

This observer was not sure any policy would have worked with Diệm but thought the soft policy would probably have had the best chance, since experience had shown the president could sometimes be persuaded but never intimidated. However, he pointed out, American public opinion in the long run would not tolerate the soft line.[94]

The Pentagon Papers tell us that on September 16, 1960, Ambassador Durbrow told the department that the Diệm government was threatened by two separate but related dangers:

> Danger from demonstrations or coup attempt in Saigon [sic] could occur earlier; likely to be predominantly non-Communistic in origin but Communists can be expected to endeavor infiltrate and exploit any such attempt. Even more serious danger is gradual Viet Cong [sic] extension of control over countryside which, if current Communist progress continues, would mean loss [of] Free Vietnam to Communists. These two dangers are related because Communist successes in rural areas embolden them to extend their activities to Saigon and because non-Communist temptation to engage in demonstrations or coup is partly motivated by sincere desire to prevent Communist takeover in Vietnam.[95]

Durbrow's message went on to acknowledge Diệm's past and probable future resentment of "frank talks" but also suggested he might act on some new American suggestions since he had apparently acted on some in the past. Anyway, prompt and drastic action was needed. Durbrow proposed he see Diệm and make certain specific suggestions intended to help him in his serious current situation. Suggestions included: assigning the vice president as minister of the interior; appointing a full-time minister to take over the National Defense Ministry from Diệm; appoint Ngô Đình Nhu to an Embassy abroad; send head of secret intelligence service, Trần Kim Tuyến, abroad in a diplomatic assignment; name one or two cabinet ministers from the opposition; disband or at least surface the Cần Lao Party; permit the National Assembly wider legislative initiative and an area of genuine debate and authorize it to conduct public investigations of any department of government; require all government officials to declare their property and financial holdings; let the press operate under a self-imposed code of conduct; and adopt a series of measures having to do with rice prices, payment for corvee labor, subsidies for agroville families, and increased compensation for the youth corps—all intended to enhance immediately peasant support of the government. The message also recommended President Eisenhower send Diệm a "letter of continued support on the fifth anniversary of the Republic of Vietnam, October 26."[96]

The final paragraph of the message read:

> We believe U.S. should at this time support Diem [sic] as best available Vietnamese leader, but should recognize that overriding U.S. objective is strongly anti-Communist Vietnamese government which can command loyal and enthusiastic support of widest possible segments of Vietnamese people, and is able to carry on effective fight against Communist guerrillas. If Diem's position in country continues [to] deteriorate as result of failure to adopt proper political, psychological economic and security measures, it may become necessary for U.S. Government to begin consideration [of] alternative courses of action and leaders in order achieve our objective.[97]

Meanwhile, more attention had been focused on Vietnamese Communist activities in Laos. As Bernard Fall reminds us in *The Two Viet-Nams*, General Giáp's first foreign invasion took place early in the spring of 1953 when he sent an estimated four divisions into Laos.[98] General Salan set up an entrenched camp in the Plaine des Jarres to stem this threat to Laos and, with the start of the rainy season, the Vietnamese Communists fell back on their major supply depots. Souphanouvong, the Pathet Lao Resistance Movement's founder (future president of the Lao People's Democratic Republic), had followed the Việt Minh unit into northern Laos on this occasion. He made a declaration broadcast over the Việt Minh radio claiming he represented the "legal authority of the Pathet Lao" but had to fall back with the Việt Minh forces when they retired. Subsequently, he set up a nominal occupation of the two provinces of Sam Neua and Phongsaly bordering North Vietnam. Subsequently, at the Geneva Conference, he succeeded in having his movement recognized under the rubric "Pathet Lao Fighting Units."[99] Article 14 of the Geneva Agreement on Laos provided that, "pending a political settlement," these Pathet Lao units should move into the provinces of Sam Neua and Phongsaly except for any military personnel who preferred to be demobilized where they were.[100] Of course, Article 13 provided that Vietnamese People's Volunteer Forces should be moved out of Laos.[101] Needless to say, this never happened. However, talks did begin between the Government of Laos and the Pathet Lao on January 3, 1955, near Xieng Khouang on the Plaine des Jarres, and, in the interim, the Pathet Lao further developed their combat units in Sam Neua and Phongsaly. Others were trained in North Vietnam.

Meanwhile, the Việt Minh carried on indoctrination and recruitment operations in Laos and the Internal Control Commission (ICC) proved helpless to stop them. In August 1956, Lao Prime Minister Prince Souvanna Phouma, responding to an invitation delivered via the Indian Chairman of the ICC, went to China and North Vietnam, ostensibly to go over the heads of the Pathet Lao negotiators who had proved unresponsive when apparently operating on their own. There followed the 1957 agreements (November 2, 1957), which seemed to represent, on the face of it, a return to Lao unity. Others, including the Department of State, saw it as a "dangerous line of conduct" which, on the basis of history elsewhere in the world, would "end tragically in penetration and seizure of the country by the Communists."[102] On November 18, Souphanouvong symbolically restored the two provinces of Sam Neua and Phongsaly to the Crown Prince of Laos, and the National Assembly voted to install Souvanna Phouma's new coalition government including, as Pathet Lao representatives, Souphanouvong, as minister of reconstruction and planning, and Phourai Vongvichit, as minister of religion and fine arts. On May 4, 1958, a supplementary election, called for in the 1957 agreements, was to be held to select 21 new members of the National Assembly, raising the membership of that body to 59. All parties were to put up candidates including the Neo Lao Hak Sat (NLHS), successor to the old Pathet Lao. The NLHS campaigned on the claim that their candidates must be elected to preserve the peace which had been restored only because they had laid down their arms. While the NLHS made common cause with another party, Santiphab, which claimed to be neutralist, the government supporters split along regional and personal factional lines into three separate groups. Consequently, NLHS won nine of the 21 contested seats. Reacting to this show of communist strength, the three nationalist elements formed the Laotian People's Rally under Souvanna Phouma, who was expected to succeed himself as prime minister after a ceremonial resignation. However, an outbreak of political assassinations, especially in Southern Laos, and the discovery of arms caches, led to criticism of Souvanna Phouma's policies of arbitration and conciliation in regard to the communists. The United States Government, which had made clear its dissatisfaction with the 1957 agreements, also began to indicate displeasure with Souvanna Phouma's policies. "By hesitating for months over the question of continuing U.S. dollar aid to Laos, Washington clearly indicated its lack of enthusiasm for an expensive program of aid to a nation dallying with its worst enemies."[103]

As a Lao politician put it, "These considerations undoubtedly figured in the choice of a new Prime Minister. Suspected of indulgence or at least softness toward the Pathet Lao, Souvanna was replaced by Phoui Sananikone, a man whose nationalism and anti-Communism seemed thoroughly reliable. Already prominent in the RPL, he soon became its leader."[104] Phoui's government was installed on August 18, 1958, and undertook a hard line towards the communist Pathet Lao. It also included in its membership not only older politicians but some of the younger elements of the Committee for Defense of National Interests (CDIN in the French acronym). This was a group of younger officials and military officers who looked upon themselves as the elite of the future and took a strong line against corruption in government as well as against communist subversion. This alliance between new and old elements was an uneasy one at least in regard to the anti-corruption campaign. However, it enjoyed the support of Crown Prince (and future King) Savang Vatthana, got through a currency devaluation intended to strike at the black market, and set up a Department of Rural Affairs. Its old and young members were united, in any event, against what they saw as the communist plans for Laos.

This attitude was reflected in a change of policy. Phoui's government abandoned Souvanna Phouma's neutralist policy and sought closer ties with Western allies in Asia. Ngô Đình Diệm's brother and political advisor, Ngô Đình Nhu, was invited to Vientiane on a visit which Phoui said, "gave proof of the identical points of view and the solid friendship between our two countries." A little later, the Lao raised their legation in Sài Gòn to the status of Embassy and then accepted a Chinese (Nationalist) Consul in Vientiane. The government also dismissed a number of "Communist sympathizers and long-time fellow travelers of the Pathet Lao" from the government service.[105] The communist reaction came in January 1959 when Việt Minh (North Vietnamese) troops entered Southern Laos and occupied three villages near Tchepone. When the Lao protested to Hà Nội, the North Vietnamese replied they had acted in retaliation for alleged Lao incursions into North Vietnam by air and ground forces and suggested negotiations. Laos refused and appealed to the United Nations, and Phoui asked the National Assembly for "full powers" for a year and permission to reshuffle his government in the interest of efficiency. He got the full powers, but the reshuffle of the cabinet may not have turned out as he had expected. After a struggle between the older and younger elements, in which the younger prevailed, he ended up with three Army officers, including Colonel Phoumi Nosavan, in the cabinet. Meanwhile, the Vietnamese Communists stayed where they were in Tchepone. Phoui announced he would not be blackmailed into appealing to the ICC on the Tchepone question because his government considered "the application of the Geneva agreements as fully accomplished," and that Laos, "as a sovereign, independent country could not tolerate interference in her internal affairs." United Nations Secretary Dag Hammarskjöld made a quick visit to Vientiane on March 9 in connection with the Tchepone affair but was unable to accomplish anything since neither Hà Nội nor Peking recognized the United Nations at the time.[106]

The next crisis was the Plaine des Jarres incident. There still remained two battalions of Pathet Lao troops, most of them mountain people, who had not yet been integrated into the Royal Army. After lengthy negotiations, one of the battalions stationed in Luang Prabang Province was integrated, but the other took to the bush to remain in existence as a guerrilla arm for the Pathet Lao. Soon after their flight in May 1959, a rebel offensive began in the northern provinces and elsewhere with the first attacks coming on July 20. These attacks came at about the same time as Chinese clashes with the Indians in the Northeast Frontier Agency and Ladakh regions. Whether or not there was any connection between the events in Laos and those on the Sino–Indian frontier, it was clear the Lao attacks had been mounted on a scale far beyond the capacity of the Pathet Lao forces; the North Vietnamese role was obvious. The Hà Nội radio output of anti-Vientiane propaganda confirmed this, and Vientiane complained to the United Nations Secretary General about Hà Nội's "barely camouflaged interference."[107]

Next, in August, the communists concentrated their military efforts in Sam Neua Province; Vientiane again appealed to the United Nations, and a U.N. debate on Laos began in September. The U.N. dispatched an investigation subcommittee composed of members from Japan, Tunis, Italy, and Argentina. Their arrival coincided with a calming of the situation and their report cited only "indirect," rather than direct, aggression. The Chinese, the Soviets, and a few Westerners took the line that there never had been an invasion by the North Vietnamese. Hammarskjöld, however, had made another trip to Vientiane and agreed to have his personal representative spend a month there studying conditions relevant to a possible technical assistance program, but coincidentally providing a sort of U.N. presence.[108]

By the end of December, the differences between young and old elements of Phoui's cabinet reached the point where a coup d'état, apparently accepted by the King but a surprise to the foreign embassies, turned Phoui out and left the High Command in charge pending the formation of the next government. The British expressed hope that the new government's policies would be consistent with international obligations contracted under the Geneva Conference and that Laos would not lose its neutrality. The State Department "had declared simply that the Royal Army had been given the task of maintaining order and security in Laos during the period between the resignation of Phoui Sananikone and the formation of the next government" and expressed the hope "that no change will be made in the policy of the Lao government which might affect the attitude of peace and neutrality which the kingdom has been observing in international affairs."[109]

The French were concerned about complications which might adversely affect the easing of East–West tensions. The French, American, and British ambassadors, and the Australian chargé d'affaires, called on the King to express their governments' concern, and Dag Hammarskjöld sent the King a telegram. In the absence of a parliament, which the Army had terminated, the King named an elderly and distinguished civilian, Kou Abhay, to form a government responsible to the Crown. This government planned to go ahead with general elections scheduled for April. Souphanouvong and his key fellow leaders of the Pathet Lao had been in jail since shortly after the Plaine des Jarres incident and Souvanna Phouma was off in Paris as ambassador.

The government tried, by gerrymandering and tightening up on the eligibility requirements for candidates, to minimize the Pathet Lao chances and the Army undertook to arrange extremely tight security for the polling which further inhibited communist chances. In the election, both the communist NLHS and the "progressive" Santiphab were completely eliminated from representation in the new National Assembly. Responding to expressions of concern from the British, French, and American ambassadors about the danger inherent in a government controlled by the military, the King reassured them Laos would remain neutral. Another civilian, Tiao Somsanith, became prime minister. Meanwhile, Prince Souvanna Phouma returned from Paris, and Souphanouvong and 15 colleagues escaped from detention and took to the bush. Souvanna Phouma became president of the National Assembly. Souphanouvong's precise whereabouts remained unknown.

On August 9, 1960, while almost all members of the government were absent in Luang Prabang for funeral ceremonies for the late King Sisavang Vona, 26-year-old Army Captain Kong Le conducted a coup d'état in Vientiane with his Second Parachute Battalion. His initial propaganda was anti-American in tone and called for reconciliation with the Pathet Lao. He appealed to Souvanna Phouma to take over the leadership of his movement. Souvanna agreed, subject to approval by the National Assembly. The Assembly, meeting with some absentees and after having been invaded by a mob, elected Souvanna Phouma. Meanwhile, General Phoumi and other members of the Somsanith Government had formed an anti-coup committee at Savannakhet. The King summoned the Assembly to Luang Prabang, the royal capital, where it agreed on a coalition government with Prince Souvanna Phouma as prime minister and General Phoumi Nosavan as vice premier and minister of the interior. Kong Le rejected the new government and Phoumi did not dare to return to Vientiane where Kong Le still had control with his paratroopers. For reasons which varied in the eyes of various beholders, the attempted reconciliation had failed. A Pathet Lao delegation arrived in Vientiane, followed shortly by a Soviet ambassador. Washington suspended military and economic aid. The Russians started an airlift of fuel, food, medical supplies, arms, and ammunition. On December 8, Vientiane area troops drove Kong Le's troops out of the city only to be driven out themselves the next day. On December 10, Phoumi's troops from Savannakhet reinforced the Vientiane troops of General Kouprasith and they jointly drove Kong Le's forces out again after three days of fighting which caused heavy military and civilian casualties. Souvanna Phouma fled on December 10 and made his way to temporary exile in Phnom Penh, Cambodia. Kong Le withdrew north of Vientiane and the Soviet airlift continued at that location.[110]

This was roughly the situation that confronted the new Kennedy Administration so far as Laos was concerned. President Eisenhower, in a talk with the president-elect on January 19, concentrated particularly on Laos, stating that if a political settlement could not be arranged, he would be ready as a last desperate hope to intervene unilaterally. Citing the experience of China and the Marshall Mission, he said it would be fatal to let the communists play any part in a new Lao regime.[111]

At the moment, the new administration found the prospects in Vietnam favorable, compared to those in Laos. President Kennedy, according to his biographer, thought neutralism was the correct policy for Laos but that American prestige had been deeply engaged and it would first be necessary to convince the Pathet Lao they could not win, and the Soviets that they should not provide further military assistance before trying for neutralization.[112] He established a Lao task force and required daily reports of its progress. After further lack of success in Phoumi's military efforts, Kennedy decided Laos must have a coalition, under Souvanna Phouma, of the type the Eisenhower Administration had rejected:

> On February 19 the King of Laos, who spent most of his time trying to stay out of politics, issued a statement, drafted in the State Department, declaring a policy of non-alignment, appealing to all countries to respect his nation's independence and neutrality and asking his three neighbors to serve as guarantors. Cambodia (despite a personal letter from Kennedy to Prince Sihanouk) and Burma both declined, however, and in any case, Moscow, Peking and Prince Souphanouvong all attacked the plan.[113]

Kennedy believed the United States was overcommitted in Southeast Asia, but he had to keep Vientiane from the communists in order to have a basis for negotiations, and he could not accept any visible humiliation over Laos. He also thought unilateral American intervention on any large scale was not feasible and would not be supported by allies. He supported a British plan to revive the ICC and hold a new Geneva Conference after verifying a cease-fire.[114]

On March 23, 1961, Kennedy held his famous press conference with maps of Laos in the background and said the United States, regardless of any past misunderstandings, now wanted a neutral Laos, that armed communist attacks from the outside would have to stop and, in effect, that the United States would have to consider its response if the attacks did not stop. He also sent the Seventh Fleet into the South China Sea, alerted combat troops in Okinawa, and moved 500 marines with helicopters into Thailand. He obtained Nehru's support for a cease-fire and Macmillan's support for limited intervention along the Mekong, if necessary. On March 27, Secretary Rusk got troop pledges from Thailand, Pakistan, and the Philippines. The president warned Soviet Minister of Foreign Affairs Andrei Gromyko not to misjudge American determination. He also converted the informal military assistance group in Laos (Program Evaluation Office) into a regular Military Assistance Advisory Group and authorized it to accompany Lao troops. The Russians agreed to an appeal for a cease-fire on April 24. Meanwhile, of course, the events of the Bay of Pigs had taken place in Cuba.[115]

The Fourteen Nation Conference on Laos opened on May 16 in Geneva. In the words of one member of the American delegation, "Agreement was finally reached on July 23, 1962, fourteen months and a billion words later. During this period, the situation in Laos, which together with Cuba represented Kennedy's most troublesome international problems, became more or less stabilized. During this period too Hanoi [sic] and Washington turned their attention increasingly toward South Vietnam."[116]

Meanwhile, the South Vietnamese had been watching the Lao story closely and with extreme interest. As one member of the United States Mission in Sài Gòn later wrote, "Washington was also aware that it had seriously damaged the security of South Vietnam by accepting the 'neutralization' of Laos at Geneva in mid-1962, more or less removing all hope of effective action against Viet Cong [sic] infiltration through Laos."[117]

In Laos itself, the "secret war" was about to begin. The signing of the Geneva Agreements on Laos was supposed to mean that "fifteen nations agreed to withdraw all their military forces, cease their paramilitary assistance to the three contending factions in Laos, and recognize neutralist Souvanna Phouma as the leader of a three part coalition government." The Americans and the Soviets stopped their supply flights and the U.S. Army training teams left. "All the nations followed the agreed script, except one: North Vietnam." Only 40 of the estimated 7,000 North Vietnamese troops in Laos at the time of the signing left and 10 years later they had increased tenfold. Assistant Secretary Averell Harriman had worked out the agreement on the basis of agreement between President Kennedy and Soviet Premier Khrushchev that they did not want a confrontation in Laos. It was hoped that if the United States and the Soviet Union could in fact draw back from a confrontation in Laos, they might be able to apply the same technique elsewhere in the world. Then, when it became clear that, despite the agreement, the North Vietnamese and their Pathet Lao subordinates were still expanding their area of control and attacking the neutralist forces in the process, the U.S. moved to the provision of supplies for defensive fighting. As it became clear the Russians were not enforcing North Vietnamese compliance with the 1962 Agreement, the Lao tribal forces supported by the CIA got the job of defending against the North Vietnamese pressure; "... and the Kennedys had no doubt that it had to be undertaken." The advantage of using the CIA for this purpose was that the Lao question did not again have to become a major confrontation between the two superpowers. "The distinction Khrushchev had made in the U-2 incident between what Moscow knew and what Washington officially admitted was applied to this field, and the USSR even kept its Embassy in Vientiane as the 'secret war' escalated."[118]

In Vietnam, Kennedy inherited what has been described as a commitment "concrete and substantial enough that American prestige in Asia—and beyond—was intimately tied to the declining fortunes of Ngo Dinh Diem [sic]."[119]

Ambassador Durbrow had pushed Diệm pretty hard on policy and organizational changes seen as necessary to meet the increasing communist threat to South Vietnam. Diệm had been neither responsive nor pleased. Observers have described Durbrow as having "worn out his welcome"[120] and as being "virtually persona non grata."[121] General Lansdale, returning from a recent visit, had reported that the situation in the countryside was precarious, Diệm's governmental structure inadequate, and his government generally unprepared psychologically to fight the kind of guerrilla war it was facing.[122]

In May 1961, Ambassador Frederick Nolting replaced Durbrow in Sài Gòn. Nolting told the BBC in 1977 that the United States Government did not regard the whole Indochina peninsula as one strategic area "as it should have done" but rather planned in terms of dealing with different countries while the communists, especially the ones in Hà Nội, saw the area as a unit. The American Embassy in Sài Gòn as well as the Government of Vietnam were more and more worried about the 1962 Agreement on Laos and foresaw its breakdown. The BBC noted that all American decisions taken subsequent to the 1962 Geneva Agreement on Laos had been taken in the knowledge the Agreement must break down. Secretary Rusk commented to the BBC that the Kennedy Administration had concentrated heavy attention on Laos because President Eisenhower had recommended to President Kennedy the day before his inauguration that he put troops in Laos, "with others if possible, alone if necessary." The Kennedy Administration had concluded after observation that the Lao themselves were a threat to nobody and fighting occurred only when the Vietnamese came in. "So, we felt the best solution there would be to get everybody out of Laos—ourselves, the North Vietnamese, the French, everybody." The idea was to get an island of peace, if possible, between North Vietnam on the one hand and Thailand and South Vietnam on the other, with the Lao left to manage and mismanage their own affairs. The United States had worked hard on the 1962 Accords but had been unable to get compliance with them. As to why the Soviets had been unable to force the North Vietnamese to withdraw their troops from Laos, Rusk supposed the Soviets had not wanted to press the North Vietnamese so hard as to drive them into the arms of Peking. He agreed that, because of the long Lao–Vietnamese frontier, the breakdown of the 1962 Agreement greatly increased South Vietnam's military difficulties.[123]

Nolting told the BBC his instructions on his assignment as ambassador flowed out of a recommendation by a task force convened in Washington to try to advise the president on policies to be pursued in Vietnam. The task force recommendation, once approved by the president, became the ambassador's instructions. They were, in Nolting's words:

> I think to give the policy a new emphasis. To continue the Eisenhower policy of supporting the South Vietnamese through their elected government short of the commitment of American combat forces. To do this in a stepped-up way, in view of the increasing violence of the Vietcong which had begun the year before in 1960 or maybe as early as 1959. To do it through various means, economic help, political support, intelligence gathering particularly the supply of weapons to South Vietnamese forces, and through a training system by the U.S. military consisting not only of logistics problems and imports to South Vietnam, but in the use of those weapons and in training and training camps. So, in order to do this, the instructions put a great emphasis on building a bridge of confidence between the U.S. Mission and the Government of South Vietnam, which was the Diem [sic] Government, which had been in office as you recall some six years then, and had just been re-elected.[124]

Nolting added it had been decided tentatively that Diệm was "the best bet" and he deserved support but that President Kennedy had indicated the success of this increased American effort would depend on Diệm, and the president wanted Nolting's frank appraisal of the Vietnamese leader. Nolting said he remained very open-minded on this question for months because he thought it was a crucial one. He had ended up feeling that Diệm "was honest, that he was dedicated, that he had the best chances of rallying the nationalist spirit of the non-Communist South Vietnamese of anyone on the political scene." Nolting agreed Diệm had his shortcomings such as stubbornness, verbosity, and lack of administrative ability but he was not a dictator, not a cruel person. "He was autocratic and paternalistic in the mandarin sense, which is quite different." Asked if the new emphasis on policy limited the autonomy Diệm had been exercising or the capacity of the South Vietnamese Government to act, Nolting replied, "No, on the contrary. That point is very important. My instructions were *not* to take over any control but to try to build up mutual confidence so that our advice would be taken seriously; but the responsibility for the action was clearly left in the hands of the Vietnamese Government."[125]

The BBC commented that President Kennedy had begun the process of committing the United States more deeply in Vietnam when he acted on some of the recommendations of the Taylor/Rostow Mission (October 1961).[126]

The publishers of the Pentagon Papers tell us that "President John F. Kennedy transformed the 'limited risk gamble of the Eisenhower Administration' into a 'broad commitment' to prevent Communist domination of South Vietnam."[127] "Moreover, according to the study, prepared in 1967–68 by Government analysts, the Kennedy tactics deepened the American involvement in Vietnam piecemeal, with each step minimizing public recognition that the American role was growing."[128] The Papers report that Kennedy made his first new commitments to Vietnam in secret when he ordered 400 Special Forces troops and 100 other military advisors sent to South Vietnam without publicity. He also, according to the Papers, directed on the same day—May 11, 1961—that a clandestine warfare campaign be undertaken against North Vietnam by South Vietnamese agents, CIA directed and trained, and some American Special Forces troops. The Papers say the president also ordered "infiltration of South Vietnamese forces into southeastern Laos to find and attack Communist bases and supply lines," and directed allied forces to "initiate ground action, including the use of U.S. advisers [sic], if necessary," against communist aerial resupply missions in the vicinity of Tchepone, in the southern Laotian panhandle. The Papers describe President Kennedy's decisions "as part of an unbroken sequence that built up to much more ambitious covert warfare under President Johnson in 1964." "The analysts handling the Kennedy period put more stress, however, on the evolution of President Kennedy's decision in November, 1961 to expand greatly the American military advisory mission in Vietnam and, for the first time, to put American servicemen in combat-support roles that involved them increasingly in actual fighting." The Papers cite a telegram of November 18 in which Ambassador Nolting explained to Diệm that the American servicemen could be exposed to enemy action in their new roles and said in reply to Diệm's question, "... that in my personal opinion these personnel would be authorized to defend themselves if attacked. I pointed out that this was one reason why the decisions were very grave from U.S. standpoint."[129]

So, during his first year in office, President Kennedy had made the sixth, seventh, and eighth American decisions in regard to Indochina. Assistant Secretary Bundy summed them up in his College Park speech:

> In Laos, President Kennedy in the spring of 1961 rejected the idea of strong military action in favor of seeking a settlement that would install a neutralist government under Souvanna Phouma, a solution uniquely appropriate to Laos ...[130]

> Although the details somewhat obscured the broad pattern, I think any fair historian of the future must conclude that as early as the spring of 1961 President Kennedy had in effect taken a seventh United States policy decision: that we would continue to be deeply engaged in Southeast Asia, in South Vietnam, and under new ground rules, in Laos as well ...[131]

We then come to the eighth period of decision—the fall of 1961. By then, the "guerrilla aggression" [Hillsman's phrase] had assumed truly serious proportions, and morale in South Vietnam had been shaken. It seemed highly doubtful that without major additional United States actions the North Vietnamese threat could be stemmed.

President Kennedy took the decision to raise the ante, through a system of advisers, pilots, and supporting military personnel that rose gradually to the level of 25,000 in the next 3 years.[132]

Assistant Secretary Bundy remarked that this eighth decision represented the policy followed from early 1962 right up to February 1965 but noted that:

Within this period, however, political deterioration in South Vietnam compelled, in the fall of 1963, decisions that I think must be counted as the ninth critical point of United States policy-making. It was decided at that time that while the United States would do everything necessary to support the war, it would no longer adhere to its posture of all-out support of the Diem [sic] regime unless that regime made sweeping changes in its methods of operation.

The record of this period had been described by Robert Shaplen and now by Hillsman. Undoubtedly, the new U.S. posture contributed to the overthrow of Diệm in November 1963.

I do not myself think that we could in the end have done otherwise; but the important historical point is that our actions tended to deepen our involvement in South Vietnam and our commitment to the evolution on non-Communist nationalism, always foreseen to be difficult, that would follow the overthrow of Diem [sic].[133]

The Papers claim President Kennedy faced three principal questions on Vietnam: "whether to make an irrevocable commitment to prevent a Communist victory; whether to commit ground combat units to achieve his ends; whether to give top priority to the military battle against the Vietcong or to the political reforms necessary for winning popular support." They find that his response during his 34 months in office was to increase American advisors from some 685 to about 16,000, to put Americans into combat and "eventually to inject the United States into the internal South Vietnamese maneuvering that eventually toppled the Diem [sic] regime."[134]

The BBC described Kennedy's decision to "raise the ante" as a compromise which resulted in the dispatch of military advisors and support units instead of a military task force, proposed as a result of a Taylor/Rostow mission that had visited Vietnam in the autumn of 1961. Ambassador Nolting told the BBC that his reaction to the compromise was, on the whole, good. If the United States had continued on that basis, "assuming American material support but no military forces," he thought the chances would have been for "a gradual improvement and a viable South Vietnamese state" although he "would not have expected a wholly satisfactory situation in South Vietnam for many years." Colby told the BBC the solution proposed by the Taylor/Rostow Mission—strengthening the government and changing politically—was at fault because "The strengthening turned out to be military strengthening," and "The urging of change turned out to be: let the opposition have a role in the government." However, the problem was not a military problem. It was a guerrilla problem at the village level and there wasn't any American machinery for handling such a problem.[135]

As if it did not have enough troubles with the communist insurgency in the rural areas, the Government of Vietnam fecklessly became engaged in a conflict with the Buddhists in Huế on May 8 by banning the display of Buddhist flags on the occasion of the 2527th anniversary of Buddha's birth. A protest demonstration led to fighting between Buddhists and troops in which nine Buddhists were killed and 15 injured. The government's failure to take quick action to remedy the grievances resulting from this episode led to further demonstrations in Huế, in Sài Gòn, and in other major cities, eventually including seven suicides by fire. In the words of one American official:

> From a western viewpoint the Buddhist upheaval was a tangle of contradictions. Buddhism was a religion of withdrawal, of inward-looking meditation, of passive indifference to world affairs. Except for resistance to western encroachment by the Buddhist emperors at Hue [sic], it had never been a primary force in Vietnamese political affairs. Its leaders for the most part were men who had spent their lives in their pagodas. Yet their campaign against the Diem [sic] regime was executed with such sophisticated skill as to suggest that they had been trained on Madison Avenue.[136]

The same officer observed that the Buddhist upheaval probably:

> ... could not have succeeded without the help of the American press and radio/TV. Expressed more bluntly, American news coverage of the upheaval contributed directly to destruction of a national U.S. policy of direct importance to the security of the United States, in an area where we had deployed nearly twenty thousand Americans, where we were spending some $500 million a year, at the only point in the world where we were engaged in support of a shooting war against a Communist enemy.

He explained that:

> This was not however a malicious achievement. There were individual newsmen in Vietnam, and editorial writers and columnists back home, who hated Diem and enjoyed writing about his difficulties. But the reporting on the Buddhist crisis, for the most part, was straight. There was little sensationalism. None was necessary.[137]

The so-called press problem in Vietnam which had led to a "breakdown of communication between the U.S. Mission, and the American newsmen and thus the American public,"[138] to say nothing of the attitude of the Vietnamese Government which "further compounded the problem,"[139] helped keep the

Buddhist upheaval going. The Buddhists told their story to the journalists who reported it, and it came back over the Voice of America (VOA), the BBC, and Radio Australia to the Vietnamese urban population who had a lot of radio receivers.[140]

On June 27, "as a first step toward resolving this dispute ... between South Vietnamese and Americans, and among Americans, over the virtues and vices of Diem [sic] and his regime," President Kennedy announced that former Republican Vice Presidential Candidate Henry Cabot Lodge would replace Ambassador Nolting in Sài Gòn. Meanwhile, in Washington, "as the Buddhist protests escalated and public opinion against the Diệm regime was stirred to a fever pitch of outrage, the State Department's view of the situation came into ascendancy ... that the war could not be won unless the Saigon [sic] government was reformed to make it more democratic and popular, so as to rally the people to the fight against the Communists." The CIA apparently believed a solution could be worked out with Diệm "to handle the Buddhists' concerns and ours, while pursuing the war against the Communists." The military apparently "followed the same line, at least to the extent that they felt the main problem was winning the war and that we should not be diverted from keeping pressure on it." However, "While each of the agencies held the official position expressed by the principals as described, none was by any means unanimous within itself on the issues."[141]

Before Nolting left Sài Gòn on August 15, he had managed to persuade Diệm to make a public statement in a press interview that conciliation of the Buddhists, which he claimed had been his policy all along, was "irreversible." This statement in an interview with Marguerite Higgins was widely disseminated by United States Information Agency [USIS]. However, on August 21, while Ambassador Lodge was in Hawaii on his way to Vietnam, the government carried out coordinated raids on pagodas in Huế and Sài Gòn, in effect declaring war on the Buddhists and inflicting great "loss of face" on the Americans.[142]

Ambassador Lodge arrived in Sài Gòn on the evening of August 22. Protests against the government's action took the form of demonstrations and rioting. Two Buddhist monks had obtained asylum in the Aid Mission during the attack on the pagodas. Two more, including one of the top leaders, Thích Trí Quảng, got into the Embassy and obtained asylum there. On August 26, the day on which Lodge was to present his letters of credence to Diệm, VOA carried news reports that high-ranking United States officials were saying America might sharply reduce aid if Diệm did not get rid of the police officials responsible for the raid and that Lodge had been instructed to tell Diệm the raids were in violation of Diệm's assurances that he would seek a peaceful settlement with the Buddhists.[143]

The Pentagon Papers claim "The Pentagon's secret study of the Vietnam war discloses that President Kennedy knew and approved of plans for the military coup d'état that overthrew President Ngo Dinh Diem [sic] in 1963."[144] Arthur M. Schlesinger wrote in *A Thousand Days*, "It is important to state clearly that the coup of November 1, 1963, was entirely planned and carried out by the Vietnamese. Neither the American Embassy nor the CIA were involved in instigation or execution."[145] The Interim Report of the Senate Select Committee on "Alleged Assassination Plots Involving Foreign Leaders" reproduces the following cable from President Kennedy to Ambassador Lodge (Deptel 272, 8/29/63):

> I have approved all the messages you are receiving from others today, and I emphasize that everything in these messages has my full support. We will do all that we can to help you conclude this operation successfully. Until the very moment of the go signal for the operation by the generals, I must reserve a contingent right to change course and reverse previous instructions. While fully aware of your assessment of the consequences of such a reversal, I know from experience that failure is more destructive than an appearance of indecision. I would, of course, accept full responsibility for any such change as I must also bear the full responsibility for this operation and its consequences.[146]

At 1:30 pm Sài Gòn time, the coup d'état against Ngô Đình Diệm was launched by a group of Vietnamese generals. Some time on November 2, after they had surrendered to the coup group's forces, President Ngô Đình Diệm and his brother and political advisor, Ngô Đình Nhu, were killed. The Senate Select Committee found:

> We find that neither the President nor any official in the United States Government authorized the assassination of Diem [sic] and his brother, Nhu. Both the DCI [Director of Central Intelligence] and top State Department officials did know, however, that the death of Nhu, at least at one point, had been contemplated by the coup leaders. But when the possibility that the coup leaders were considering assassination was brought to the attention of the DCI, he directed that the United States would have no part in such activity, and there is some evidence that this information was relayed to the coup leaders.[147]

As the Pentagon Papers put it, "By supporting the anti-Diem [sic] coup, the analyst asserts, the U.S. inadvertently deepened its involvement. The inadvertence is the key factor."[148] Twenty days after Diệm's death, President Kennedy was assassinated in Dallas on November 23, 1963. As the BBC put it:

> The Americans had both desired and inspired the coup which overthrew Diem ... The overthrow of Diem [sic] had changed both in nature and degree, therefore, the American involvement in Vietnam ... In this sense, by the time Lyndon Johnson took the oath of office, Vietnam had already become an American war.[149]

U.S. Ambassadors to Vietnam/Thailand/Laos/and Cambodia[1] (1950–1975)

Ambassadors to Vietnam/South Vietnam

Donald R. Heath[2]	October 22, 1950 – June 25, 1952[3]
Donald R. Heath	July 11, 1952 – November 14, 1954
MG J. Lawton Collins[4]	November 8, 1964 – May 10, 1955
G. Frederick Reinhardt	May 28, 1955 – February 10, 1957
Elbridge Durbrow	April 16, 1957 – May 3, 1961
Frederick E. Nolting Jr.	May 10, 1961 – August 15, 1963
Henry Cabot Lodge Jr.[5]	August 26, 1963 – June 28, 1964
Maxwell D. Taylor[5]	July 14, 1964 – July 30, 1965
Henry Cabot Lodge Jr.[5]	August 25, 1965 – April 25, 1967
Ellsworth F. Bunker[5]	April 28, 1967 – May 11, 1973
Graham A. Martin	July 20, 1973 – April 29, 1975

Ambassadors to Siam/Thailand

Edwin F. Stanton	July 4, 1946 – April 10, 1947[6]
Edwin F. Stanton	May 9, 1947 – June 30, 1953
William J. Donovan[5]	September 4, 1953 – August 21, 1954
John E. Peurifoy	December 3, 1954 – August 12, 1955 (Died near Hua Hin)
Max Waldo Bishop	January 9, 1956 – January 6, 1958
U. Alexis Johnson	February 14, 1958 – April 10, 1961
Kenneth Todd Young[5]	June 22, 1961 – August 19, 1963

---

1 Unless otherwise noted, each person named held the title of "Ambassador Extraordinary and Plenipotentiary" and also was a career State Department officer ((FSO) Foreign Service Officer.)
2 Donald Heath was accredited to Vietnam, Laos, and Cambodia, first as Envoy Extraordinary and Minister Plenipotentiary (EEMP), then as Ambassador Extraordinary and Plenipotentiary (AEP) when the legation was raised to embassy status. He was resident in Saigon.
3 Edmund A. Gullion was serving as Chargé d'affaires ad interim when the Legation in Saigon was raised to Embassy status on Jun 25, 1952 and Edwin Stanton was promoted from EEMP to AEP.
4 Special U.S. Representative with personal rank of Ambassador.
5 Political Appointee.
6 The legation in Bangkok was raised to embassy status March 18, 1947. At the same time the envoy was promoted to ambassador. Hereafter ambassadors were commissioned to Thailand rather than Siam, as previous envoys had been.

84 • TURNING POINTS

Graham A. Martin   November 7, 1963 – September 9, 1967
Leonard S. Unger   October 4, 1967 – November 19, 1973
William R. Kintner[5]   November 29, 1973 – March 15, 1975
Charles S. Whitehouse   May 30, 1975 – June 19, 1978

U.S. Ambassadors to Laos

Paul L. Guest[7]   August 1950 – December 1950
Donald R. Heath   December 29, 1950 – November 1, 1954
Charles Yost   November 1, 1954 – April 27, 1956
J. Graham Parsons   October 12, 1956 – February 8, 1958
Horace H. Smith   April 9, 1958 – June 21, 1960
Winthrop G. Brown   July 25, 1960 – June 28, 1962
Leonard S. Unger   July 25, 1962 – December 1, 1964
William H. Sullivan   December 23, 1964 – March 18, 1969
G. McMurtrie Godley   July 24, 1969 – April 23, 1973
Charles S. Whitehouse   September 20, 1973 – April 12, 1975
Thomas J. Corcoran[7]   August 1975 – March 1978

U.S. Ambassadors to Cambodia/Khmer Republic

Donald R. Heath   July 11, 1950 – October 2, 1954
Robert McClintock   October 2, 1954 – October 15, 1956
Carl W. Strom   December 7, 1956 – March 8, 1959
William C. Trimble   April 23, 1959 – June 8, 1962
Philip D. Sprouse   August 20, 1962 – March 3, 1964
Randolph A. Kidder   September 18, 1964
                          (*did not present credentials*)
Vacant   1964–1970
Emory C. Swank   September 15, 1970 – September 5, 1973
John Gunther Dean   April 3, 1974 – April 12, 1975

Credits: Wikipedia, Foreign Relations of the United States (FRUS), Foreign Service Lists and State Department Register

---

7 Chargé d'affairs *ad interim*

PART III

Deepening U.S. Involvement (1964–1968)

When Lyndon B. Johnson rose to the presidency on November 22, 1963, he promised himself to devote his efforts during the remainder of President Kennedy's "unfulfilled term" to achieving the goals he had set, including "seeing things through in Vietnam." He was convinced the broad lines of Kennedy's policy in Southeast Asia had been right and consistent with the goals the United States had set for itself in the world since the end of World War II. He shared President Kennedy's belief in the United States' commitment to Southeast Asia's security under the Southeast Asia Treaty Organization (SEATO) Treaty and noted Kennedy had, by late 1963, sent about 16,000 American troops to South Vietnam "to make good our SEATO pledge."[1]

The next day the new president met with Ambassador Henry Cabot Lodge who had returned for scheduled consultation with President Kennedy. Secretaries Rusk and McNamara, and Under Secretary of State George Ball, as well as CIA Director John McCone and National Security Advisor McGeorge Bundy (younger brother of William), were present. President Johnson found Ambassador Lodge optimistic regarding the prospects for the new military government which had succeeded Diệm but McCone much less encouraging. The president set forth his own "serious misgivings." He found many people critical of the removal of Diệm and shocked by his murder.[2] At about this time, Vice President Hubert Humphrey quoted Johnson as remarking while passing a portrait of Ngô Đình Diệm in a building, "We had a hand in killing him. Now it's happening here."[3] Richard Helms' biographer (Thomas Powers) much later wrote that Helms was one of a group which heard Johnson claim that. Kennedy's death had been caused "by unnamed persons seeking vengeance for the murder on November 1, 1963, of the President of South Vietnam, Ngo Dinh Diem [sic]."[4] C. L. Sulzberger wrote that he was startled to hear Johnson say in a 1966 conversation "Think back to when we assassinated

Diem [sic]…"[5] However, Johnson wrote that he told the meeting all that was in the past and the current task was to get the new Vietnamese Government on its feet and performing effectively.[6]

He also told Lodge there had been too much dissension in the American Mission in Sài Gòn earlier in the year and he wanted it to become a strong team working together under the ambassador as "the sole boss." He promised full support in Washington and soon sent Lodge a new deputy chief of mission, a new (CIA) station chief, a new United States Information Service Director, replacements for certain other officers, and, by the middle of the year, General William C. Westmoreland to replace General Paul Harkins as head of the Military Assistance Command, Vietnam (MACV).[7]

The president set forth his opinion:

> We had spent too much time and energy trying to shape other countries in our own image. It was too much to expect young and undeveloped countries to establish peace and order against well-trained and disciplined guerrillas, to create modern democratic political institutions, and to organize strong economies all at the same time. We could assist them with all three jobs, I said, but the main objective at present was to help them resist those using force against them. As for nation-building, I said that I thought the Vietnamese, Thai and other peoples of Asia knew far better than we did what sort of nations they wanted to build. We should not be too critical if they did not become thriving, modern twentieth century democracies in a week.[8]

Johnson also took up with Rusk, McNamara, McGeorge Bundy, and others the report of the Honolulu meeting originally prepared for President Kennedy. This report addressed the importance of strong American support for the new inexperienced government that had taken over in Sài Gòn, the problem of dealing with an expected $100 million deficit in the South Vietnamese budget in 1964, and the need for full consultation and united action among and by the members of the United States Mission in Vietnam. Although Rusk and McNamara had some reservations, Johnson found that most of his advisors believed the United States would be able to start withdrawing some of the military advisors by the end of the year (1963) and a majority of them by the end of 1965. Most of the people at the meeting thought that, over the next two years, it would be possible for the South Vietnamese to take over the training, supply, and support functions which the United States forces were currently performing.[9]

Although the Honolulu Conference had not changed the overall assessment which President Kennedy's principal advisors had earlier held on Vietnam, they recommended President Johnson "Underline, especially within government circles, the continuity of policy and direction under the new President." He agreed and approved National Security Action Memorandum (NSAM) 273 on November 26. He described this as his first important decision on Vietnam as president. It was "important not because it required any new actions but because it signaled our determination to persevere in the policies and actions in which we were already engaged." NSAM 273 read:

> It remains the central objective of the United States in South Vietnam to assist the people and government of that country to win their consent against the externally directed and supported Communist conspiracy. The test of all United States decisions and actions in this area should be the effectiveness of their contribution to this purpose.[10]

Johnson described NSAM 273 as restating the goal of withdrawing United States advisory forces earlier announced in an October 2 White House statement following the McNamara–Taylor report. It also reiterated the president's expectation that "All senior officers of the government will move energetically to insure [sic] the full unity of support for established United States policy in South Vietnam," assigned various specific actions to appropriate departments or agencies, and "defined the Mekong Delta as the area of greatest potential danger in the coming months." Johnson recorded that this was the view of Vietnam he had received during his first few days in office and was "shared by the top levels of the Mission in Saigon and by my principal advisers [sic] in Washington." He himself had an important reservation regarding this rather hopeful prognostication. He still thought Diệm's assassination had brought more problems than it had solved. He could not see much sign of men of experience and ability on hand in Sài Gòn among the Vietnamese ready to help their country. He also knew McNamara's October estimate about the withdrawal of United States advisors assumed political confusion in South Vietnam would not affect military operations. This same assumption, of increasingly questionable validity, underlay the Honolulu conclusions.[11]

Vietnam, in short, was well on the way to becoming what Richard Helms' biographer was to describe as "Lyndon Johnson's obsession and nemesis."[12]

Johnson and his advisors still felt, nevertheless, that increasing American assistance was improving Vietnamese morale and performance and that, while American expenditures for military and economic aid would have to increase as the Vietnamese Government increased its efforts against the Việt Cộng, the major American advisory effort could be terminated by the end of 1965.[13] Johnson recalled in *The Vantage Point* the history of the periods before, during, and after World War II. He "felt strongly that World War II might have been avoided if the United States in the 1930's [sic] had not given such an uncertain signal of its likely response to aggression in Europe and Asia." He cited the refusal by the House of Representatives to vote funds for the strengthening of

Guam in 1939 and 1940, the fight over the Selective Service Act in 1940 and "the 1-vote margin [203–202] in the House by which the length of service for draftees was extended half a year only four months before Pearl Harbor."[14]

Referring to his trip to East Asia, including Vietnam, as vice president at President Kennedy's request in May 1961, Johnson quoted the main conclusion he had presented to the president on his return:

> The fundamental decision required of the United States—and time is of the greatest importance—is whether we are to attempt to meet the challenge of Communist expansion now in Southeast Asia by a major effort in support of the forces of freedom in the area or throw in the towel. This decision must be made in a full realization of the very heavy and continuing costs involved in terms of money, of effort and of United States prestige. It must be made with the knowledge that at some point we may be faced with the further decision of whether we commit major United States forces to the area or cut our losses and withdraw should our other efforts fail. We must remain master of this decision. What we do in Southeast Asia should be part of a rational program to meet the threat we face in the region as a whole. It should include a clear-cut pattern of specific contributions to be expected by each partner according to his ability and resources. I recommend we proceed with a clear-cut and strong program of action. [15]

He remarked that President Kennedy agreed with this estimate and "regarded our commitment to Southeast Asia as a serious expression of our nation's determination to resist aggression. As President he [Kennedy] was determined to keep the promises we had made. He understood what they meant and what they might mean in the future."[16]

As the weeks went on, Johnson concluded that the Vietnamese problem was a more serious one than earlier reports had indicated. Early in December, he read a review of the military situation "developed by the State Department's intelligence analysts," which "concluded that the military effort had been deteriorating in important ways for several months." At about the same time, Ambassador Lodge forwarded a report of increased Việt Cộng influence, operations, and control in a northern delta province. Johnson thought mission reporting earlier in 1963 had reflected too much wishful thinking on the part of some observers and too much reliance on Vietnamese statistics and information. He asked McNamara to return from a December NATO meeting by way of Sài Gòn. McNamara spent December 18–20, 1963, in Vietnam and, on December 21, made a gloomy report to the president. He thought that, unless they were reversed in the next two or three months, current trends would lead to "neutralization at best and more likely to a Communist-controlled state." Johnson commented that "neutralization" at the time meant application of the de Gaulle formula for unification and neutralization of both Vietnams with withdrawal of all foreign forces. He wrote that most thinking people "recognized that the De Gaulle [sic] formula for neutralization would have meant the swift Communization of all Vietnam, and probably of Laos and Cambodia as well." He noted that President Kennedy had brushed the French proposal aside as irrelevant in a CBS interview on September 2, 1963.[17]

McNamara thought the new Vietnamese government was "indecisive and drifting" and that United States Mission reporting was very weak. He told the president, "Viet Cong [sic] progress has been great during the period since the coup [November 1], with my best guess being that the situation has in fact been deteriorating in the countryside since July to a greater extent than we realize because of our undue dependence on distorted Vietnamese reporting."[18] Ambassador Lodge, General Harkins, and Vietnamese General Dương Văn Minh ("Big Minh") were less pessimistic but Johnson had more confidence in McNamara's estimate of the situation. He accepted recommendations by McNamara and CIA Director McCone for improvement of intelligence reporting. The Embassy "refined and expanded province reporting" and Ambassador Lodge initiated a weekly personal report to the president describing problems as well as progress. In *The Vantage Point*, Johnson wrote that all the reporting, plus those observations he received from individual travelers inside and outside the government, and from press and television reports, gave him more complete and balanced information than could be realized by those "outside the mainstream of official reporting."[19]

Nevertheless, with the year 1964 there was more and more bad news. As Assistant Secretary Bundy put it in his "Path to Vietnam" speech, Vietnam "wallowed in confusion" for a year and a half after the overthrow and death of Ngô Đình Diệm.[20] In an article published in the *Foreign Service Journal* of July 1968,[21] former Ambassador Frederick E. Nolting was to express the opinion that errors committed in the last months of the Kennedy Administration, inherited by President Johnson, and, in Nolting's view, compounded during Johnson's administration, were so great as to be practically non-redeemable. In his article, Ambassador Nolting cited a letter he had written to President Johnson on February 25, 1965, regretting his inability to get an appointment to see the president and stating that his decision to retire from the Foreign Service "has been influenced by my strong disapproval of certain actions which were taken last fall in relation to Vietnam, with predictable adverse consequences ..." Nolting went on in the article to make several points from his own recollections in elaboration of his theme:

> [President Kennedy] and his government decided on a negotiated settlement in Laos and at the same time a substantial increase in American support to the Government and people of South Vietnam. This must have seemed rather strange to the strategists in Moscow, Peking,

and Hanoi [sic], who despite their differences, tended to look upon the whole of Indo-China [sic] as one strategic area. They saw their opportunity and did not fail to take advantage of it.

The treaty on Laos, negotiated by Averell Harriman, signed in Geneva in 1962 and never lived up to by the Communist signatories, promptly turned the Ho Chi Minh trail into the "Harriman Memorial Highway" (I did not coin the phrase). The treaty on Laos gave immunity to the North Vietnamese to take control of the Northern Provinces of Laos and to infiltrate South Vietnam while tying the hands of our side.

Meanwhile the Viet Cong attempt to undermine progress in South Vietnam and to paralyze its government was making alarming headway. South Vietnamese government officials, non-military assassinated or kidnapped by the Viet Cong in 1960 … minor officials, for the most part, who were carrying on the work of the Diem [sic] government, the agricultural extension agents, road engineers, dredge foremen, district chiefs, school teachers, doctors and nurses, anti-malaria teams and others—2,000 of them were killed or kidnapped in one year. Was this a popular uprising against an unpopular government as some would have us believe?

An evident rapport was established between Vice President Johnson and President Diệm on the former's visit to Vietnam in May 1961. President Kennedy promptly approved an agreement worked out between Diệm and Nolting after General Maxwell Taylor's visit providing for "vigorous new programs of action to protect the Vietnamese people and to win them solidly to the government's side—without enlarging the area of conflict, without inviting outside interference, without undercutting the essential spirit of Vietnamese nationalism and without the use of American combat forces." Nolting's instructions were to build "a bridge of confidence strong enough to carry the load of advice and aid which we were giving."

In Nolting's view, this program of help and advice worked well for two years. The change in the policy of supporting Diệm to one which would have the Kennedy Administration "turn on its proven ally and connive in his overthrow" was, he thought, sudden and disastrous. He believed the causes for the change against which, he said, Vice President Johnson had warned, were:

> First, the press—the overwhelming weight of public information on Vietnam was prejudiced and slanted towards the editorial line of the reporters' papers. This had a profound effect on American public opinion.
>
> Second, in the State Department and even in the White House staff there was a small group who had been against Diem [sic] for years. They had been squelched and silenced for a while by President Kennedy's earlier forthright decisions but they remained unconvinced.
>
> Third, there came in mid 1963 the Buddhist crisis. A clever and inhumane political plot came through to the American public as a genuine revolt against religious persecution exactly as the Buddhist agitators had intended.

Nolting went on to write that after his recall from Vietnam in August 1963 he had asked Secretary Rusk, "Why the State Department had turned so sharply against the Diem [sic] government?" Rusk had replied, "We cannot stand any more burnings." Nolting interpreted this to mean the policy makers in Washington were lacking in farsightedness. He wrote that "For them to yield to popular misconceptions and encourage a coup d'état was in my judgment unjust to an honorable ally and irresponsible to the American people."

For some other observers too, ever after, Diệm's fate kept turning up in any discussion of the American problem in Vietnam, sort of like King Charles' head in the studies of David Copperfield's friend Mr. Dick.[22] To Ellen Hammer:

> The overthrow of the Diem [sic] government marked the end of nine years of stability and relative calm in this turbulent area of the world. His administration, in spite of its mistakes and its failure to promote healthy political life in the country had finally evolved into a coherent national regime. And Diem's overthrow was considered by his formidable opponents Ho Chi Minh [sic] and Mao Tse-tung as marking the end of the attempt to create an independent state in South Vietnam free of Communist interference.[23]

Hammer also noted the abrupt removal of Diệm, bringing down the framework of authority which "for better or worse, had held the nation together," led to anarchy. The National Assembly and the constitution were abolished by the military coup group. Arbitrary purges which upset the administration, a collapse of the strategic hamlet program, and desertions from the Army and militia were followed by an extension of Việt Cộng control over large areas in Central Vietnam theretofore considered secure.[24] "In the countryside Diem's [sic] overthrow meant to the still Confucianist population that his policy of resistance to the Viet Cong had failed, and that the 'mandate of Heaven' had passed to the Communists."[25]

Guenter Lewy cites a *New York Times* editorial of November 3, 1963, which "hailed the new rulers of South Vietnam as a group of dedicated anti-Communists, saying that if the new regime identified itself with the aspirations of the people it would have 'taken a long step towards repulsing further Communist inroads throughout Southeast Asia.'" In fact, he wrote, "the overthrow of Diem [sic] did not lead to a regime more responsive to the needs of the people of South Vietnam and it brought with it a dangerous degree of instability."[26] Chapter 5 of Former Prime Minister Nguyễn Cao Kỳ's book is entitled: "1964: The year of the seven coups."

Neither the "remnants of the VNQDD" (Vietnam Nationalist Party) party nor the "deeply divided Dai Viet" party could exercise political power effectively as some people in Washington had hopefully expected because neither party had a popular base and because feuds, factions, and personal conflicts split the military and civilian elite.[27]

Hammer wrote that, for some two years after the fall of Diệm, nine coup-generated governments followed in succession with a constant increase in governmental corruption and no real attempt to replace the 1956 constitution. The original coup group lasted only three months, being in turn overthrown by General Nguyễn Khánh whose erratic tenure lasted a few months longer and saw communal violence between Buddhists and Catholics in Sài Gòn and in northern towns. It also saw the emergence of the "Committee of Public Salvation" in Central Vietnam which appeared to try, under the inspiration of Buddhist layman Lê Khắc Quyến, to keep Khánh from setting up a military dictatorship. However, by June 1965, after ostensibly civilian interludes under President Phan Khắc Sửu and Prime Ministers Trần Văn Hương and Phan Huy Quát, a new military junta took over with the agreement of the civilian politicians. General Nguyễn Văn Thiệu was head of state and Air Vice-Marshal Nguyễn Cao Kỳ was prime minister.[28]

President Johnson found all this Vietnamese political turmoil discouraging and thought "the South Vietnamese often seemed to have a strong impulse toward political suicide."[29] Discouraged as he was by the South Vietnamese, who seemed to be their own worst enemies, he "felt even more impatient with those who were always ready only to criticize." He thought the South Vietnamese "needed and deserved understanding and patience, not constant vilification."[30]

As Air Vice-Marshal Kỳ saw it, two factors thwarted all American efforts to resolve the political chaos in post-Diệm South Vietnam. First, the Americans, by keeping the "hated" President Diệm in power so long, and then dumping him so suddenly, had created a political vacuum which only the communists could exploit. The non-communist Vietnamese were incapable of filling the vacuum. They did not know how. Going from French colony to American dependency, they had never learned how to govern themselves on their own. Secondly, the Americans had no clear-cut ideas of what they wanted; "… they arrived full of good intentions but without any real understanding of the problems involved, without any real policy, and so took refuge in makeshift accommodations." "They tried to run the Saigon Government by Capitol Hill methods. They never understood that it is impossible to impose a western mask on an eastern face." The revolution against Diệm was never a real revolution. It was a coup carried out by "opportunists rather than idealists." They were never able to unite sufficiently "to select effective leaders and give them complete support."[31]

On the other hand, President Johnson and other Americans might have been forgiven some bemusement over the coup attempt which started on February 19, 1965.

Kỳ, in his book, admits that a few days earlier he had decided to organize a coup against Khánh which fell through. When the February 19 General Lâm Văn Phát coup started, Kỳ first helped Khánh to flee to Đà Lạt and then had him flown back to Biên Hòa near Sài Gòn to confer with the other generals, and then once again sent Khánh back to Đà Lạt after obtaining his consent to support Phát or anyone else. Kỳ then forced Phát to abandon his coup under threat of aerial bombardment. The generals then named Khánh a roving ambassador and sent him out of the country. The preceding September (1964), Phát had supported a coup attempt by General Dương Văn Đức. Kỳ had concluded that Đức had started this earlier coup because he had over-interpreted a remark by Kỳ to the effect that something would have to be done about Khánh. Đức had taken over most of Sài Gòn, including the Army headquarters and the radio station. Then General Phát had gone on the air to support General Đức. Phát's line sounded to Kỳ like too much of a return to Diệm's ideas, so he forced Đức to back down under threat of air bombardment. In the February 1965 coup, Phát enjoyed the support of one Colonel Phạm Ngọc Thảo, a Catholic who was also an ex-Việt Minh officer and, by the way, assigned to the Vietnamese Embassy in Washington. Thảo had ostensibly gone AWOL from the Embassy and turned up in Sài Gòn to help, or perhaps push, Phát. When initial reports indicated the coup was succeeding, the Vietnamese ambassador to the United States, General Trần Thiện Khiêm, held a press conference in Washington announcing his support of Phát. When the coup failed, everybody wondered what would happen to Ambassador Khiêm. In the event, the authorities in Sài Gòn decided Khiêm had made no official statement to the government on the subject, and they really could not take notice of press conferences. Ambassador Khiêm later served in high posts including as ambassador to Taiwan and prime minister of Vietnam. Colonel Thảo, in the aftermath of the coup, was shot, wounded, escaped, and was shot again, this time fatally, according to all reports.

Johnson did observe that the communists were profiting from the damage done to South Vietnamese morale and leadership by the political confusion.

He asked Secretary McNamara and General Maxwell Taylor to go to Vietnam again in March 1964 for another look at the situation and preparation of recommendations on how to improve it.[32] They reported "things had been getting worse, particularly in matters of security, morale and political effectiveness and that Hanoi's [sic] involvement in the insurgency, always significant, has been increasing." McNamara again reviewed the disastrous consequences to be anticipated if South Vietnam went under to the communists and recommended that "The U.S. at all levels must continue to make it emphatically clear that we are prepared to furnish assistance and support for as long as it takes to bring the insurgency under control."[33] He also recommended some specific actions including assisting the South Vietnamese to increase their forces by 50,000 men, improving the quality and quantity of military supplies being sent to the South Vietnamese, and "providing several forms of budgetary support to help the Vietnamese bear the costs of an expanding war." McNamara ended his report by stating:

> If the Khanh [sic] government can stay in power and the above actions can be carried out rapidly it is my judgment that the situation in South Vietnam can be significantly improved in the next four to six months. The present deterioration may continue for a part of this period, but I believe it can be levelled out and some improvement will become visible during the period. I therefore believe that this course of action should be urgently pursued while we prepare such additional actions as may be necessary for success.[34]

McNamara further recommended that "we by ready to carry out, on three days' notice, certain border control actions as well as retaliation against North Vietnam. We should also be in a position, the Secretary said, to conduct a program of graduated military pressure against the north on a month's notice. The Defense Secretary specified that he was not in favor of these actions 'at this time' but was recommending that we be prepared if they should prove necessary in the future."[35]

Johnson wrote that McNamara reported that Ambassador Lodge and the members of the country team in Sài Gòn (including the senior representatives of the Agency for International Development AID, CIA, Defense, and the United Stated Information Agency) favored his proposals. He remarked that all concerned departments and agencies in Washington also favored them and that nobody opposed any of the military recommendations in the National Security Council (NSC) meetings. He did note "the Joint Chiefs of Staff thought the proposed actions might not be sufficient and favored taking immediate measures against the north." Johnson shared two principal objections of his senior advisors when the question of such action was raised then and later in the year. He feared the South Vietnamese political and military base was too fragile to permit measures which would invite increased action by the "enemy," and he feared that striking the North might lead to involvement by the Chinese or Soviets or both. He "approved the twelve actions on the McNamara list and instructed the Executive Departments to carry them out but rejected proposals to do more than that."[36]

The president concluded the leaders in Hà Nội had decided in the summer of 1964 that it was time to develop their military operations from a guerrilla-warfare level to a more conventional general offensive. They had developed large units in the South and by the end of 1964 were sending North Vietnamese regulars into South Vietnam to take part in the war. They clearly intended, he thought, to smash the South Vietnamese Army, provoke a political collapse in Sài Gòn, and "take over."[37]

Assistant Secretary Bundy, in his "Path to Vietnam" speech, recalled that intensification of North Vietnamese and Việt Cộng terrorist and military action had started almost immediately upon Diệm's overthrow and "demonstrated—if it needed demonstrating—that the struggle was not over Diem [sic], despite Communist claims and honest liberal qualms, but was an attempt to destroy non-Communist nationalism of any sort in South Vietnam."[38] Bundy said that "In early 1964 President Johnson expressly reaffirmed all the essential elements of the Kennedy administration policies publicly through every action and through firm internal directives."

"It is simply not true to say there was any change in policy in this period toward greater military emphasis, much less major new military actions. Further actions were not excluded—as they had not been in 1954 or 1961—but President Johnson's firm object right up to February 1965 was to make the policy adopted in late 1961 work if it could possibly be done, including the fullest possible emphasis on pacification and the whole political and civilian aspect."[39]

Commenting on the developments of the summer of 1964 described by President Johnson and cited above, Bundy noted the period brought a new phase but not a change in policy. That was not to come until the following year after the North Vietnamese had markedly increased infiltration of troops, including native Northerners, into the South.

Meanwhile, at the beginning of August 1964, there was the Gulf of Tonkin episode. Bundy told the BBC interviewers that this incident in which "American naval ships on patrol in the Gulf of Tonkin were attacked, and there were two responding United States attacks on North Vietnamese naval bases,"[40] "was totally unexpected and unpremeditated on the part of the Johnson administration."[41]

President Johnson recorded for his part that Blair Seaborn, the new Canadian leader of his country's delegation to the International Control Commission for Vietnam, en route to Hà Nội June 17, 1964, had been briefed on Johnson's first peace suggestion and asked to:

> ... sound out the authorities in North Vietnam regarding the chances for peace. We told him he could assure Ho Chi Minh [sic] and his colleagues that the United States had no intention of trying to overthrow their regime. We had no wish to retain military bases or a military position in the south. We were, of course, aware of Hanoi's [sic] control of

> the Viet Cong [sic]. We asked only that the leaders in Hanoi abide by the agreements reached with the French at Geneva in 1954 and in the Laos settlement in 1962: keep their men inside their own territory and stop sending military supplies into the south. If our peace proposal was accepted, we would assist all the countries of the area in their economic development. North Vietnam could benefit from that improvement along with her neighbors.[42]

Johnson noted that Seaborn, who both presented the American views and listened to the North Vietnamese views as a "dispassionate intermediary," got nothing from the leaders in Hà Nội but propaganda to the effect that the United States should withdraw totally, that a "neutral" regime should be set up under the National Liberation Front's program and that "the front would have to take a leading role in determining the future of the country."[43]

Johnson interpreted the North Vietnamese reply, and a similar reply given again in August, as slamming the door shut on the peace offer. He concluded the North Vietnamese did not want "to limit their actions or to negotiate; they were interested in only one thing, victory on the battlefield. This experience of trying to open an avenue to peace negotiations and coming up against a roadblock was repeated dozens of times over the next several years."[44] Recalling he was not going to "take charge of the war or carry out actions that would risk a war with Communist China," Johnson also denied in *The Vantage Point* that he was the "peace" candidate, as opposed to "war" candidate Goldwater, in the presidential election of 1964. He claimed:

> The American people knew what they were voting for in 1964. They knew Lyndon Johnson was not going to pull up stakes and run. They knew I was not going to go back on my country's word. They knew I would not repudiate the pledges of my predecessors in the presidency. They knew too that I was not going to wipe out Hanoi [sic] or use atom bombs to defoliate the Vietnamese jungles. I was going to do what had to be done to protect our interests and to keep our promises. And that is what I did.[45]

The editors of the Pentagon Papers claim that for six months before the Tonkin Gulf incident the Johnson Administration "had been mounting clandestine attacks against North Vietnam while planning to obtain a Congressional resolution that the Administration regarded as the equivalent of a declaration of war." The editors go on to state that the administration did not reveal these clandestine attacks when the incident occurred and actually pushed the resolution through Congress on August 7. Then, according to the editors, the administration, "again drawing on a prepared plan," secretly sent a Canadian emissary to Hà Nội to warn "Premier Pham Van Dong [sic] that the resolution meant North Vietnam must halt the Communist-led insurgencies in South Vietnam and Laos or suffer the consequences."[46]

The editors maintained that "The magnitude of this threat to Hanoi [sic], the nature and extent of the covert military operations and the intent of the administration to use the resolution to commit the nation to open warfare, if this later proved desirable, were all kept secret."[47] They remarked that the Papers portrayed the period from the beginning of 1964 to the clashes in the Gulf of Tonkin in August "as a critical period when the groundwork was laid for the wider war that followed."[48]

The Papers spoke of:

> ... an elaborate program of covert military operations against the State of North Vietnam under the code name Operation *Plan 34A*. President Johnson ordered the program, on the recommendation of Secretary McNamara, in the hope, held very faintly by the intelligence community, that "progressively escalating pressure" from the clandestine attacks might eventually force Hanoi to order the Viet Cong guerrillas in Vietnam and the Pathet Lao in Laos to halt their insurrections.[49]

The Papers also refer to American destroyer patrols in the Gulf of Tonkin "as a show of force" and intended to collect "the kind of intelligence on North Vietnamese warning radars and coastal defenses that would be useful to *34A* raiding parties, or, in the event of a bombing campaign to pilots." The Papers state that:

> ... although the highest levels of the administration sent the destroyers into the gulf while the *34A* raids were taking place, the Pentagon study, as part of its argument that a deliberate provocation was not intended, in effect says that the administration did not believe that the North Vietnamese would dare to attack the ships.
>
> ...
>
> But the study makes it clear that the physical presence of the destroyers provided the elements for the Tonkin clash.[50]

President Johnson put it all quite differently:[51]

- Early Sunday morning August 2, 1964, the White House situation room told him USS *Maddox* had been attacked by three Democratic Republic of Vietnam (DRV) PT (patrol torpedo) boats some 300 miles off the North Vietnamese coast in the Tonkin Gulf.
- *Maddox* had returned fire with its 5-inch battery and called for air support from USS *Ticonderoga*. The aircraft carrier's jets had left one PT dead in the water and the other two damaged and retiring. No casualties to *Maddox*.
- *Maddox* was on DESOTO (DeHaven Special Operations off Tsingtao[52]) patrol to spot evidence of Hà Nội's infiltration of men

and material into South Vietnam by sea and to gather electronic intelligence like the Soviet trawlers operating off the American coast.
- Johnson and his advisors attributed the attack to an over-eager North Vietnamese commander and decided against retaliation but to continue the patrol reinforced by another destroyer and provided with air cover.
- Operation *34A* strikes by the Vietnamese Navy were not connected with DESOTO and were intended to interfere with Hà Nội's deployment of men and supplies to the south by sea. Members of House and Senate designated to oversee intelligence operations had been briefed on *34A* in January, May, June (twice), and early August 1964. McNamara briefed members of Senate Foreign Relations Committee in a closed session on August 3, 1964.
- One *34A* attack occurred July 30 when *Maddox* was 120 miles away. A second *34A* attack took place on the night of August 3 when the DESOTO patrol was 70 miles away. DESOTO commanders did not know locale or timing of the attacks. Nevertheless, after the first attack on *Maddox*, its track was moved further north to gain even further separation from Vietnamese activity.
- Although deciding to treat the first North Vietnamese attack on *Maddox* as an accident, the U.S. sent a warning via the Voice of America about "grave consequences which would inevitably result from any further unprovoked offensive military action against United States Forces."
- On August 4, 1964, mid-morning Washington time, "the North Vietnamese struck again at our destroyers." Johnson consulted Rusk, McNamara, Vance, McCone, and Bundy at lunch. "The unanimous view of these advisers [*sic*] was that we could not ignore this second provocation and that the attack required retaliation."
- In the light of a report from *Maddox* questioning "whether the many reports of enemy torpedo firings were all valid [during the second attack—August 4], Johnson ordered McNamara to investigate and clarify." "Admiral Sharp called McNamara to report that, after checking all the reports and evidence, he had no doubt whatsoever that an attack had taken place. McNamara and his associates reached the same conclusion. Detailed studies made after the incident confirmed this judgment."
- Johnson summoned the NSC for a meeting at 6:15 pm "to discuss in detail the incident and our plans for sharp but limited response."

At 7:00 pm, he "met with the Congressional leadership in the White House for the same purpose."
- He told the leadership that he "believed a Congressional resolution of support for our entire position in Southeast Asia was necessary and would strengthen our hand." He recalled he had given the same advice to President Eisenhower who had followed it in the Middle East and Formosa crises, in both of which Congress had backed him with resolutions. He thought President Truman could easily have obtained such a resolution when he had gone to the defense of South Korea and that his one mistake had been in not asking for it.
- Johnson's first major decision on Vietnam, he said, had been to reaffirm Kennedy's policies. His second was to retaliate for the Tonkin Gulf attacks and to seek a Congressional Resolution in support of U.S. Southeast Asia policy.
- He announced the attacks at about 11:30 pm, Washington time. They damaged or destroyed 25 boats and 90 percent of the oil storage tanks at Vinh for a loss of two planes (and Lieutenant (junior grade) Alvarez, the first American pilot shot down and taken prisoner in North Vietnam in this war).
- The next day he approved a draft "Southeast Asia Resolution" which Secretary Rusk and Under Secretary Ball had worked out with Congressional leaders. In his message transmitting it to Congress, Johnson "made it clear that I was asking the support of the Congress not merely to reply to attacks on our own forces, or simply to carry out our obligations in South Vietnam but to be in a position to do what had to be done to fulfill our responsibilities in all of Southeast Asia."[53]
- Johnson wrote he had "urged free hearings of the Committees on Foreign Relations and Armed Services in the Senate and the Committees on Foreign Affairs and Armed Services in the House. He wrote that he had also asked the leadership to insist on roll calls both in committees and on the floors of both houses so that the record would be complete and indisputable." "The vote in the Senate was 88 to 2 [Ernest Gruening, Alaska, and Wayne Morse, Oregon] and in the House unanimous 416–0." [There was in fact a minimum of discussion in the Senate and the House took only 40 minutes to make its decision.][54] However, as Johnson accurately observed, the exchange on the Senate floor between Senator Cooper of Kentucky

and Senator Fulbright spelled out clearly that the resolution gave the president advance authority to act as he might deem necessary in regard to the defense of South Vietnam or any other country covered by the SEATO Treaty unless the Senate should withdraw its approval at a later date by concurrent resolution.[55]

Former Secretary of State Dean Rusk told the BBC interviewers that the Tonkin Gulf Resolution was an exercise of the war powers of Congress. The interviewers remarked, "And yet one is also very impressed with the senators who still seem to be convinced that they were given the impression that a much more limited intention was made or intended when it came to implementing those words despite the wording given to them." Rusk replied:

> In 1966 Senator Morse, a man for whom I had a high regard but who was an opponent throughout, made a motion to rescind the Tonkin Gulf Resolution. He only had the support of five Senators, four besides himself, in 1966. It's my personal view that Senators ought to vote, and that the Executive branch of the government has a right to rely upon the way they vote without all the whining around the edges. Let them bring the matter up and vote on it so we will know where they stand.[56]

The text of the Southeast Asia Resolution (Public Law 88–408 [H. J. Res 1145] 78 Stat. 384], approved Aug. 10, 1964), especially the second section thereof, cited by Assistant Secretary Bundy in his "Path to Vietnam" speech, seems clear enough to justify Rusk's impatience with any legislators who claimed at a later date they had not known what they were agreeing to.[57] Guenter Lewy discussed the charges of duplicity involving "the second attack on the *Maddox* on 4 August which allegedly never took place and is said to have been manufactured by the administration, in order to have an excuse to expand the war and obtain congressional approval for it." He judged that:

> It is true that the president seized upon the incident in order to approve and carry out measures that had been recommended to him earlier, but this does not establish that the attack was deliberately provoked, let alone that it rests on a fabrication. While the sonar and radar readings and the visual sightings of torpedoes can be questioned as unbelievable and inconclusive, there is other unambiguous evidence which leaves no doubt of the fact of an attack. As McNamara told the Senate Foreign Relations Committee in closed session in February 1968, the *Maddox* was able to intercept uncoded North Vietnamese orders to patrol boats to attack the American ships as well as transmissions from the North Vietnamese boats to their headquarters reporting on the progress of the sea battle.[58]

It was quite clear at the end of 1964, as noted above, that things were going badly in Vietnam. The editors of the Pentagon Papers tell us the administration had reached a "general consensus" in September 1964 that air attacks against North Vietnam would probably have to be conducted early in 1965.[59]

They report that new reprisal strikes were, in fact, ordered against North Vietnam on February 8, 1965, and that the president ordered the start of *Rolling Thunder* (sustained bombing of North Vietnam), on February 13. The editors saw Johnson as "moving and being moved toward war, but reluctant and hesitant to act until the end."[60]

As noted earlier, General Westmoreland had replaced General Harkins as COMUSMACV (Commander U.S. Military Assistance Command, Vietnam) on June 20, 1964. General Maxwell Taylor replaced Henry Cabot Lodge as ambassador on July 7. The editors of the Pentagon Papers report that, on August 18, Ambassador Taylor had cabled from Sài Gòn that he agreed with an "assumption" held by the administration in Washington that the Việt Cộng "could not be defeated and the South Vietnamese Government preserved by a counter guerrilla war confined to South Vietnam itself."[61] He recommended, according to the Papers, "a carefully orchestrated bombing attack on NVN [North Vietnam], directed primarily at infiltration and other military targets" with "January 1, 1965, as a target D-day."[62] The Papers report the ambassador suggested the bombing effort could serve either to "persuade the regime of Gen. Nguyen Khanh [sic] to achieve some political stability and get on seriously with the pacification program or to prevent 'a collapse of national morale' in Saigon [sic] whatever progress Khanh made." Reflecting doubts about the longevity of the Khánh government, Taylor said that "before bombing the North the United States would also have to send Army Hawk anti-aircraft missiles to the Saigon and Danang [sic] areas to protect the airfields there against retaliatory Communist air attacks—assumed possible from China or North Vietnam—and to land a force of American Marines at Danang [sic] to protect the airbase there against possible ground assaults."[63]

President Johnson wrote that the idea of striking at North Vietnam, either in reprisal actions or in a sustained campaign, had been long discussed in Washington, in Sài Gòn, and in the press. The Joint Chiefs had argued that certain proposals Secretary McNamara had made in March 1964 might not be strong enough and that immediate attacks on military targets in the North would be preferable. The president recalled that CIA Director McCone "felt strongly that increased action in the South should be accompanied by intensive air and naval action against the North." He stated that:

> ... during my first year in the White House no formal proposal for an air campaign against North Vietnam ever came to me as the agreed suggestion of my principal advisers [sic]. Whenever the subject came up, one or another of them usually mentioned the risk of giving Communist China an excuse for massive intervention in Vietnam. Rusk was concerned that

putting direct pressure on North Vietnam might encourage the Soviets to raise the level of tension around Berlin, in the Middle East, or elsewhere. I fully concurred. Our goals in Vietnam were limited, and so were our actions. I wanted to keep them that way.[64]

Johnson also recalled that many people in State and Defense feared heavy air attacks against the North might cause Hà Nội to undertake an open invasion of South Vietnam or at least step up the guerrilla war. American officials in Sài Gòn and in Washington felt, politically and militarily, the South Vietnamese could not survive such an escalation by the communists.[65] Johnson called Ambassador Taylor back to Washington on consultation early in September "to hear in detail his estimate of internal political weaknesses." He also wanted to discuss further steps to take or get the Vietnamese to take. "Finally, I thought those in Washington who were urging military action against the North should hear from our man on the scene just how uncertain the base we were operating from would be if their advice was taken."[66]

On September 9, President Johnson met with Ambassador Taylor, Secretaries Rusk and McNamara, General Earle Wheeler, CIA Director McCone, Assistant Secretaries of State William P. Bundy and Robert J. Manning, and Assistant Secretary of Defense John T. McNaughton. Johnson heard "a recommendation for several specific actions developed by the Departments of State and Defense after consulting with Taylor." These included resumption of patrols in the Gulf of Tonkin and preparation to retaliate against North Vietnam should there be an attack on U.S. units or "special," presumably new in kind or intensity, Việt Cộng action against South Vietnam. Although Secretary McNamara told the president the Joint Chiefs of Staff supported the proposals, he pointed out that the chief of staff of the Air Force and the commandant of the Marine Corps "thought it would also be necessary to carry out extensive air strikes against the North." The chairman and the Army and Navy chiefs had been persuaded by Ambassador Taylor that any drastic action, presumably such as extensive air strikes against the North, might produce a communist reaction that would be too much for the South Vietnamese to handle. Johnson wrote that, after listening to such gloomy positions, he asked whether anyone present had doubts about Vietnam being worth all the effort contemplated and whether anyone had a different view on the military recommendation presented to him. Ambassador Taylor quickly replied that "we could not afford to let Hanoi [sic] win in the interests of our overall position in Asia and in the world." General Wheeler said loss of South Vietnam would mean, eventually, the loss of Southeast Asia. CIA Director McCone agreed and, "So did Secretary Rusk, with considerable emphasis." Johnson approved the recommendation, "After serious consideration and a great deal of discussion."[67]

According to the editors of the Pentagon Papers, the president "ordered a number of interim measures in National Security Action Memorandum 314." They report the final paragraph read:

> These decisions are governed by a prevailing judgement that the first order of business at present is to take actions which will help to strengthen the fabric of the Government of South Vietnam; to the extent that the situation permits, such action should precede larger decisions. If such larger decisions are required at any time by a change in the situation, they will be taken.[68]

The interim measures, according to the Papers, included:

- Resumption of DESOTO patrols in the Tonkin Gulf, initially well beyond the 12-mile limit, clearly disassociated from *34A* operations but with air cover from aircraft carriers;
- Reactivation of *34A* operations with the GVN (Government of Vietnam) ready to admit, justify, and legitimize them on the basis of the facts of Việt Cộng infiltration by sea;
- Arrangement with the Lao Government of Souvanna Phouma to permit "limited GVN air and ground operations into the corridor areas of [Southeastern] Laos, together with Lao air strikes and possible of U.S. armed aerial reconnaissance";
- Preparation to launch "tit for tat" reprisal air strikes against the DRV.[69]

President Johnson recorded that, on November 1, after a Việt Cộng attack damaging U.S. aircraft at Biên Hòa near Sài Gòn, and one on Christmas Eve which killed Americans and Vietnamese, he turned down requests by the Joint Chiefs and Ambassador Taylor for retaliatory bombing because he was worried not only about the South Vietnamese Government's ability to handle communist reaction but also about the possibility the communists would strike back in turn against American dependents in Sài Gòn. However, he "was persuaded increasingly that our forces deserved the support that air strikes against the source of aggression would represent." He also observed that infiltration of arms and men into the South continued steadily and that, by the end of 1964, "We were picking up North Vietnamese Army troops wearing regulation uniforms and carrying full field equipment," and that "These regulars were not just replacements for Viet Cong units, as they had been in the past, but members of organized battalion formations."[70]

Assistant Secretary Bundy addressed the circumstances attending the decisions soon to be made about the taking of new military measures in his "Path to Vietnam" speech. He said a review was undertaken at the end of 1964, as the situation declined politically and militarily. It appeared the administration could choose:

- To continue the existing policy, improving it in every way possible within its limits;
- To take "new and major military measures" while sticking with the original basic objectives;
- To move toward withdrawal.

Circumstances, he said, convinced all concerned that the first choice was no longer a valid one and would amount to acceptance for South Vietnam "of Communist control achieved through externally backed subversion and aggression." "This was," he added, "a straight practical judgment. It ran against the grain of every desire of the President and his advisers [sic]." Bundy was "sure it was a right judgment—accepted at the time by most sophisticated observers and, the light of reflective examination now accepted [1967], I believe, by virtually everyone who knows the situation at all at first hand." In short, Bundy believed the choices had narrowed to two—move toward withdrawal or do much more to have a military effect and also to buck up South Vietnamese morale and will to continue.[71]

Bundy stressed that the basis for the decisions, starting in February (1965) to start bombing, in March to introduce small numbers of combat forces, and in July to send in major United States combat forces, "depended on an overall view of the situation and on an overall view that what had been going on for years was for all practical purposes aggression—and indeed this term dates from late 1961 or early 1962 in the statements of senior administration spokesmen." He also refuted the charge it was the United States which had "unilaterally changed the character of the war in the direction of a conventional conflict," a charge based on the allegation Hà Nội was refraining from sending in its regulars in units with the tacit understanding America would not bomb North Vietnam in exchange for such restraint. He stated that evidence available from the spring of 1965 onward showed that:

> ... one North Vietnamese regiment entered South Vietnam by December 1964, and we know that several other regiments entered in the spring of 1965 on timetables of infiltration that can only have reflected decisions taken in Hanoi [sic] prior to the beginning of the bombing ... The point is that Hanoi, as we suspected then and later proved, had taken major steps to raise the level of the war before the bombing began.[72]

President Johnson wrote that in late January 1965 he gave General Westmoreland permission, which the general had requested, to use American jet aircraft against the Việt Cộng in support of Vietnamese troops "when he considered it absolutely necessary," and that Westmoreland first used this authority late in February. Early in January, Ambassador Taylor had told the president that failure to take positive action would mean acceptance of defeat in the fairly near future and the president's "civilian advisors were driven to the same conclusion by the hard facts." McGeorge Bundy, in a memorandum of January 27, told the president that he and Secretary McNamara had concluded current policy could lead only to disastrous defeat and that "the time had come to use more power than we had thus far deployed." They saw a choice between using our military power in the Far East to force a change of communist policy or concentrating resources on a negotiations track in order to salvage "what little can be preserved with no major addition to our present military risks." They were inclined to favor the use of more military power, the first alternative, but thought both courses should be looked into carefully, and programs for the pursuit of each developed and argued out in the president's presence. McGeorge Bundy and McNamara pointed out Secretary Rusk did not agree with their assessment. Rusk thought the consequences of both escalation and withdrawal were so bad a way had to be found to make the current policy work. Bundy and McNamara believed this was not possible.[73]

Consequently, the president asked Secretary Rusk "to instruct his experts once again to consider all possible ways for finding a peaceful solution." He also asked Bundy to go to Sài Gòn with a team of military and civilian experts for a "hard look at the situation on the ground." Bundy was to report back on February 7. Meanwhile, on February 2, CIA Chief McCone predicted a serious political crisis for General Khánh in Sài Gòn and pointed out that Soviet Chairman Kosygin would soon be in Hà Nội, would give the North Vietnamese greatly increased economic and military aid, and would encourage Hà Nội "to step up its subversion and military and guerrilla warfare in South Vietnam." McCone, in response to the president's request for recommendations, suggested bombing selected targets in North Vietnam.[74] On February 6, in the afternoon, word came of communist attacks on a number of targets in South Vietnam, including the U.S. Army advisor's barracks in Pleiku and a nearby U.S. Army helicopter base, killing a total of 9 Americans and wounding over one hundred, and destroying five U.S. aircraft and damaging 15. Johnson summoned the NSC that evening, including Secretary McNamara, his deputy Cyrus Vance, General Wheeler, Under Secretary of State Ball (in place of Secretary Rusk who was out of town), Llewellyn Thompson and William Bundy of State, Treasury Secretary

Douglas Dillon, Carl Rowan of USIA, and Marshall Carter from the CIA. House Speaker McCormick and Senator Mansfield were also present.[75]

The president wrote, "My advisers [sic] strongly urged that we answer the attacks by striking four targets in North Vietnam immediately. United States planes would handle three; the South Vietnamese Air Force would strike the fourth. The targets were army barracks associated with North Vietnam's infiltration system into the South."[76] McGeorge Bundy in Sài Gòn reported, by secure telephone, the concurrence of Ambassador Taylor and General Westmoreland. The president asked George Ball, as the senior State Department man present, what he thought. "'We are all in accord that action must be taken,' Ball replied. 'We do need to decide how we shall handle the air strikes publicly. We must make it clear that the North Vietnamese and the Viet Cong are the same. We are retaliating against North Vietnam because Hà Nội directs the Viet Cong, supplies arms and infiltrates men.'"[77]

Johnson, who had long been concerned about the danger of communist retaliation against American dependents in Sài Gòn, now decided to begin evacuating them at once.

He found, in going around the table, that only Senator Mansfield opposed the air strikes. "'We should be cautious,' he warned. 'We might be getting into a war with China. We might be healing the split between Moscow and Peking. He strongly opposed the idea of retaliation but he proposed no alternative.'"[78]

President Johnson thought for his part that a sudden and effective air strike might convince the Hà Nội leadership the United States was serious and that they could not be sure of continued immunity if they kept attacking in the South. He knew there were risks of Soviet or Chinese involvement but noted neither of the two was "trying to bring peace or even urging restraint and doubted that either wanted direct involvement." "After long discussion," he authorized the strikes subject to South Vietnamese Government approval, which was hardly in doubt. In the event, only one of the American targets was hit because of bad weather. The Vietnamese hit their target, or, according to Nguyễn Cao Kỳ, a target of opportunity—an antiaircraft regiment headquarters, but the Americans did not try again for the remaining two to avoid giving the impression of beginning a sustained air offensive. "That decision had not yet been made."[79]

McGeorge Bundy's report on his trip to Sài Gòn "found the situation in Vietnam going downhill," recommended major action against the North to reverse the trend and expressed the opinion that without such action defeat seemed inevitable within the next year or so. Bundy's party had included John McNaughton, assistant secretary of defense; Leonard Unger, deputy assistant secretary of state; General Andrew J. Goodpaster, assistant to the chairman of the Joint Chiefs, and Chester Cooper of the NSC staff. The report found:

> ... the international prestige of the United States and a substantial part of our influence directly at risk in Vietnam. There is no way of unloading the burden on the Vietnamese themselves and there is no way of negotiating ourselves out of Vietnam which offers any serious promise at present ... a negotiated withdrawal of the United States at that time would mean "surrender on the installment plan."

Bundy said a policy of "graduated and continuing reprisal," as outlined in the annex to his report, was the "most promising course available." All the members of his team agreed with him and so, he thought, did all members of the Country Team in Sài Gòn.[80] An annex to the report predicted the costs of the plan would be real in terms of significant American air losses and casualties that would be "higher—and more visible to American feelings—than those sustained in the struggle for South Vietnam." It also maintained, however, that the risks were acceptable and the cost cheap "measured against the costs of defeat in Vietnam."

Johnson recalled several planning exercises on bombing the North including the 94 Target Plan which had been renewed in August 1964 by the Joint Chiefs of Staff but opposed by his civilian advisers, notably McNamara and Rusk. It had been rejected again in September and December. Now, however, things had changed. The president met on February 8, 1965, with most of the NSC members and some of their principal aides, plus Speaker McCormick, House Republican Leader Gerald Ford, and Senators Mansfield and Dirksen.

> McNamara briefed the Congressional leaders on the results of the air strikes of the previous two days. George Ball dealt with the diplomatic side. He pointed out that we had explained our case in full to the Secretary General of the United Nations. We had also advised the Russians of the reasons for our retaliation and had assured them that Kosygin's visit to the Far East had no connection with our timing. The North Vietnamese had chosen the time by attacking our men and installations.[81]

The president explained that earlier proposals for action against the North had been turned down in the hope the South Vietnamese would build a stronger political base and because of concerns about American dependents. "Now we had decided to go forward with the kind of program we had earlier studied and postponed. We were evacuating all dependents." It was believed necessary to respond to deliberate and flagrant North Vietnamese attacks on men and installations, but we were reacting not to specific incidents but rather to the whole pattern of terrorism and aggression recently accelerated by Hà Nội. Johnson instructed Ambassador Taylor to explain our views to the South

Vietnamese and tell them we hoped to be able to plan and act with a "unified and going government."[82]

Two days later, the Việt Cộng "blew up an enlisted men's barracks in Qui Nhon, killing twenty-three Americans and seven Vietnamese, and wounding twenty-one American soldiers." Johnson again summoned the NSC on February 10. All present agreed to a response in some form but differed as to kind and timing. Things were complicated by Kosygin's travel. He was in North Korea, expected to stop in Peking en route back to Moscow. George Ball and Llewellyn Thompson wanted the reprisal strike held up until Kosygin had left the Far East. Vice President Humphrey also had doubts, but the others agreed with McNamara and the chiefs on going ahead. The attack was conducted on February 9 but the target closest to Hà Nội (a bridge 75 miles to the south was deleted from the plan). On February 13, the president had Ambassador Taylor and MACV informed of his approval of a "three point plan of immediate action:"

- Intensify the pacification program by all available means;
- Carry out measured and limited air action jointly with the GVN against targets in North Vietnam south of the 19th Parallel;
- "Go to the U. N. Security Council and detail the case against Hanoi's [sic] aggression."[83]

As the Việt Cộng continued their activities, and after Johnson had consulted ex-President Eisenhower on February 17, bombing began again on March 2, stopped for 11 days and thereafter became more frequent.

As Johnson put it:

> The policy of gradual but steady reprisal against North Vietnam for its continuing aggression in the South had been put into action. This was my third Vietnam decision. The decision was made because it had become clear gradually but unmistakably, that Hanoi [sic] was moving in for the kill.[84]

> My advisers [sic] had long agreed that a weak government in Saigon [sic] would have difficulty surviving the pressures that might be exerted against the South if we bombed the North. Now concluded that political life in the South would soon collapse unless the people there knew that the North was paying a price in its own territory for its aggression. There were strong military reasons for our action, as the Joint Chiefs had long argued. Now the weight of the political argument as well had shifted to support intensified action.[85]

Johnson recorded that, starting with the first air attack on a military target in North Vietnam, Hà Nội, Peking, and Moscow opened a growing propaganda barrage to "stop the bombing" and voices in some non-communist countries "joined the Chorus," as did some American public figures. But, as Johnson saw it, "They all ignored the vital fact that we were bombing the North because Hanoi was stepping up its war in the South."

By February 27, 1965, the Department of State had prepared for release the White Paper, "Aggression from the North: The Record of North Vietnam's Campaign to Conquer South Vietnam." As Guenter Lewy commented later:

> The 1965 White Paper did not make as good a case for aggression from the north as would have been desirable. The presence in South Vietnam of an enemy unit had to be confirmed through prisoner interrogation or analysis of captured documents and this meant that such confirmation usually did not become available until six to nine months after the unit had infiltrated. Moreover, the most persuasive evidence on the infiltration of men and supplies was derived from intelligence sources which could not be revealed publicly without compromising their future usefulness. The White Paper, therefore was criticized as being inconclusive.[86]

However, he noted that:

> More complete information than that available in 1965 and 1966 ... confirms the basic argument of the 1965 White Paper. As I mentioned earlier, the decision to assume the offensive was taken by the VWP [Vietnam Workers Party] in Hanoi [*sic*] in December 1963. As the level of the fighting increased during 1964 and an early South Vietnamese collapse became likely, North Vietnam decided to send in reinforcements in order to hasten victory and guarantee Hanoi's political control after the triumph. The supply of Southerners having been exhausted, elements of the 325th People's Army of Vietnam [PAVN] Division began to prepare in April 1964 for the move south. The first regular North Vietnamese infantry regiment departed the North in September or October 1964, another followed in October and a third in December ... The initial escalation, through the introduction of North Vietnamese combat forces, thus, was carried out by the Communists, well before the American decision to bomb North Vietnam.[87]

Lewy went on to observe:

> More basically, the argument over the issue of North Vietnamese regulars in the South directs attention from the larger pattern of North Vietnamese intervention, which, as we have seen, goes back at least to 1959. Contrary to Communist propaganda, the southern insurgency was never a spontaneous uprising but from the beginning was a deliberate campaign directed and supported from Hanoi.[88]

The Department of State produced a memorandum on March 8, 1965, entitled, "Legal Basis for United States Actions Against North Vietnam."[89] The memorandum considered the question whether United States–South Vietnamese actions against military targets in North Vietnam were justified in international law, particularly in light of the United Nations Charter and the 1954 Geneva Accords on Vietnam. It concluded these actions were fully justified. It cited "Aggression from the North" as establishing beyond question that North Vietnam was carrying out a careful conceived plan of aggression against the South. It cited an earlier paper issued by the department in December 1961, entitled "A Threat to the Peace," and a Special Report of the International Control Commission in Vietnam in June 1962 which concluded there was "sufficient evidence to show beyond reasonable doubt" that North Vietnam was sending arms and men into South Vietnam to carry out subversion there in violation of the 1954 Geneva Accords.

The department's 1965 memorandum stated that "to meet the threat created by these violations of the Geneva Accords and by North Vietnam's aggressive intervention contrary to international law, the Government of the Republic of Vietnam requested United States Assistance." The memorandum traced the history of United States economic and military assistance from 1950–51, its continuation under the 1954 Geneva Accords, and its increase at Vietnamese request in 1961, "proportioned with the design of sustaining Vietnam in its defense against aggression without extending the conflict beyond the borders of the country." It stated that "the Communists, however, increased their intervention without regard to obligations under international law and agreements by which they were bound," violating in the process the 1962 Geneva Agreement for the Settlement of the Laotian Question. It cited sharp increases in North Vietnam's infiltration of men and equipment in recent months and noted virtually all the personnel coming in were natives of North Vietnam. It cited the right of Vietnam and the United States to act under Article 51 of the United Nations Charter (Self Defense) and under Article 2, paragraph 4 of the Charter (Threat or Use of Force Against Territorial Integrity or Political Independence of Any State). Finally, citing North Vietnam's violations of both the 1954 Geneva Accords and the 1962 Geneva Agreement, it recalled that "In these circumstances, international law recognizes the principle that a material breach of a treaty by one party entitles the other parties at least to withhold compliance with an equivalent corresponding or related provision until the other party is prepared to observe its obligations." The memorandum closed by stating, "Both South Vietnam and the United States have made clear that the actions they have taken will no longer be necessary if North Vietnam would comply with the Accords."

President Johnson decided to use the occasion of an invitation from President Milton Eisenhower of Johns Hopkins University in Baltimore to speak there on April 7, 1965, "to explain United States policy as clearly as possible, to urge Hanoi [sic] once more to join us in trying to reach a peaceful settlement and to describe what peace and cooperative effort could do for the economic development of all of Southeast Asia."[90]

Meanwhile, leaders from 17 non-aligned nations—Afghanistan, Algeria, Cyprus, Ceylon, Ethiopia, Ghana, Guinea, India, Iraq, Kenya, Nepal, Syria,

Tunisia, Uganda, The United Arab Republic, Yugoslavia, and Zambia—met in Belgrade in the middle of March, with Vietnam, among other items, on their agenda. Hoping to get peace talks started, they sent an appeal "to the United States, North and South Vietnam, other interested parties and governments as well as to the Secretary General of the United Nations."[91] The essence of their proposal, delivered to Secretary Rusk on April 4 by ambassadors of four of the non-aligned nations, "was a call for negotiations among interested parties 'as soon as possible without any preconditions.'"

Secretary Rusk described the appeal to a National Security Council meeting convened on April 2 to hear a report by Ambassador Taylor. Rusk "urged that our reply be 'serious, restrained and positive.'" The president agreed and decided to include the main elements of the U.S. reply in his Johns Hopkins address.

In the speech, Johnson laid out the essential elements, as he saw them, of a "just peace":

- an independent South Vietnam, "securely guaranteed and able to shape its own relationships—free from outside interference—tied to no alliance—a military base for no other country."
- United States readiness for unconditional discussions.
- Association of the countries of Southeast Asia in a greatly expanded cooperative effort for development with the hope "North Vietnam would take its place in the common effort just as soon as peaceful cooperation is possible."
- A request for the Secretary General of the United Nations to use the prestige of his office to launch a plan for cooperation in economic development.
- An offer to "ask the Congress to join in a billion dollar American investment in this effort as soon as it is under way" and the hope that all other industrialized countries, including the Soviet Union, would join in this effort.[92]

On April 8, the United States delivered its formal reply to the Belgrade Conference proposal, incorporating the substance of the Johns Hopkins Speech; "The United States would negotiate without preconditions." Johnson considered the dispatch of this response his fourth major Vietnam decision. Peking, Moscow, and Hà Nội rejected the American offer and, on April 20, North Vietnam declared that the 17 Belgrade Conference nations were "not accurately informed." As Johnson read this reaction: "They [Hà Nội] had no interest in cooperating with their neighbors in a peaceful way; they preferred to take them over by force."[93]

He also saw Hà Nội's military campaign against South Vietnam as part of a broader communist strategy. The Chinese Communists had set off their first nuclear explosion in October 1964 and were not only voicing support for Hà Nội but pushing "wars of liberation" in general. They were training Thai guerrillas, and a "liberation front" for Thailand enjoyed Chinese backing. Chinese influence in Indonesia was increasing and Sukarno had pulled out of the United Nations (January 1965) and was carrying on his "confrontation" with Malaysia. "By the end of 1966 Cambodia's main port, Sihanoukville, had become a principal supply point for Chinese military equipment going to the Viet Cong and North Vietnamese. Other supplies moving down through Laos were also fed into Cambodia for transshipment to the Communist forces in Vietnam." The Ho Chi Minh Trail in Laos had become the principal North Vietnamese supply line into South Vietnam. The Indonesians were training troops for Lao General Kong Le who was in opposition to the neutralist government of Souvanna Phouma in Laos. The North Koreans were training North Vietnamese fighter pilots. "Thus, what we saw taking place rapidly was a Djakarta–Hanoi–Peking–Pyongyang Axis with Cambodia probably to be brought in as a junior partner and Laos to be merely absorbed by the North Vietnamese and Chinese."[94]

On May 10, Johnson agreed to a bombing halt for a limited period. He was reacting largely to criticism from those "at home and abroad," who "argued that only by stopping the bombing or reducing it drastically could we hope to persuade Hanoi [sic] to talk about peace." He asked the Russians to inform the North Vietnamese of his decision, but they declined to act as intermediaries and the Vietnamese declined messages sent for delivery to them in Moscow and Hà Nội. The message indicated:

> ... we would be watching during the pause for signs of "significant reduction in ... armed actions."
>
> ...
>
> Hanoi [sic] never answered directly but infiltration into the South continued as did Viet Cong [sic] attacks. Then Hanoi denounced the pause and Peking even alleged there was no pause. Once again, we had tried to open the door; once again Hanoi had slammed it shut. In the face of Hanoi's continued hostility, we renewed bombing on May 18.[95]

As Johnson put it, "My fifth, and by far the hardest, Vietnam decision lay ahead." Recapitulating President Kennedy's decisions, which had increased the military advisory force from 700 to more than 16,000 by the time he

(Johnson) became president, he noted the number of advisors had been further increased to nearly 23,000 by the end of 1964 but emphasized the situation in Vietnam at the beginning of 1965 was "as different from 1963 as 1961 had been from 1959." The North Vietnamese had sent in three regiments. It was clear to Johnson "Hanoi [sic] was deploying major forces, trying for a military victory." He was hardly exaggerating. General Westmoreland, in his book *A Soldier's Story*, wrote that, in 1964, "Indeed, concerned lest the hawks force acceptance of harsh measures, the Johnson administration long withheld from the public the information that North Vietnamese troops were entering South Vietnam."[96] Johnson was also concerned, once the bombing of the North had begun on a sustained basis, the communists would go after the air base at Đà Nẵng. He therefore approved, in March, General Westmoreland's request for two marine battalions to guard the air base.[97] The marines were not supposed to engage in day-to-day actions against the Việt Cộng[98] and Secretary Rusk said so on "Face the Nation" the day before they went in. He was later criticized for "misleading" the public. However, Lewy suggests the decision to send in these marines, "watershed in the history of American involvement" that it turned out to be, was "made without very much discussion and planning" and was "seen by official Washington as a one shot affair to meet a specific situation," i.e., early North Vietnamese reaction to the bombing of the North.[99]

Late in March, just after Ambassador Taylor left Sài Gòn for consultation in Washington, the Việt Cộng set off a large explosive charge in an automobile in front of the American Embassy in Sài Gòn, killing two Americans and 15 Vietnamese, and wounding many people including Deputy Ambassador U. Alexis Johnson.[100]

President Johnson met with Ambassador Taylor and others to consider various recommendations for action that had been made. Johnson noted that, "The proposals that came to me were a compromise among the views of three groups: those [especially in the armed forces] who wanted to move fast and in strength; my civilian advisers [sic] and Ambassador Taylor, who thought we should proceed, but more deliberately; and a few who opposed any significant involvement in the ground war."[101]

The meeting took place April 1 and 2 at the White House and produced decisions on:

> ...a detailed program of non-military actions submitted by Taylor; programs in the information and psychological warfare field; an elaborate military program submitted by General Johnson [Chief of Staff of the Army] with special emphasis on aircraft and helicopter reinforcements.[102]

The Chiefs of Staff and the CIA Director wanted to increase the level of the air attacks against North Vietnam. Mr. McCone believed that:

> "...by limiting our attacks to targets like bridges, military installations and lines of communication, in effect we signal to the Communists that our determination to win is significantly modified by our fear of widening the war ..."

Johnson, however, agreed with "most of his advisers" to follow the plan of the "slowly ascending tempo" rather than accept the risks of "deeper Chinese and Soviet involvement" that was feared might accompany any sharp escalation of the air war. The United States would remain ready to increase or decrease the air effort depending upon what the communists did. The president also approved:

- An 18,000 to 20,000-man increase in U.S. logistic and support forces;
- Deployment of two additional battalions (for a total of four) and one Marine air squadron to the Đà Nẵng–Huế area, with one of the battalions to go to Phu Bai, near Huế to protect communications facilities and the airport there;
- A change in mission for the marines to permit "their more active use" under rules to be approved by the secretaries of state and defense.[103]

At that time, Johnson wrote, the approved U.S. force level in Vietnam was just over 40,000, of whom 33,500 were actually on the ground. He thought it was time for a new assessment and sent McNamara to Honolulu to hold a meeting of Washington, Sài Gòn Mission, and CINCPAC (Commander in Chief, Pacific Fleet) representatives. McNamara reported back on April 21 the conference view that communist failure in the South would have as much or more to do with achieving a settlement in Vietnam than any pain inflicted on North Vietnam. They thought it would take a year or two to convince the communists they could not win a military victory in the South and they anticipated no "dramatic improvement in the South in the immediate future."[104] The conference envisaged a strategy of breaking the will of the DRV and the Việt Cộng by denying them victory or, as Ambassador Taylor put it, by "a demonstration of Communist impotence." They saw "slow improvement in the South" but considered it critically important to avoid the severe psychological damage that would follow from any "spectacular defeat" of the GVN or U.S. forces. They proposed to stiffen the GVN forces, while they were building up, by sending in, in addition to the 33,500 Americans and 2,000 South Koreans then in Vietnam, reinforcements including two

U.S. Army brigades, three Marine battalions and three Marine air squadrons, plus logistics troops, raising the approved level to 82,000. McNamara also wanted the Vietnamese to ask South Korea and Australia for more troops. The president approved only some of these recommendations: the 173rd Airborne Brigade to secure the air base at Biên Hòa and the Third Marine Amphibious Brigade to secure a new airfield site at Chu Lai. By the end of April, there were more than 40,000 U.S. troops in Vietnam.

On May 4, the president asked, and in three days got, from Congress a supplemental appropriation of $700,000,000 for increasing costs in Vietnam. He announced this bill meant to the Vietnamese that "America keeps her promises. And we will back up those promises with all the resources that we need." To the American "boys" it meant "We are going to give you the tools to finish the job."[105] Up to about this time, the mission of the U.S. forces in Vietnam had been, in the president's view, to secure the base areas to which they were assigned. He had broadened that mission somewhat to permit active and aggressive patrolling near those bases. On June 9, he granted General Westmoreland's request "to use his forces in combat support if it became necessary to assist a Vietnamese unit in serious trouble." This authority applied to "support of Vietnamese forces faced with aggressive attack when other effective reserves are not available and when, in his judgment, the general military situation urgently requires it." Later in the month, the president extended this authority to permit Westmoreland to commit U.S. troops to combat "independently of or in conjunction with" Vietnamese troops if asked and if he judged their use "necessary to strengthen the relative position of GVN forces."[106]

> The first major ground combat operation by U.S. Forces in Vietnam occurred from June 27 to June 30, 1965 when troops of the 173rd Airborne Brigade went into War Zone D, northwest of Saigon [sic]. Also, in action there were the Vietnamese 48th Regiment, two battalions of Vietnamese airborne troops and an Australian battalion that had arrived early in June.[107]

Meanwhile, the South Vietnamese Army had suffered a number of defeats in fighting with the North Vietnamese and the Việt Cộng. General Westmoreland estimated early in June that most, if not all, of the North Vietnamese 325th Division was in the South Vietnamese Highlands. The 304th Division was in the Laos panhandle and could get into South Vietnam quickly. South Vietnamese morale was sagging. Westmoreland told the Joint Chiefs there was no alternative to rapid reinforcement by U.S. or third country forces. This was the period of the political crisis that brought to power the National Leadership Committee with General Nguyễn Văn Thiệu as chief of state and Marshal

Nguyễn Cao Kỳ as prime minister.[108] According to Ambassador Taylor, Kỳ saw the need for additional U.S. ground combat forces. He was "impressed with the need for injection of additional U.S. (or other third country) forces to tide over the monsoon offensive period and to take off Viet Cong pressure while mobilization measures are being taken."[109]

Kỳ wrote in his book that, when he took office, he was unaware of President Johnson's April 2 decision "that American ground troops should go over to offensive action." Kỳ said Johnson had taken this decisive step "because it was apparent that the month-old bombing offensive could not alone stave off the collapse of South Vietnam with its ever-changing governments," and because "Johnson did not dare to increase the bombing and risk Chinese intervention." In Kỳ's opinion, "The decision was taken none too soon," because "by June the Communist summer offensive was in full flow."

In Kỳ's view, the fact that the president's decision on the use of ground forces became public knowledge at the same time as news of 200 U.S. Marine casualties, and that White House statements simply defined Westmoreland's authority along the lines set forth above while denying (he said) any recent change in the mission of U.S. ground combat units in Vietnam, combined to widen the "credibility gap" in the United States. He thought that when the 173rd Airborne Brigade went into action with the Australian battalion and the South Vietnamese north of Sài Gòn on June 27, "the gap became a chasm."[110]

Johnson wrote that he was not prepared to send additional men to Vietnam without careful study. Consequently, he again sent McNamara to the scene in Vietnam to consult Vietnamese and American officials. He wanted to know, he said, if the Vietnamese Government was doing as much as it could on its own, if the Vietnamese and Americans on the spot thought American forces could deal effectively with the Việt Cộng in the mountains and the jungles, and if their appearance would recall the colonial period and thus "arouse anti-foreign sentiments." Thiệu and Kỳ told McNamara:

> That they were convinced that Americans and perhaps other foreign forces would be needed to hold back the Communist attackers. When McNamara asked for their estimate of how many might be needed, the Vietnamese leaders said they thought that in addition to the forty-four battalions they had already requested, there should be another combat division. Their total estimate called for about 200,000 Americans in all categories.[111]

McNamara recommended a choice among three courses of action:

- Cut our losses and withdraw under the best conditions that can be arranged;

- Continue at about the present level, with the U.S. force level limited to say, 75,000, holding on and playing for the breaks; and
- Expand promptly and substantially the U.S. military pressure against the Việt Cộng in the South and maintain the military pressure in the North while launching a vigorous effort on the political side to lay the groundwork for a favorable outcome by clarifying our objectives and establishing channels of communication.

McNamara recommended the third alternative as "The course involving the best odds of the best outcome with the most acceptable cost to the United States," even though he observed "it would imply a commitment to see a fighting war through at considerable cost in casualties and material and would make any later decision to withdraw even more difficult than would be the case today."[112]

Johnson wrote that "The Secretary believed that after the recommended ground forces had been deployed and certain actions had been taken in the bombing program in the North, we should consider a diplomatic initiative toward peace, including a bombing pause of perhaps six to eight weeks."[113]

He summarized the recommendations on ground forces:

- There were 15 American combat battalions in Vietnam, or on the way, with a total force level of 75,000. McNamara wanted to increase these to 34 or, if the South Koreans did not come through with nine battalions they had promised, 43. The force level would then be 175,000, or 200,000 if the Koreans did not participate.
- McNamara warned that deployment of perhaps 100,000 more men would be needed early in 1966 and possibly even more thereafter.
- McNamara suggested asking Congressional authority to call up 235,000 men in Reserves and the National Guard and increasing the regular forces by 235,000. The total increase in military forces would be 600,000 men by mid-1966 and an additional supplementary appropriation would be necessary.[114]

Johnson discussed these recommendations, which he described as a "major undertaking," with his top advisors at Camp David on Sunday, July 25. Under Secretary Ball outlined his views at the president's request:

> His basic thesis was that we could not win a protracted war against local guerrillas in Asian jungles. He thought there was great danger of intrusion by the Chinese Communists. In his opinion, we were losing friends and influence in Europe and elsewhere because of our commitment in Asia. The best thing to do, he thought, was to cut our losses and pull away. He foresaw many problems in that course, but he believed they were outweighed by the advantages of the action he proposed.

After long and detailed discussion, the president "felt the Under Secretary had not produced a sufficiently convincing case or a viable alternative."[115] Johnson also remarked that Secretary Rusk had put into words a key consideration that was much on the his mind. "If the Communist world finds out that we will not pursue our commitments to the end," he said, "I don't know where they will stay their hand."[116]

As the review continued the "military commanders" "refined their estimates" to indicate they could get by for the immediate future with 50,000 men. Johnson said he was rejecting such choices as: bringing the enemy to his knees by using Strategic Air Command; packing up and going home; staying there as we were, losing territory and taking casualties; or going on a war footing with all that that implied. He concluded, rather, that "Finally, we can give our commanders in the field the men and supplies they say they need." Johnson believed:

> ... we should do what as necessary to resist aggression but that we should not be provoked into a major war. We would get the required appropriation in the new budget and would not boast about what we were doing. We would not make threatening noises to the Chinese or the Russians by calling up reserves in large numbers. At the same time, we would press hard on the diplomatic front to find some path to a peaceful settlement.

He said that all present at an NSC meeting on July 27, 1965, agreed to the course of action he had described.[117]

The president next met with Congressional leaders of both Houses and both parties at the White House that evening. He laid out the five alternatives and expressed the opinion that the real choice lay between "to go the full congressional route now," or "to give the congressional leadership the story now and the bill later." In the course of lengthy discussions, Johnson "explained that we were thinking of increasing our forces in three phases and that I thought our total force would be doubled by November 1." He noted:

> In the entire group the only expression of serious doubt and opposition to the proposed course again came from Mike Mansfield [Senate Majority Leader]. As always, he expressed his opinion candidly. He spoke of the deepening discontent in the country. He thought the best hope was "a quick stalemate and negotiations." But he concluded by saying that as a Senator and Majority Leader he would support the President's position.[118]

On July 28, 1965, President Johnson told the White House Press Corps:

> I have asked the commanding general, General Westmoreland, what more he needs to meet this mounting aggression. He has told me. We will meet his needs. I have today ordered to Vietnam the Air Mobile Division and certain other forces which will raise our fighting strength from 75,000 to 125,000 men almost immediately. Additional forces will be needed later, and they will be sent as requested.[119]

As the president put it in his book, "now we were committed to major combat in Vietnam."[120]

Johnson recorded in *The Vantage Point* that he had reached the conclusion by the summer of 1965 that the United States and other nations would have to engage their own fighting forces if South Vietnam were to survive. He saw the United States, South Vietnam, and third countries engaged over the next three-and-a-half years in a triple effort of "defeating aggression, building a nation and searching for peace." He reported that only a very few of his closest advisors knew of the many attempts being made in pursuit of the third part of this effort:

> The fact is that from 1965 until January 1969 we were in virtually continuous contact, either directly or through intermediaries, with leaders in Hanoi [*sic*] or their representatives. Hardly a month passed throughout that period in which we did not make some effort to open the gateway to peace. Until March 31, 1968, every attempt we made was ignored or rejected by the North Vietnamese.[121]

In pursuing the first part of the effort, however, Johnson seemed to have forgotten his own observation that President Truman's one mistake in Korea had been in not asking for a Congressional resolution backing his dispatch of American forces to the rescue of the South Koreans. Perhaps he had changed his mind or more likely had concluded over-optimistically that the Southeast Asia Resolution (Tonkin Gulf Resolution) would suffice to cover the deployment of considerable ground forces. The BBC interviewers observed that "The shift from bombing to an expeditionary force of combat troops without the further approval of Congress undoubtedly helped to sow the whirlwind of hostile protest in the United States."[122] They speculated that he believed "Congress would force a choice between the Great Society to which he was summoning the nation, and the war; and he was in little doubt that the Great Society would be the casualty." He also feared, they believed, an open debate at that particular time would lead the communists to doubt the United States would stand by its guarantees.[123]

The interviewers asked former Assistant Secretary Bundy what had happened to bring about intensive bombing of the North and the presence of half a million United States troops in the South if the original policy had not called for either measure. Bundy replied that neither measure had resulted from a specific decision. Circumstances had stretched earlier, more measured decisions on bombing and troops further than anyone had foreseen at the time. They next asked how the administration had approached the dilemma of dealing openly with public opinion in the United States, and thus accepting a public debate which would destroy the basis of its strategy "to convince the North Vietnamese of your unyielding will and resolution." Bundy replied:

> Well let me say that at my level, I always assumed that there would be very full Presidential statements and Congressional action. And the key period to look at is July 1965 when the initial course of action recommended by Secretary of Defense McNamara to the President called for the calling up of reserves, which required Congressional action; and called for a very heavy immediate supplemental financial appropriation to meet the costs of the war. Then in a very dramatic way that I wasn't party to, and after there'd been consultation with some of the Congressional leaders—particularly recall Gerald Ford being in the room in his capacity as House Minority Leader—President Johnson changed the signals and opted for the lowest possible key Presidential announcement, and opted for not presenting the course to Congress and so on.

Asked whether this was an honest approach, Bundy expressed the opinion it was "at least as honest as many things that Franklin Roosevelt did in the course of 1941. The trouble was that this turned out badly and therefore looks much worse in history."[124]

Bundy also recalled that public opinion polls and Congress itself supported the president's policy at that time.[125]

Senator Eugene McCarthy told the BBC interviewers that, at the time of the 1968 Democratic Party Convention in Chicago:

> Insofar as the Congress was concerned, there were only I suppose really fifteen Senators who had made some position of criticism of the war by the time of that convention—Senator Morse and Senator Gruening and Senator Hughes and Senator Hart—and there were a few others who were quite outspoken against the war like McGovern. Mansfield was against the war but he didn't do anything about it at Chicago. Fulbright was against it; he didn't make any overt commitment.[126]

President Johnson thought the May 1965 bombing pause had been a total failure, producing nothing except criticism it had been too short.[127] McNamara proposed another bombing halt "to reinforce our diplomacy" before sending more troops to the South or stepping up the bombing pressure in the North. He thought it would be "easier for us to carry out necessary additional military measures in the future if we first made a serious peace move." Johnson, McGeorge Bundy, and Secretary Rusk were skeptical. Rusk thought the leaders in Hà Nội might simply dangle the possibility of talks before the U.S. with no intention of moving to serious negotiations. He thought a halt which produced only extended talks while the communists continued fighting with full force would have a bad effect. However, he also believed in continued probing of Hà Nội through diplomatic efforts and "If the North Vietnamese give some firm sign that they would lower the level of fighting or enter into serious negotiations ... we should then end the bombing." Ambassador Lodge reported to the President, "An end of bombing of the North with no other quid pro quo than the opening of negotiations would load the dice in favor of the Communists and demoralize the GVN. It would be effect leave the Communists free to devastate the South with impunity while we tie our hands in the North."[128] General Westmoreland, Admiral Sharp (CINCPAC), and the Joint Chiefs of Staff all opposed a bombing halt "on military grounds."[129]

Probing and discussion continued, wrote the president, and in November the Soviet ambassador told McGeorge Bundy that a pause of "twelve to twenty" days would lead to "intense diplomatic activity." A Hungarian told Secretary Rusk that "a few weeks would be enough." Gradually, opinion in the administration moved towards the idea of a "pause." Even Secretary Rusk thought it would be worth trying. "Resistance centered mainly in the military services and in our Embassy in Saigon [sic]."[130] Johnson had his doubts but was moving "reluctantly" towards acceptance of the idea with its attendant risks. Rusk, McNamara, and McGeorge Bundy, he said, assured him there would be no serious trouble in resuming the bombing if Hà Nội failed to respond. "As it turned out, of course, we received little credit for stopping the bombing and heavy criticism for renewing it."[131]

In a meeting on December 18 with Rusk, McNamara, McGeorge Bundy, George Ball, and Alexis Johnson, and with Clark Clifford and Justice Abe Fortas present, Johnson reviewed the pros and cons of a bombing halt. Secretary Rusk spoke of the importance of demonstrating to the American people "That we had done everything we could to find the way to a peaceful settlement." He also said the pause should be tried even if there were only one chance in 10 or 20 it "could lead to a settlement [on the basis of] the Geneva Agreements and the 17th parallel." "Finally the Secretary of State said that he thought a bombing pause would place the responsibility for continuing the war where it rightly belonged, on Hanoi [sic] and on those who were saying that only our bombing of the North stood in the way of peace." McNamara agreed, adding that "... he felt that there was no assurance of military success in Vietnam and that we had to find a diplomatic solution." Justice Fortas thought, in the absence of any evidence other governments with influence in Hà Nội would encourage the North Vietnamese to respond to a pause, the arguments made in favor of a pause were not convincing. Clark Clifford thought the leaders in Hà Nội would not talk until such time as they knew they were not going to win, and they were not at that point yet.[132]

However, Johnson decided to extend a 30-hour Christmas Eve truce, already planned with South Vietnamese agreement, "for several more days, possibly into the middle of next week." He informed American allies, the U.N. Secretary General and, in a widespread diplomatic campaign involving Vice President Humphrey, Secretary Rusk, Averell Harriman, and Assistant Secretaries G. Mennen Williams, and Tom Mann, made "clear that similar restraint by Hanoi [sic] would be welcome and would influence our future actions."[133] Simultaneously, messages were sent to the North Vietnamese through diplomatic channels in Rangoon and Moscow. The North Vietnamese rebuffed all these overtures insisting "that we accept their four point plan—including withdrawal of all American forces—as the only basis for peace.[134] Radio Hanoi, on January 28, broadcast a tough letter Hồ Chí Minh had addressed to many governments accusing the United States of deceit and hypocrisy and insisting "we pull all our troops out of Vietnam and that we accept the Communist-run National Liberation Front of South Vietnam as 'the sole genuine representative of the people of South Vietnam.'" Meanwhile, the traffic of North Vietnamese men and supplies towards the Demilitarized Zone and the Ho Chi Minh Trail continued apace. "It was obvious that nothing good had happened as diplomats friendly to Hanoi [sic] had forecast; nor was anything good going to happen." Johnson resumed the bombing on January 31, 1966.

There followed a hue and cry from the communist world and from some other quarters to stop the bombing altogether since only such a definitive halt, it was said, would produce any real opportunity for serious talks. Johnson noted the bombing had been stopped eight times from 1965 to the beginning of 1968 and, at five other times, targets in and around Hà Nội and Hải Phòng were excluded for lengthy periods. "The net result of all those bombing pauses was zero. Indeed, it was less than zero because the enemy used every pause to strengthen its position, hastily pushing men and supplies and equipment down the roads of North Vietnam for massive infiltration into the South."[135]

On February 7 and 8, 1966, President Johnson and some of his senior advisors met at Honolulu with Thiệu and Kỳ and their "principal aides." The meeting was to give special emphasis to the political and economic future of South Vietnam; "… the principal advisers [sic] from both delegations divided into smaller specialized groups, some to discuss ways to find a path to negotiations, others to consider how to make pacification and rural development more effective." The participants issued a joint statement, the "Declaration of Honolulu," in which the Vietnamese expressed their intentions to "defeat the Viet Cong [sic] and those illegally fighting with them on our soil …"; their dedication "to the eradication of social injustice …"; and the importance of establishing and maintaining "a stable, viable economy … a better material life for the people" and of building "true democracy for our land and for our people." They invited those on the other side of the conflict to "join in this national revolutionary adventure, and to come and work through constitutional democracy to build together that life of dignity, freedom and peace those in the North would deny the people of Vietnam." The Americans "promised to support the goals and programs the Vietnamese had advanced."

Johnson "ordered a reorganization of our Mission in Saigon [sic] to reflect this new emphasis on non-military programs"; Deputy Ambassador Porter was to take charge of this effort in the field with Robert W. Komer of the NSC coordinating and supervising "Washington support for pacification and other non-military Campaigns." Vice President Humphrey went off to Vietnam for another "first hand look at the situation there" and on to a number of other Asian capitals to explain what had been agreed to at Honolulu and to ask "these other free nations" for their support.[136]

By this time, early in 1966, the broad lines of the administration's policy and actions in Vietnam for the next two years had been laid down. They formed a triple effort to:

- meet the military threat posed by the communists;
- assist the Government of Vietnam in moving towards constitutional democracy and a stable, viable economy; and
- achieve an honorable and lasting agreement for a peaceful settlement.

The whole effort was to be delayed by a political crisis starting in March when the removal of the I Corps Commander, General Nguyễn Chánh Thi, was used by the militant Buddhists of Thích Trí Quảng to advance their own political ambitions. As Kỳ put it, Trí Quảng's "attempts to control power from behind the scenes was [sic] seriously hampering the war effort." Demonstrations occurred in Huế, Đà Nẵng, Sài Gòn, and elsewhere. Many soldiers in the First Division openly sided with the Buddhists.[137] The First Division's commander was reduced to an ineffectual role. The Buddhist chaplain issued orders to the division and eavesdropped clumsily when the American consul-general called on the division commander to try unsuccessfully to get assurances of protection for U.S. lives and property. The commander explained in French, which the chaplain apparently could not understand, that he was helpless.[138] The police chief, Nguyễn Chí Cảnh, refused to disperse the mob which wrecked, for the second time, the United States Information Service's bi-national center. They subsequently burned the U.S. Consulate General building and a staff house. Hue Radio output was indistinguishable from Radio Hanoi in its anti-Americanism. The police chief was later identified in the press as a "ranking member of the Communist infrastructure."[139]

As Kỳ saw the situation, the First Division had practically joined the Buddhists as had some Special Zone Forces in Quảng Nam and Quảng Da. He thought that if this trend continued:

> ...even for two weeks longer, the whole of the central area would fall into Buddhist hands and be proclaimed an autonomous territory. Already the radio station, municipal buildings and army headquarters in Danang [sic] were in Buddhist hands. Already the insurgents were using Communist guerrilla methods of infiltration, distributing weapons to the people of Danang, dividing the populace into groups and committees, each group spying on the other.[140]

Acting on his own without consulting the Americans, Kỳ flew troops to Đà Nẵng and reestablished government authority there after some fighting. A couple of weeks later, government authority was reestablished in Huế without bloodshed. The swift and secret nature of Kỳ's operation led to a certain contretemps with the U.S. Marines at Đà Nẵng, described variously by General Walt, General Westmoreland, and Air Marshal Kỳ in their respective books, but that was smoothed over.[141]

As General Westmoreland put it, "The crisis in the North had temporarily set back the war against the Viet Cong [sic]."[142]

National elections were held on September 11 to elect members of a constituent assembly. In October, Johnson flew to Manila at the invitation of President Marcos for a conference with Thiệu, Kỳ, the president of Korea, and the prime ministers of Australia, New Zealand, and Thailand "for a review of the war and of non-military programs of development." It produced three documents.[143] The first set forth the "goals of freedom":

- To be free from aggression.
- To conquer hunger, illiteracy and disease.
- To build a region of security, order and progress.
- To seek reconciliation and peace throughout Asia and the Pacific.

The second, a communiqué, included a declaration by the South Vietnamese Government that it would ask its allies to withdraw their forces as soon as peace was restored, and the allies replied:

> They shall be withdrawn, after close consultation, as the other side withdraws its forces to the North, ceases infiltration and the level of violence thus subsides. These forces will be withdrawn as soon as possible and not later than six months after the above conditions have been fulfilled.[144]

The third document, the Declaration of Peace and Progress in Asia and the Pacific concluded with the statement:

> We do not threaten the sovereignty or territorial integrity of our neighbors, whatever their ideological alignment. We ask only that this be reciprocated. The quarrels and ambitions of

ideology and the painful frictions arising from national fears and grievances should belong to the past. Aggression rooted in them must not succeed. We shall play our full part in creating an environment in which reconciliation becomes possible for in the modern world men and nations have no choice but to learn to live together as brothers.[145]

The Guam Conference followed in March 1967. Ellsworth Bunker took over as ambassador from Henry Cabot Lodge, with Eugene Locke as his deputy; Robert Komer became General Westmoreland's deputy for Civil Operations and Revolutionary Development Support. A new Vietnamese Constitution was approved. General Creighton Abrams was appointed Deputy to General Westmoreland in May and succeeded Westmoreland as COMUSMACV on June 10, 1968. On August 3, President Johnson approved deployment of an additional 45,000 to 50,000 U.S. troops for a new ceiling of 525,000 men in the year ahead.[146] Elections were held on September 6 in which "more than 70 percent of all eligible South Vietnamese citizens registered and 4 out of 5 of these voted.[147]

On September 29, 1967, in San Antonio, President Johnson offered what was to be known as the San Antonio formula:[148]

> The United States is willing to stop all aerial and naval bombardment of North Vietnam when this will lead promptly to productive discussions. We, of course, assume that while discussions proceed, North Vietnam would not take advantage of the bombing cessation or limitation.

Meanwhile, from June 18, 1964, to October 31, 1967, seventy-two major peace initiatives had accumulated. There had been 17 U.S. contacts with North Vietnam involving 17 "peace channels."[149]

As the BBC interviewers put it, "By 1968 and three years of search and destroy operations conducted by General Westmoreland the Communist guerrillas had taken disproportionately vast casualties, sometimes in the ratio of six or ten to one. Nevertheless, their will to go on appeared unbroken." "By 1968, General Westmoreland was fighting far from the population centers, near the borders of Cambodia and Laos, and on the demilitarized zone at the 17th Parallel. He was claiming victory in sight and envisaging being able to lower the number of American troops. This confident hope was suddenly reduced to dust. In February, the Communists launched their TET offensive and by appearing within the ring now being held by Westmoreland on the frontiers of South Vietnam and attacking forty provincial towns and cities they in effect overthrew the assumptions of the American Vietnam policy."[150]

The former Assistant Secretary of Defense for International Security Affairs, Paul Warnke, expressed it a bit differently:

> I think you have to recognize that the TET [sic] offensive did two things. In the first place it very seriously eroded the strength of the Viet Cong [sic] and the North Vietnamese, but

at the same time it destroyed the entire myth that existed about the fact that the United States position in Vietnam was very well established and that eventually victory was going to be secure. So that the military aspects of the TET offensive were entirely favorable to our side but the psychological consequences of TET made our eventual withdrawal from Vietnam inevitable.[151]

As President Johnson himself put it:

> I did not expect the enemy effort to have the impact on American thinking that it achieved. I was not surprised that elements of the press, the academic community and the Congress reacted as they did. I was surprised and disappointed that the enemy's efforts produced such a dismal effect on various people inside government and others outside whom I had always regarded as staunch and unflappable. Hanoi [sic] must have been delighted. It was exactly the reaction they sought.[152]

On March 31, 1968, President Johnson announced on television from the oval office, "Accordingly, I shall not seek, and I will not accept, the nomination of my party for another term as your President."[153]

On May 10, 1968, after predictable haggling about the venue for the talks, the American delegation to the "Paris talks" made its first contact with the North Vietnamese delegation and scheduled the first full meeting for May 13.[154]

PART IV

Conclusion of U.S. Involvement (1968–1975)

Writing of the 1968 presidential primaries, Richard M. Nixon observed that the Vietnam war was the dominant issue in the New Hampshire primary and remained so throughout the campaign. For his part, he said he wanted the war to end, but in a way that "would save the South Vietnamese people from military defeat and subjection to the domination of the North Vietnamese Communist regime." He thought there were still a number of ways, yet untried, to look into and seek an end to the war. He also thought the United States could use its armed strength more effectively than it already had to persuade the North Vietnamese of the impossibility of a military victory for their side. He thought that we were not fully exploiting our considerable diplomatic resources and that the "heart of the problem lay more in Peking and Moscow than in Hanoi [sic]." We could train and equip the South Vietnamese so as to improve their capability for self-defense. He had no particular plan to offer and would not have made it public even if he had one.[1]

On July 26, 1968, President Johnson gave him, and, separately, Governor Wallace, the other candidate, an intelligence briefing which centered on Vietnam. Secretary Rusk, present at the briefing stressed the "panic" that would be created in the rest of Asia if the United States withdrew from Vietnam "without an honorable peace settlement." Johnson said he was awaiting Soviet and North Vietnamese reaction to another bombing halt proposal even though "previous halts had produced nothing." Nixon assured President Johnson that although he would not undercut the negotiating position "just in case" the communists accepted Johnson's conditions for a new halt, he would be critical of some of the Johnson Administration's tactics.[2]

On October 31, Johnson telephoned Nixon in New York to tell him he was going to announce a total bombing halt in two hours' time. Johnson added he had not been able to persuade the South Vietnamese to go along and, therefore, they would not join in the announcement. Nixon, Wallace, and Humphrey all promised to support the president in this step. Nixon was a bit frustrated, however, since he felt Johnson was doing something which might "determine the outcome of the election." He recalled Johnson's earlier contemptuous description of those pushing for a bombing halt and his insistence he was not going to let the communists send ammunition freely into the South "to kill American boys." Nixon was not really surprised by the announcement, which he had known about for some time. He thought only that its timing "so close to the election was utterly callous if politically calculated and utterly naive if sincere." He had been warned by Kissinger through John Mitchell that "something big was afoot regarding Vietnam."[3] On October 16, in a telephone conference call briefing of the presidential candidates, Johnson had said he was "maintaining that three points had to be met: (1) Prompt and serious talks must follow any bombing halt; (2) Hanoi [sic] must not violate the demilitarized zone, and (3) The Vietcong [sic] or the North Vietnamese would not carry out large scale rocket or artillery attacks against South Vietnam's major cities." Nixon was ready to support any arrangements Johnson might make under these conditions. In Rochester on October 17, he said, "If a bombing pause can be agreed to in Vietnam … one which will not endanger American lives, and one which will increase the chances for bringing a peaceful and honorable solution to the war, then we are for it." He added he did not want to play politics with peace, "But," he wrote in his memoirs, "that was inevitably what was happening."[4] Nixon heard from "someone in Johnson's innermost circle" that Johnson was driving hard for a deal with North Vietnam and would accept almost any arrangement as an excuse to order a bombing halt so as to help Hubert Humphrey's candidacy. Nixon "immediately decided that the only way to prevent Johnson from totally undercutting my candidacy at the eleventh hour was for me to make public the fact that a bombing halt was imminent. In addition, I wanted to plant the impression—which I believed to be true—that his motives and his timing were not dictated by diplomacy alone."[5]

Accordingly, on October 26, Nixon issued a statement on the peace talks:

> In the last thirty-six hours I have been advised of a flurry of meetings in the White House and elsewhere on Vietnam. I am told that top officials in the administration have been driving very hard for an agreement on a bombing halt, accompanied possibly by a cease-fire, in the immediate future. I have since learned that these reports are true.
>
> I am … told that this spurt of activity is a cynical, last minute attempt by President Johnson to salvage the candidacy of Mr. Humphrey. This I do not believe.
>
> At no time in the campaign have I found the President anything but impartial and candid in his dealings with the major presidential contenders about Vietnam.

...

> In every conversation I have had with him he has made clear that he will not play politics with this war.[6]

At the Madison Square Garden rally on October 31, Nixon reacted to the announcement of the bombing halt simply by saying neither he nor his running mate would say "anything that might destroy the chance to have peace." He did believe, and stated that later studies confirmed, the announcement and the hope it inspired for a peace settlement caused "massive voter shifts to Humphrey." However, Thiệu deflated things somewhat on November 2 when he announced he would not participate in the negotiations Johnson was talking about. Nixon followed up by having Robert Finch indicate to the press that peace prospects were not as far along as Johnson's statement indicated and state that, "I think this will boomerang. It was hastily contrived." Johnson was infuriated and Nixon telephoned to calm him down but also told a Texas rally the same day, "In view of the early reports that we've had this morning, the prospects for peace are not as bright as they looked only a few days ago."[7]

Five days after the election, Nixon wrote, he attended a briefing with President Johnson in the cabinet room with Secretaries Rusk and Clifford, General Wheeler, Richard Helms, and Walt Rostow present, the chief subject being Vietnam. Nixon wrote that all present "emphasized that the United States must see the war through to a successful conclusion—with negotiations, if possible, but with continued fighting if necessary. They agreed that an American bug-out, or a negotiated settlement that could be interpreted as a defeat, would have a devastatingly detrimental effect on our allies and friends in Asia and around the world."[8]

In describing the formation of his cabinet, Nixon wrote, "Bill Rogers, a strong administrator, would have the formidable job of managing the recalcitrant bureaucracy of the State Department."[9] He also wrote, "When Eisenhower selected Foster Dulles as his Secretary of State, he wanted him to be his chief foreign policy adviser, a role Dulles was uniquely qualified to fill. From the outset of my administration, however, I planned to direct foreign policy from the White House. Therefore, I regarded my choice of a National Security adviser [sic] as crucial."[10] After a meeting with Henry Kissinger in the Hotel Pierre in New York on November 25, Nixon asked him if he would like to head the National Security Council (NSC); Kissinger accepted. Nixon "knew that we were very much alike in our general outlook in that we shared a belief in the importance of isolating and influencing the factors affecting worldwide balance of power. We also agreed that whatever else a foreign policy might be, it must be strong to be credible—and it must be credible to be successful." He thought "we needed to rethink our whole diplomatic and military policy in Vietnam." He was also "determined to avoid the trap Johnson had fallen into, of devoting virtually all my foreign policy time and energy to Vietnam, which was really a short-term problem." He recalled:

> Kissinger [noting that] Kennedy had replaced NSC strategic planning with tactical crisis management and Johnson, largely because of his concern with leaks, had reduced NSC's decision-making to informal weekly luncheon sessions with only a few advisers ... recommended that I structure a National Security apparatus within the White House that, in addition to coordinating foreign and defense policy, could also develop policy options for me to consider before making decisions.[11]

When, on December 12, Nixon informed President Johnson of his intention to "revive the 'moribund' National Security Council," the outgoing president doubted the wisdom of this decision:

> Let me tell you, Dick, I would have been a damn fool to have discussed major decisions with the full cabinet present, because I know that if I said something in the morning, you could sure as hell bet it would appear in the afternoon papers. It's the same thing with the National Security Council. Everybody there's got their damned deputies and note-takers with them sitting along the wall. I will warn you now, the leaks can kill you. I don't even let Hubert sit in on some of these meetings for fear his staff might let something out. And even with all the precautions I take, things still leak out.[12]

Kissinger, for his part, wrote that Nixon said he wanted a good negotiator as secretary of state rather than a policy maker because he reserved the latter role for himself and his assistant for National Security Affairs, "and because of his distrust of the Foreign Service, Nixon wanted a strong executive who would ensure State Department support of the President's policies." He regarded William Rogers as the ideal choice; "As a negotiator he would give the Soviets fits and 'the little boys in the State Department' had better be careful because Rogers would brook no nonsense."[13]

Kissinger went on to observe that lack of substantive knowledge is a problem for any cabinet member and "a particular problem for the Secretary of State." Kissinger thought that able, intelligent, competent, and hardworking as Foreign Service Officers might be, they had:

> ... the conviction that a lifetime of service and study has given them insights that transcend the untrained and shallow views of political appointees ... When there is not a strong hand at the helm, clannishness tends to overcome discipline. Desk Officers become advocates for the countries they deal with and not spokesmen of national policy. Assistant Secretaries push almost exclusively the concerns of their areas. Officers will fight for parochial interests with tenacity and a bureaucratic skill sharpened by decades of struggling for survival. They will

carry out clear-cut instructions with great loyalty, but the typical Foreign Service Officer is not easily persuaded that an instruction with which he disagrees is really clear-cut.[14]

Kissinger also considered the State Department's procedures "well-designed to put a premium on bureaucratic self-will." "Despite lip service to planning," he wrote, "there is a strong bias in favor of making policy in response to cables and in the form of cables." He later "discovered that it was a Herculean effort even for someone who had made foreign policy his life's work to dominate the State Department cable machine." He found it ironic that "Nixon's decision to choose as Secretary of State someone with little substantive preparation was that he thereby enhanced the influence of the two institutions he most distrusted—the Foreign Service and the Press." Kissinger thought that "Since he tended to identify the public and Congressional mood with the editorial position of leading Eastern newspapers, and since these also powerfully influenced his subordinates, Rogers at critical junctures found himself unwilling to do battle for the President and often sponsored positions at variance with Nixon's."[15]

Consequently, according to Kissinger, the president and he, acting for the president, dealt more and more with foreign leaders "through channels that directly linked the White House Situation Room to the field without going through the State Department—the so-called back channels. This process started on the day after Inauguration."[16]

> Nor was the President above dissociating himself from State Department foreign policy ventures. Thus in March 1969, Nixon asked me to inform Ambassador Dobrynin privately that the Secretary of State in his first lengthy talk on Vietnam with the Soviet envoy had gone beyond the President's thinking ... There can be no doubt, however, that the conduct of both the White House and the State Department made the Soviets aware of our own internal debate and that they did their best to exploit it. Nixon kept his private exchange with North Vietnam's President Ho Chi Minh in July–August 1969 from Rogers until forty-eight hours before he revealed it on television in November.[17]

Later, after his own experience as both national security advisor and secretary of state, Kissinger was to "... become convinced that a President should make the Secretary of State his principal adviser [sic] and use the National Security Adviser primarily as a senior administrator and coordinator to make certain that each significant point of view is heard."[18]

The president also ordered the dismantling of the Senior Interdepartmental Group (SIG) established in 1967 under the under secretary of state as chairman and including his opposite numbers in Defense and Treasury, the deputy chief of the CIA, and the chairman of the Joint Chiefs of Staff. Its function was to review the options to be passed up to the National Security Council and to follow up on the execution of decisions made. "Firmly persuaded of the Foreign Service's ineradicable hostility to him, Nixon flatly refused to consider preserving the SIG."[19] Kissinger observed that Former President Eisenhower and General Goodpaster, the latter being temporarily on Nixon's transfer staff, argued abolition of the SIG on the grounds the Pentagon "would never willingly accept State Department domination of the National Security process. It would attempt end-runs or counter-attack by leaking ... and for all his admiration for Dulles, he had always insisted on keeping control of the NSC machinery in the White House."[20]

As Kissinger noted, the SIG had not had much of a role in the Johnson Administration because the NSC met so rarely. Its abolition, therefore, was essentially a symbolic blow at "the Department's role in foreign policy."[21] The department tried unsuccessfully to fight back and National Security Decision Memorandum 2—signed on January 19, 1969, and issued shortly after Inauguration (January 20)—established a new NSC structure with final review "under White House chairmanship as it had been in the Eisenhower administration."[22]

Kissinger commented:

> To be sure the organization made White House control easier. It gave me a means to involve myself and my staff in early stages of policy formulation. Though this was not envisaged at the beginning, it also made possible the secret negotiations in which as time went on, I was increasingly involved. Nixon and I could use the interdepartmental machinery to educate ourselves by ordering planning papers on negotiations that, as far as the bureaucracy was concerned, were hypothetical; these studies told us the range of options and what could find support within the government. We were then able to put departmental ideas into practice outside of formal channels. Strange as it may seem, I never negotiated without a major departmental contribution even when the departments did not know what I was doing.[23]

Kissinger thought that since the influence of a presidential assistant really grows out of the confidence the president has in him, "the control of the interdepartmental machinery and the right to present options at NSC meetings were useful but not decisive." As he summed it up:

> Eventually, though not for the first one and a half years, I became the principal adviser [sic]. Until the end of 1970 I was influential but not dominant. From then on, my role increased as Nixon sought to bypass the delays and sometimes opposition of the departments. The fact remains that the NSC machinery was used more fully before my authority was confirmed, while afterward tactical decisions were increasingly taken outside the system in personal conversations with the President.[24]

As the BBC interviewers saw it, President Nixon had been elected at a time when there had been 20 years of war in Vietnam. President Johnson's refusal to send an additional 200,000 troops to Vietnam was seen as "a recognition that the strategy adopted since 1965, of seeking a military victory, was no longer achievable within a time and at a cost which was politically acceptable to enough Americans at home." They also judged that his decision not to run again in 1968, while pretty much ending the bombing in the North, had induced the communists to agree to start talking in Paris. It looked to them as if, "For the first time since World War II it seemed that America was in retreat," having been forced to look for a negotiated settlement. President Nixon's administration was therefore limited in its choice of actions by the state of American opinion and the results of the anti-war movement. Throughout the campaign it had become clear the role of American fighting forces would have to be reduced. Nixon was therefore obliged to start withdrawing troops. The level of American forces was to go down from 500,000 to 70,000 in two years; the American casualty rate reduced dramatically. "But the political commitment to the survival of a non-Communist South Vietnam remained." Nixon had told David Frost "more recently" (after leaving office) that "the reason for our being in Vietnam had not been adequately understood by the American people." He thought Kennedy and Johnson had been right in going into Vietnam but that they, especially Johnson, could have run the war in a much more effective manner. Nixon had his doubts, but he was not going to take the easy way of "bugging out" and blaming it all on his predecessors. Such a course of action might have been very popular, but the consequences would have been costly to the United States and even more costly to the free world.[25]

Nixon had started disengagement of the American forces, but he did not want to have to make "a humiliating exit from Vietnam," because of the harm that would do to "America's guarantees elsewhere in the world." Opinions diverged as to South Vietnam's possibilities of survival as an independent nation. Nixon's appointee as Assistant Secretary of Defense for International Security Affairs, Warren Nutter, told the BBC interviewers that "The question of winning militarily was really ruled out. There was no way at that point in time to bring to bear the kind of military force that would have been necessary to conclude the war." The remaining options were:

- Try to negotiate a settlement which we were already doing.
- Just abandon Vietnam—or "bug out."
- Try to train the Vietnamese to take over their own defense and gradually pull out our own forces remaining involved only to the extent of providing materiel, equipment, and "know-how."

He said the decision made at the time was to try a combination of negotiations and what was later called "Vietnamization," which was more or less the third alternative described above. He thought there was no movement at all being made at the negotiations because the communists insisted all along that we would have to give up militarily and also throw out the Government of Vietnam which was "absolutely contrary to our commitment." He thought that when we had first become involved in Vietnam, we had thought in terms of helping the South Vietnamese "to defend themselves and maintain a separate state."

> But then for a period of four years, that had been completely abandoned and in fact the opposite course had been taken and we imposed on them our own way of handling the military affairs and had removed them from all responsibility for any military action. They had virtually no responsibility left. And then suddenly, after TET [sic] we decided to train them at least to protect against the Viet Cong [sic], against the internal threat, but never against the external threat.

The BBC interviewers suggested it had become unrealistic to suppose a viable state could be made in South Vietnam, but Nutter thought we had been more optimistic than that.[26]

The BBC interviewers thought such optimism had been encouraged by those who believed the military strategy theretofore followed had established wrong priorities. They also observed that, after the Tet Offensive, it was better understood that the communists had taken "crippling casualties" and that while they had been politically successful in bringing about American disengagement, they were too weak to exploit their advantage on the ground. Sir Robert Thompson told the interviewers there was an alternative strategy that would have permitted continued American troop withdrawals.[27]

Thompson thought that instead of depending on fighting the North Vietnamese in a war of attrition, however necessary that might have been, the real priority should have been given to a containment of the North Vietnamese forces while rebuilding the South. He thought, "That is where the Americans failed absolutely between 1965 and 1968." He had given this advice to Kissinger even before Nixon's election. That is, the Americans should go back to emphasis on pacification and Vietnamization and if they did that, they could still withdraw 100,000 troops in the first year because of the resultant improvement in the internal situation. He said the Tet Offensive had destroyed most of the Việt Cộng regular and regional units in South Vietnam and that the South Vietnamese had, in fact, regained control in the countryside very rapidly between 1969 and 1970.[28]

Nixon in 1977 told the BBC interviewers he considered, during his first term of office, that it was possible to negotiate "a mutual withdrawal of all American forces and all foreign forces, including of course, North Vietnamese forces—within twelve months of an agreement, and a supervised election and a supervised ceasefire." There was no progress on this track. The communists stayed with their tough line until October 8, 1972. He thought the United States should continue to negotiate, combining negotiations, if they became deadlocked, with increased military pressure, combining such military pressure with training the South Vietnamese forces to take over more of the burden of the war.[29]

The BBC interviewers thought the North Vietnamese were not alone in thinking the United States would run out of patience. The South Vietnamese were worried about this possibility; Thiệu remarked in 1970:

> So, we have no reason to retain them forever here, and we have to replace them; that's quite normal. But the replacement of U.S. troops by Vietnamese troops should be gradual and very progressive. It takes years and years, but we are now feeling more and more confident and we try to do our best to alleviate the burden of U.S. people. And I think if the Vietnamization plan is very well done, it's the best solution for us, and for the Americans too.[30]

Vietnamization had two parts to it, strengthening the South Vietnamese Armed Forces and trying again "to police and pacify the villages of South Vietnam." The strategy of attrition had been "largely discredited." "President Nixon sent Colby out to Vietnam in 1969 with Ambassadorial rank to take personal charge of the new priority—pacification." Colby told the BBC interviewers that "the real war was still at the village level."[31] The interviewers thought the Americans were aware of the likelihood the communists would launch a major attack when ready to upset the pacification effort. They thought that:

> In an attempt to forestall that and also to give a forewarning of the response to be expected from him, President Nixon had sent American forces into Cambodia in 1970, into the sanctuaries where the Communist guerrillas trained and rested and which they used as jumping-off points for major military actions. Some of these were only fifty miles or so from Saigon [sic].

The anti-war reaction, including the Kent State affair, had reminded the president "There would be violent constraints at home to his use of American forces in ground fighting."[32]

Sir Robert Thompson thought the North Vietnamese and the Việt Cộng understood the pacification and Vietnamization effort was working even if the critics did not. They knew they were losing ground in the South and the government was getting stronger in all respects. They had to react and their only effective instrument was the North Vietnamese Army. So, they used it in March 1972, twelve divisions of it. They had some initial successes, but the South Vietnamese held and made it possible for American air power to intervene, inflicting heavy casualties on the North Vietnamese who, equipped with tanks and artillery, presented remunerative targets.[33]

The BBC interviewers observed that, in the months before this communist attack, Henry Kissinger had been engaged in secret diplomacy "in which he and President Nixon sought to change the whole context in which Vietnam had been viewed." Kissinger had been meeting, secretly at the home of Jean Sainteny in Paris, with a member of the North Vietnamese Politburo. "Also, in July 1971 the White House had announced that Kissinger had been to Peking secretly to see Zhou Enlai and Mao Tse-tung and that President Nixon himself would visit Chairman Mao in 1972." It seemed to the interviewers that Nixon and Kissinger were beginning to look at Vietnam "as an episode rather than an all-consuming concern. In which case, was Vietnamization at heart a fig leaf concealing another and more fundamental change?" Warren Nutter answered that:

> With hindsight it's become more and more clear to me that probably the leader of the Executive Branch, President Nixon, was more interested in finding some, as you call it, fig leaf to cover a fundamental change in our posture in the world than anything else; and I am not at all sure that wasn't the main interest of Henry Kissinger at that time.[34]

He added:

> Moreover, leading up to the second election of President Nixon it became more and more clear that the timetable that was set for various bench marks in foreign policy was geared almost exclusively to the elections so that it was imperative that Vietnam be settled by 1972. There was no doubt that that had to happen because otherwise it would be an election issue that would not be favorable to the President. Similarly, the whole unwinding, or the beginnings of the policy of detente and so on, the haute politique—all of that fitted into what now, as one looks back, seems to be a timetable designed primarily to ensure a reelection with a mandate.[35]

But that is getting ahead of the story.

Nixon wrote that, during the transition period in 1968, he and Kissinger had developed the concept of "linkage," in recognition of the widespread and overlapping interests of the two superpowers. This meant that progress in areas of concern to the Soviets, such as strategic arms limitation and increased trade, would be linked with progress in areas important to the United States, such as Vietnam, the Mideast, and Berlin. He said it took two years of hard effort on the American side before the Soviets would accept the idea.[36]

The most pressing foreign problem Nixon anticipated having to cope with was, of course, Vietnam; Kissinger began working out a review of all possible policies reduced to the form of "specific options" that ran the gamut from massive military escalation to immediate unilateral withdrawal. There was, for example, the escalation option which involved removal of the Johnson restrictions on military operations permitting bombing of the North, the threat of an invasion of North Vietnam, mining of Hải Phòng Harbor, and free pursuit of communist forces into Laos and Cambodia. Nixon wrote, "It was an option we ruled out very early."[37] The anticipated United States casualty rate made this option impracticable. Bombing the irrigation dikes in North Vietnam with very heavy civilian casualties or using tactical nuclear weapons would have caused an unacceptable "domestic and international uproar."[38] At the other extreme was the possibility of simply assuring the quick and orderly withdrawal of all American forces. Nixon thought that despite "some undeniably compelling political arguments to recommend this particular course" of action it was an option that had "long since been foreclosed." It would have meant abandonment of "17 million South Vietnamese, many of whom had worked for us and supported us, to Communist atrocities and domination ... We simply could not sacrifice an ally in such a way ... we would not be worthy of the trust of other nations and we certainly would not receive it."[39] Nixon said that, as far as he was concerned, "almost everything involving a Vietnam settlement was negotiable except two things: I would not agree to anything that did not include the return of all our ... [prisoners of war] and an accounting for our missing in action; and I would not agree to any terms that required or amounted to our overthrow of President Thieu [sic]."

As he saw it, there was no more enlightened or more tolerant or more democratic alternative to Thiệu but only someone weaker who would not be able to hold the various factions in South Vietnam together.[40] He saw the commitment to Thiệu, therefore, as a commitment to stability in South Vietnam. He wrote that "For three and a half years, until the fall of 1972, the North Vietnamese insisted upon our willingness to overthrow or sacrifice Thieu as a sine qua non for a settlement. Once they dropped this demand serious negotiations began."[41]

In Nixon's mind, he started out in office with three basic premises on Vietnam:

- He "would have to prepare public opinion for the fact that total military victory was no longer possible."
- He "would have to act on what my conscience, my experience and my analysis told me was true about the need to keep our commitment."
- He "would have to end the war as quickly as was honorably possible."

Since there was no chance of a military victory he had, he believed, to try for a negotiated settlement preserving the independence of South Vietnam and he was prepared to devote most of his first year as president to reaching such an arrangement.[42]

He decided in December to send such a message to the North Vietnamese through Jean Sainteny whom he and Kissinger had both met. Nixon's first message "set forth in conciliatory terms our proposals for a negotiated settlement." The reply, 11 days later, attacked the South Vietnamese for holding up the opening of the peace talks and the United States for supporting the South Vietnamese demands. However, it also expressed readiness to receive more information on the U.S. position. Nixon in turn replied he was ready to negotiate in good faith. In his inaugural address, he again spoke of his desire to reach a peaceful settlement but also said, "To all those who would be tempted by weakness, let us leave no doubt that we will be as strong as we need to be for as long as we need to be."[43]

As Nixon saw it, his problem was complicated by the fact, unprecedented in American history that "Many of the most prominent liberals in both parties in Congress, having supported our involvement in Vietnam under Kennedy and Johnson, were now trying to back off from their commitment." In 1969, he retained only a bare majority in Congress on war matters and was not at all sure how long this majority would hold. He also noted that "The American news media had come to dominate domestic opinion about its [the war's] purpose and conduct and also about the nature of the enemy." He wrote:

> The North Vietnamese were a particularly ruthless and cruel enemy, but the American media concentrated primarily on the failings and frailties of the South Vietnamese or of our own forces. In each night's TV news and in each morning's paper the war was reported battle by battle, but little or no sense of the underlying purpose of the fighting was conveyed. Eventually this contributed to the impression that we were fighting in military and moral quicksand, rather than toward an important and worthwhile objective.[44]

He also noted he "was the first newly elected President since Zachary Taylor 120 years earlier to take office with both houses of Congress controlled by the opposition party." Obviously, he required "a coalition of bipartisan support."[45]

Believing he was taking over as commander in chief "at what was perhaps the most troubled time in the history of our armed forces," concerned about the effects of the antiwar movement on the morale and discipline of the armed forces, seeing the problem getting worse as more and more draftees "infected by antiwar attitudes" entered the forces, he introduced in 1969 a plan for an all-volunteer force which, by 1973, ended the draft.[46]

On February 17, Nixon received the Soviet ambassador on his first official call and got the impression the Soviets "were prepared to move forward on a whole range of topics, including the Middle East, Central Europe, Vietnam and arms control."⁴⁷ On February 23, he started an eight-day visit to Europe, seeing the NATO Council, Queen Elizabeth, Prime Minister Harold Wilson, the Pope, and, especially, General de Gaulle. The Frenchman told him "the only way to end the war was by conducting negotiations on political and military issues simultaneously and by establishing a calendar for the departure of our troops." American power and wealth were so great they could make such a settlement with dignity, and direct conversations with the North Vietnamese would be the best way to go about it.⁴⁸

In February, the North Vietnamese started a small offensive against South Vietnam which Nixon regarded as an attempt to take his measure at the very beginning of his term. He and Kissinger were inclined to agree he must retaliate or lose the ability to deal with the communists "from a position of equality, much less one of strength." They thought Johnson had made the mistake of not so reacting. General Abrams and Ambassador Bunker agreed, calling for B-52 attacks on the communist supply line in the Cambodian sanctuaries. Secretary of State Rogers and Secretary of Defense Laird opposed the B-52 recommendation. The president wrote, "They feared the fury of Congress and the media if I expanded the war into Cambodia." He agreed with Kissinger that the fear of media objections should not affect his decision but decided to postpone action until his return from Europe in order to avoid the risk of antiwar demonstrations which might have marred his European visit. He did, however, alert General Abrams to continue contingency planning for B-52 strikes.⁴⁹

The communists intensified their offensive and, on March 14, opened a new one against the demilitarized zone (DMZ). Nixon met with Rogers, Laird, Kissinger, and General Wheeler on March 16. He reviewed U.S. casualty figures, noted intelligence reports of 40,000 communist troops massed "in a zone ten to fifteen miles wide just inside the Cambodian border," and considered the fact that "the state of play in Paris was completely sterile." He thought the only way to get the negotiations moving was to act on the military front. He decided to order the bombing under the codename *Menu* and recorded, "It was the first turning point in my administration's conduct of the Vietnam War."⁵⁰

Great precautions were ordered to keep the bombing secret. It was known that Prince Sihanouk greatly resented the North Vietnamese Army's presence in his country. "As early as 1968, he had asked the United States to retaliate against the North Vietnamese, either with 'hot pursuit' on the ground or by bombing the sanctuaries." Of course, because of his neutral status, he could not officially approve of such action. "Therefore, as long as we bombed secretly, we knew that Sihanouk would be silent; if the bombing became known publicly however, he would be forced to protest it publicly." We also expected the North Vietnamese, who were denying they had any troops in Cambodia at all, would have a problem in protesting. The domestic antiwar protest was another factor. The president did not want to touch off a great public outcry at the beginning of his administration. "In order to preserve the secrecy of the bombing, we informed only Richard Russell and John Stennis, the Chairman and the ranking member of the Senate Armed Services Committee. Although Russell was beginning to have doubts about the war in general, both men said that they would back me up in the event that it became public."[51]

President Nixon soon decided his predecessor's warnings about the dangers of "leaks" were well founded. Such leaks had started almost at once after he assumed office. "In the first five months of my presidency, at least twenty-one major stories based on leaks from materials in the NSC files appeared in New York and Washington newspapers. A CIA report listed forty-five newspaper articles in 1969 that contained serious breaches of secrecy." Details of the first NSC meeting on the Middle East were leaked to the press within a few days. Former President Eisenhower, who had been briefed by Nixon on the meeting, warned Kissinger to "tighten up" his operation. On May 9, an article in *The New York Times*, entitled "Raids in Cambodia by U.S. Unprotested," blew the Cambodian bombing exercise; "… the reporter attributed his information to Nixon administration sources." Nixon thought the Cambodian bombing had worked well, saving American lives, causing the enemy to suffer, and building pressure to negotiate, and now the "leak" threatened the whole thing. His reaction was interesting:

> Kissinger was enraged, and I was as well. He immediately speculated that the leak must have come from State or Defense. We knew that State Department bureaucrats routinely leaked. But in this particular case, Rogers was the only person at State who had been told about the bombing, and I was certain that he would never leak secret information.

They also suspected the Pentagon but apparently thought that since this leak would embarrass Secretary Laird it did not come from him. Nixon told Kissinger to take a hard look at his own staff and Kissinger consulted J. Edgar Hoover. Wiretaps were undertaken, but "unfortunately none of these wiretaps turned up any proof linking anyone in the government to a specific national security leak." So, as in the Johnson Administration, "When our efforts to discover the source of the leaks failed, we began conducting our foreign policy planning in small groups. It is an ironic consequence of leaking that instead of producing more open government, it invariably forces the government to operate in more confined and secret ways."[52]

Nixon thought in the early months of his first term that, despite the communist February 1969 offensive and the lack of movement in the Paris talks, military pressure resulting from the secret bombing and public opinion pressure resulting from his many invitations to talk would combine to make the communists respond. In March, as he told the cabinet, he thought the war would be over in a year.[53] He had proposed, at Paris, the restoration of the DMZ as a boundary between North and South Vietnam and had spoken of a simultaneous withdrawal of American and North Vietnamese troops from South Vietnam. President Thiệu had said he was ready to talk to the North Vietnamese about a political settlement and had offered free elections. However, the North Vietnamese stood fast, insisting political and military issues could not be separated, the United States would have to withdraw its troops unilaterally, and Thiệu would have to go before there could be serious talks.[54]

In April, Nixon and Kissinger tried to pressure the Soviets through Ambassador Dobrynin to get the North Vietnamese to meet with the U.S., separately from the Paris talks if necessary, to get moving on a discussion of general principles of a settlement. Kissinger told Dobrynin "that U.S.–Soviet relations were involved because, while we might talk about progress in other areas, a settlement in Vietnam was the key to everything."[55] Dobrynin argued that Soviet influence on Hà Nội was limited and the Soviets could never threaten to cut off Hà Nội's supplies. But he did say the proposals would be sent to Hà Nội "within twenty-four hours." In the absence of any reply as the weeks went by, Nixon made a speech on television on May 14 offering "our first comprehensive peace plan for Vietnam." He "proposed that the major part of all foreign troops—both U.S. and North Vietnamese—withdraw from South Vietnam within one year after an agreement had been signed. An international body would monitor the withdrawals and supervise free elections in South Vietnam." There was no real response. Nixon admitted that while he had never thought peace would come easily, he now had to realize "it might not come at all."[56]

The administration had decided early on that "withdrawing a number of American combat troops would demonstrate to Hanoi [sic] that we were serious in seeking a diplomatic settlement; it might also calm domestic public opinion by graphically demonstrating that we were beginning to wind down from the war." Secretary Laird, who "had long felt that the United States could 'Vietnamize' the war," returned from a visit to South Vietnam in March with an optimistic report about the possibilities of training the Vietnamese to defend themselves and, "largely on the basis of Laird's enthusiasm," Nixon undertook the "Vietnamization" policy, thus passing "another turning point in my administration's Vietnam strategy."[57]

Not too surprisingly, President Thiệu "was among those who objected to the proposed plan for American withdrawals from South Vietnam." Nixon assured him through Ambassador Bunker of our steadfast support and proposed a meeting on Midway Island on June 8 to reinforce this assurance. After the meeting, Nixon announced that "as a consequence of Thieu's [sic] recommendation and the assessment of our Commander in the field, I have decided to order the immediate redeployment from Vietnam of approximately 25,000 men. This involved some diplomatic exaggeration, because both Thieu and Abrams had privately raised objections to the withdrawals."[58] Nixon said he would consider further withdrawals on the basis of progress in training and equipping the South Vietnamese, the progress of the Paris talks, and the level of communist military activity.

Writing of Vietnamization in his book, Marshall Kỳ claimed he had for years "begged the Americans to allow the Vietnamese Army to shoulder more responsibility, to have more say in the planning and execution of the war, for if one wants to build a great army there is no better kind of on the job training than fighting in the field of battle." He wrote that he had asked President Johnson in Honolulu if it wouldn't be possible for the United States "to keep out of the picture" while helping the Vietnamese. Johnson had agreed to consider it but, in Kỳ's opinion, "Johnson feared that South Vietnam could never win the war." When Kỳ took the same line with Vice President Spiro Agnew, he said Agnew replied, "It sounds like a great idea, but do you think your boys can fight? I have heard reports they're not that good." Kỳ was inclined to agree Agnew was partly right but believed the problem was the Vietnamese troops had been too long part of an American machine; "... the morale of the armed forces would be much higher if our officers had more responsibility and felt they were fighting their own battle."[59]

Kỳ thought the Americans had been inhibiting the natural process of development which would have led the South Vietnamese to take over a more significant fighting role. He cited a speech he said he had made in July 1969 to a group of "nineteen former South Vietnamese generals," when he had said:

> The Americans have all along been wrong in their evaluation of the abilities and capacities of the Vietnamese people. According to reports by American advisers [sic], a number of Vietnamese units are ineffective and it will be difficult for them to replace American units. But I told the advisers that when there is a possibility of our doing the job, they should let us do it, so we can win the respect of the people.[60]

Kỳ, in his book, described Vietnamization as he saw it. General Westmoreland had told the Americans on television in 1967 that the United States could perhaps start pulling out its troops in 1969 if the bombing and the military program went on but this would also depend on whether or not the South Vietnamese could take on a larger share of the fighting. President Nixon had made Vietnamization the keystone of his Indochina policy. To bring the GIs home he would have to bolster the South Vietnamese forces sufficiently to preserve a non-communist regime. Kỳ claimed the idea was his although Westmoreland and Abrams had supported it. With $10,000,000 made available, General Abrams had begun a crash program to step up training. The Vietnamese had ordered a general mobilization of men from 18 to 38 with the seventeen-year-olds and those in the 39-to-43-year bracket available for the village protection forces.

He wrote that, by the end of 1970, the South Vietnamese had added 400,000 men to their services and accumulated 1,100,000 under arms. They had received, in three years, "nearly a million light weapons, 46,000 vehicles and 1,100 aircraft and helicopters."[61]

Kỳ thought, however, that the Americans had, while carrying on Vietnamization, unconsciously imposed an "American way of fighting" marked by squandering of ammunition, excessive use of air power and fire power in general, and excessive luxuries for the troops in the "PX" system, the products of which the Americans had shared with their Vietnamese allies, but which would vanish with Vietnamization.[62]

Guenter Lewy wrote that the idea of Vietnam eventually taking over its own struggle had been repeatedly emphasized since the beginning of American involvement, but that Vietnamization did not really get under way seriously until after the Tet Offensive and did not begin to produce results until later still.[63] The war had become Americanized for many reasons. American advisors had in many cases just found it easier and quicker to do things themselves. The big infusion of American troops in 1965 accentuated this process and, there was some reason to believe, further inclined the South Vietnamese to let the Americans "do the job for them."[64] Superior resources in weapons and in artillery, air, and helicopter support enjoyed by the Americans in relation to the Vietnamese also delayed the process. American production shortages were partly responsible but there was also an impression MACV (Military Assistance Command, Vietnam) was concentrating on building up American rather than Vietnamese forces because, as Marshal Kỳ, at least, believed, the Americans, who should have started Vietnamization in 1965, did not because they thought their firepower would bring about a quick victory.[65] Starting "in the summer of 1967—after the establishment of CORDS [Civil Operations and Revolutionary Development Support] under [Robert W.] Komer and the new emphasis on pacification and after President Johnson in July had decided to limit the further input of American troops," Vietnamization was accelerated after the Tet Offensive and the Clifford Task Force report. Plans (Phase I) to add more artillery, armor, and helicopters to the Vietnamese ground forces were approved in October 1968. In December, the Plan (Phase II) was approved for "creation of a self-sufficient RVNAF [Republic of Vietnam Armed Forces] capable of coping with the internal insurgency after a U.S.–North Vietnamese withdrawal." The Government of Vietnam, in the wake of Tet, was readier than it had been to mobilize more troops and 1968 "ended with the armed forces at the all time high of 819,200, up 176,000 from 1967," despite the 116,000 desertions during the year.[66]

By the beginning of 1972, the RVNAF, with almost four hundred twenty-nine thousand men in the Army, 43,000 sailors in the Navy, with 1,680 naval craft, and 51,000 airmen and well over one thousand aircraft, including about five hundred helicopters, "had taken over completely the combat on the ground." There were also about three hundred thousand Regional Forces and twenty-five thousand Popular Forces.[67]

It was generally agreed that "during these years of American disengagement the effectiveness of RVNAF increased significantly."[68] It was also quite clear that, at the beginning of the Nixon Administration, Vietnamization "became an essential ingredient of the policy of lightening the American combat burden while the U.S. gradually disengaged from Vietnam."[69] There was, however, a certain degree of optimism reflected in the rating of the Vietnamese units.[70] Leadership problems remained and were complicated by a shortage of officers.[71] Desertions continued. Another problem arose from the fact, already cited by Kỳ, the South Vietnamese Army had developed on the American model with great dependence on armor, artillery, air support, all kinds of sophisticated equipment, and lavish expenditure of ammunition,[72] making it unsuited for operations and survival without assured massive logistics support from the outside.

On his return from Midway, Nixon told the people who welcomed him on the White House lawn that the combination of his May 14 peace plan and the troop withdrawal decided at Midway had opened the door to peace; he said, "And now we invite the leaders of North Vietnam to walk with us in through that door."[73] He thought by the end of June that Hà Nội might be responding. There appeared to be a lull in military activity and there were intelligence reports of some North Vietnamese troop withdrawals from the South. Lê Đức Thọ, Politburo member and special advisor to the North Vietnamese Delegation in Paris, returned suddenly to Hà Nội, perhaps, it was speculated, to get instructions. Although he wrote that he remained aware of the danger of seeming over-anxious to negotiate, Nixon "decided to 'go for broke' in the sense that I would attempt to end the war one way or other—either by negotiated agreement or by an increased use of force."[74] Other considerations were pressing on him. He expected "a massive new anti-war tide would sweep the country during the fall and winter" after Congress and the colleges had returned from summer vacations. The dry season in Vietnam would almost certainly bring a new communist offensive in February. Pressures linked to the 1970 elections would produce Congressional demands for more troop withdrawals. He felt that "after half a year of sending peaceful signals to the Communists I was ready to use whatever military pressure was necessary to prevent them from taking over South Vietnam by force. During several long sessions Kissinger and I developed an elaborate orchestration of diplomatic, military and publicity pressures we would bring to bear on Hanoi [sic]."[75]

The president set the November 1, 1969, "anniversary of Johnson's bombing halt" as the deadline for an "ultimatum" he intended to issue to North Vietnam. He sent a letter on July 15 to Hồ Chí Minh via Jean Sainteny whom he received in the White House. He told Sainteny to let Hồ know that "unless some serious breakthrough had been achieved by the November 1 deadline, I would regretfully find myself obliged to have recourse 'to measures of great consequence and force.'" In the letter, he said:

> I realize that it is difficult to communicate meaningfully across the gulf of four years of war. But precisely because of this gulf, I wanted to take this opportunity to reaffirm in all solemnity my desire to work for a just peace ...
>
> As I have said repeatedly, there is nothing to be gained by waiting ...
>
> You will find us forthcoming and open-minded in a common effort to bring the blessings of peace to the brave people of Vietnam. Let history record that at this critical juncture, both sides turned their faces toward peace rather than toward conflict and war.[76]

The North Vietnamese soon proposed a secret meeting between Kissinger and Xuân Thủy. When, on July 23, Nixon went to the Pacific for the Apollo 11 splashdown and an onward tour, including visits to Guam, the Philippines, Indonesia, Thailand, South Vietnam, India, Pakistan, Romania, and Great Britain, he decided Kissinger should split off from the presidential trip and go on to Paris under the pretext of briefing French officials on the president's contacts during his travels. At Guam, Nixon enunciated the Guam Doctrine, later better known as the Nixon Doctrine. Nixon soon found some people, including Senator Mansfield, had misinterpreted the Nixon Doctrine as "signaling a new policy that would lead to total American withdrawal from

Asia and from other parts of the world as well." He wrote that he explained to Mansfield, as he had to Asian leaders, that "The Nixon Doctrine was not a formula for getting America out of Asia but one that provided the only sound basis for America's staying in and continuing to play a responsible role in helping the non-Communist nations and neutrals as well as our Asian allies to defend their independence."[77] In Romania, he took the occasion to tell President Nicolae Ceausescu that if there was no response to his recent message to Hà Nội "We must re-evaluate our policy," and that "In order to get peace we might have to open another channel of communication between the two states." Ceausescu promised to be helpful.

Kissinger meanwhile was approaching his secret meeting with Xuân Thủy, "the first negotiation in which I participated as a principal."[78]

In his "Foreign Affairs" article of January 1969, Kissinger had proposed the "two-track" approach in negotiations with the Vietnamese Communists. This meant the United States and Hà Nội would discuss the military issues and the Vietnamese parties would discuss the political issues. Harriman and Vance had endorsed this approach when they were President Johnson's negotiators. Quickly exposed to "the maddening diplomatic style of the North Vietnamese," Kissinger concluded, "It would have been impossible to find two societies less intended by fate to understand each other than the Vietnamese and the Americans."[79]

Kissinger had found the president skeptical of the chances for progress in negotiations until some military progress had been made on the ground and was therefore inclined to favor a policy of maximum pressure. He found Secretary Rogers and the State Department "at the other extreme." He thought the secretary's "primary objectives were to avoid domestic controversy and the charge of rigidity." Kissinger also thought, "Many in the State Department shared the outlook advocated by the leading newspapers or the more dovish figures in the Congress partly out of conviction, partly out of fear. The practical result was that we were deluged by State Department proposals whose main feature was that they contained elements the other side had vaguely hinted it might accept." He reported "constant pressure from our Paris delegation to initiate private talks with the North Vietnamese based on all sorts of compromise schemes" even though the communists remained rigid in their demands. Kissinger thought that Rogers had made a mistake, a "gaffer," in conversation with Ambassador Dobrynin in which he "unilaterally abrogated the two track approach" by expressing willingness to discuss political and military actions simultaneously and proposed immediate private talks with Hà Nội despite the shelling of Sài Gòn and without requiring "an end of attacks on major population centers as a condition."⁸⁰ He thought Secretary Laird had done something similar with a unilateral announcement of a 10-percent reduction in B-52 bomber sorties, "effective June 30, because of budgetary considerations."⁸¹

Sainteny, unable to get a visa for Hà Nội from the North Vietnamese, turned the president's letter over to Mai Văn Bộ, Hà Nội's representative in Paris. Since Lê Đức Thọ had left Paris, Kissinger was to meet Xuân Thủy, Hà Nội's plenipotentiary at the Paris talks, in Sainteny's apartment on August 4. Kissinger "still half believed that rapid progress would be made if we could convince them of our sincerity." He presented "the most comprehensive American peace plan yet. I had gone far beyond the most dovish position then being advocated within the Washington bureaucracy by offering the total withdrawal of all American troops with no provision whatever for residual forces. I had proposed the de-escalation of military operations." In Xuân Thủy's position:

> Hanoi [sic] continued to insist that the United States establish a new government under conditions in which the non-Communist side would be made impotent by the withdrawal of the American forces and demoralized by the removal of its leadership. If the United States had the effrontery to withdraw without bringing about such a political upheaval, the war would go on and our prisoners would remain.

Kissinger added that:

> Over the years we moved from position to position, from mutual to unilateral withdrawal, from residual forces to complete departure. But Hanoi never budged. We could have neither peace nor our prisoners until we achieved what Hanoi apparently no longer trusted itself to accomplish: the overthrow of an ally ... Our refusal to overthrow an allied government remained the single and crucial issue that deadlocked all negotiations until October 8, 1972, when Hanoi withdrew the demand.⁸²

Referring to Nixon's hints that "if no progress had been made in Paris by November 1, he would take strong action," Kissinger wrote, "The first I heard of the deadline was when Nixon uttered it to Yahya Khan in August 1969. And because Nixon never permitted State Department personnel [and only rarely the secretary of state] to sit in on his meetings with foreign leaders, no one else in our government ever knew that a threat had been made."⁸³

Nixon let Dobrynin know through Kissinger that Vietnam was the critical issue in Soviet–American relations and Kissinger added that "The next move was up to Hanoi [sic]."⁸⁴ On October 6, Nixon, meeting with Secretary Rogers:

> ... prohibited any new diplomatic initiative on Vietnam until Hanoi [sic] responded in some way; for the first time he mentioned his deadline of March 1. Rogers took the threat seriously because, as he told me on October 8, he was convinced the President would in fact make some move on November 1, though he was evidently no clearer than I just what it was.⁸⁵

"On October 13, the White House let it be known Nixon was planning a speech for November 3 to review Vietnam policy." In the meantime, Nixon told Dobrynin that in the absence of any progress soon the U.S. "would have to pursue its own methods for bringing the war to an end. On the other hand, if the Soviet Union cooperated in bringing the war to an honorable conclusion we would 'do something dramatic' to bring the war to an end."[86]

Diplomatic efforts to press the Soviets and the North Vietnamese continued as the antiwar movement, marked by the Vietnam Moratorium (October 15), gathered strength. Nixon noted that "My real concern was that these highly publicized efforts aimed at forcing me to end the war were seriously undermining my behind the scenes efforts to do just that." His concern was increased by Phạm Văn Đồng's letter, broadcast by Radio Hanoi, to the American people wishing splendid success to "A broad and powerful offensive throughout the United States to demand that the Nixon administration put an end to the Vietnam aggressive war and immediately bring all American troops home."[87]

As his November 1 "deadline" approached, Nixon said he considered three factors:

- American casualty figures in Vietnam had been reaching new lows and he thought this might be a communist ploy to make it difficult for him to escalate the fighting.
- The death of Hồ Chí Minh might have created new opportunities for reaching a settlement.
- Sir Robert Thompson had told him escalation would risk a major American and worldwide furor and still not address the central problem of whether the South Vietnamese were sufficiently confident and prepared to defend themselves against a renewed communist offensive.

In consideration of these factors, and because he recognized the moratorium had undercut the credibility of his November 1 ultimatum, Nixon said he began to think in terms of stepping up Vietnamization and holding the fighting at its current level instead of increasing it. He decided to use a meeting with Dobrynin on October 23 to make the U.S. position "absolutely clear" to the Soviets. In summary, he told Dobrynin the U.S. could not let a "talk–fight strategy continue without taking action."[88]

As the time for the speech approached, Nixon received "much conflicting advice," about how he should cast his speech. Secretaries Rogers and Laird urged him to concentrate on the hopes for peace. "Kissinger was advocating a very hard line." Senator Mansfield sent him a memorandum listing "actions that amounted to a unilateral cease-fire and withdrawal."[89]

In the event, as Nixon wrote:

> The message of my November 3 speech was that we were going to keep our commitment in Vietnam. We were going to continue fighting until the Communists agreed to negotiate a fair and honorable peace or until the South Vietnamese were able to defend themselves on their own—whichever came first. At the same time, we would continue our disengagement based on the principles of the Nixon Doctrine: the pace of withdrawal would be linked to the progress of Vietnamization, the level of enemy activity and developments on the negotiating front. I emphasized that our policy would not be affected by demonstrations in the streets.

Although "the comments and analyses broadcast by the network news correspondents criticized both my words and my motives," Nixon wrote, "... there were signs that the critics and the commentators were unrepresentative of public opinion ... I began to realize that the reaction to the speech was exceeding my most optimistic hopes."[90]

> By morning the public reaction was confirmed. The White House mail room reported the biggest response ever to any presidential speech. More than 50,000 telegrams and 30,000 letters had poured in, and the percentage of critical messages among them was low. A Gallup telephone poll taken immediately after the speech showed 77 percent approval.[91]

> The outpouring of popular support had a direct impact on Congressional opinion. By November 12, 300 members of the House of Representatives—119 Democrats and 181 Republicans—had co-sponsored a resolution of support for my Vietnam policies. Fifty-eight Senators—21 Democrats and 37 Republicans—had signed letters expressing similar sentiments.[92]

On November 13, Vice President Agnew made his Des Moines, Iowa, speech attacking the "unaccountable power in the hands of the 'unelected elite' of network newsmen." On November 15, the November Moratorium took place in Washington with "scattered episodes of violence."[93]

When he sized things up at the beginning of 1970, Nixon recalled:

> As I sat in my study in San Clemente on New Year's Day thinking about these problems, I actually allowed myself a feeling of cautious optimism that we had weathered the worst blows from Vietnam and had only to hold firm until time began to work in our favor. I suppose that in some respects the Vietnam story is one of mutual miscalculation. But if I underestimated the willingness of the North Vietnamese to hang on and resist a negotiated settlement on other than their own terms, they also underestimated my willingness to hold on despite the domestic and international pressures that would be raised against me.[94]

Kissinger thought Nixon's November 3 speech had had:

> ... a shock effect since it defied the protesters, the North Vietnamese, and all expectations by announcing no spectacular shift in our negotiating position and no troop withdrawals.

It had appealed to the "great silent majority" of Americans to support the Commander-in-Chief. For the first time in a presidential statement, it had spelled out clearly what the President meant when he said he had "a plan to end the war"—namely, the dual-track strategy of Vietnamization and negotiations. And it made the point that Vietnamization offered a prospect of honorable disengagement that was not hostage to the other side's cooperation.[95]

In short, as Kissinger saw it, the administration had gained some maneuvering room but would need something more than that to deal with the tenacious and persistent leaders in Hà Nội. What these leaders had been doing was hardly negotiation. "Hanoi [sic] was determined to break our will at home and to achieve this it could not permit a flicker of hope or the appearance of progress. As the last convinced Leninists in the world, the North Vietnamese had no intention of sharing power."[96]

Former President Johnson, meeting with President Nixon in the White House on December 11, 1969, said his own major mistake as president had been in "trusting the Russians" too much. He thought all the bombing pauses had been mistakes and that each of them had been undertaken because of assurances received from the Russians or other sources that the Vietnamese Communists would react positively.[97] Nixon and Kissinger had, as noted above, become a bit disillusioned as to the Soviet ambassador's usefulness as a channel to the North Vietnamese.

Nixon, in his book, was also quite frank in describing differences of outlook and clashes of personality in his own administration. Speaking of Kissinger and Secretaries Laird and Rogers, among whom he said the most important differences and clashes had occurred, he remarked that fireworks were inevitable when "three such distinctive personalities and temperaments were added to the already volatile institutional mix of the State Department, the NSC and the Pentagon." He noted that Rogers and Laird sometimes undertook sensitive dealings and negotiations without coordinating them with the White House and that sometimes they did it, not inadvertently but to head off objections by the president or Kissinger or "to show themselves, their departments and the press that they were capable of independent action." He noted that, in some cases, the results threatened "to undercut our policy and credibility with foreign nations." The president wrote that, "Rogers felt that Kissinger was Machiavellian, deceitful, egotistical, arrogant and insulting. Kissinger felt that Rogers was vain, uninformed, unable to keep a secret and hopelessly dominated by the State Department bureaucracy."[98]

At the beginning of 1970, in light of intelligence reports on the increased North Vietnamese infiltration of men and equipment into Laos and Cambodia, as well as into South Vietnam, Nixon began to think about what could be done to convince the communists we still took our commitment in Vietnam seriously. Kissinger had his second secret meeting with the North Vietnamese in Paris on February 21, 1970, and Nixon thought the American position was much stronger this time because of favorable reaction at home to his November 3 speech, and because we were now talking to both the Soviets (Bonn) and the Chinese (Warsaw). He noted also that Politburo member Lê Đức Thọ had joined Xuân Thủy. Although Thọ took the line that the people and the press of the United States, as well as most of the people of Vietnam, opposed the Sài Gòn government of "Thieu–Ky–Khiem," he indicated willingness to meet again on March 16. In preparing for the next meeting, Nixon told that, "We need a break-through on principle—and substance." On March 16, Kissinger told the North Vietnamese that, in the event of a settlement being reached, we could get all of our troops out of Vietnam within 16 months. Two days later, however, came the surprise Lon Nol coup against Prince Sihanouk of Cambodia, who was in Moscow on a trip.[99]

Kissinger met again with the North Vietnamese on April 4 but found that, "In short, Hanoi's [sic] position as it emerged in the three meetings with Le Duc Tho [sic] was preemptory and unyielding." He recorded that "The first series of secret negotiations with Le Duc Tho ended with his statement that unless we changed our position, there was nothing more to discuss." In examining the record later, Kissinger was astonished by his "own extraordinarily sanguine reporting." He wrote:

> The record leaves no doubt that we were looking for excuses to make the negotiations succeed, not to fail. Far from being determined on a military solution as our critics never tire of alleging, we went out of our way to give the benefit of every doubt to the pursuit of a negotiated settlement. Nixon shared this positive attitude despite his greater pessimism.[100]

Nixon's immediate reaction to the news from Cambodia had been to want to do everything possible to help Lon Nol, but Secretaries Rogers and Laird advised caution, as did CIA Director Helms. The two secretaries thought that Moscow, Peking, and Hà Nội might use the provision of U.S. military or economic aid as a pretext for a full-scale invasion of Cambodia. Helms reported that the Lon Nol Government was unlikely to survive and might be overthrown even before aid could be rushed to it. So, Nixon decided to wait and see for at least a week during which time the Cambodians fought very well and closed the Port of Sihanoukville, cutting off a major source of communist supplies.[101]

Despite the disturbing Cambodian military situation and the deadlock in the Paris talks, Nixon decided to go ahead with the withdrawal of American troops from Vietnam, scheduled for April 20. It would be useful in dealing with the building antiwar protest. The fact the president announced the withdrawal of 15,000 men over the next year, instead of a smaller figure over a shorter period of time, came as a "dramatic surprise."

Meanwhile, the communists had taken control of over a quarter of Cambodia and were moving on Phnom Penh. Nixon saw South Vietnam being outflanked, and the U.S. troop-withdrawal program being jeopardized by this communist move, and prepared to discuss aid for Lon Nol in an NSC meeting on April 22. He prepared a memorandum to Kissinger expressing the opinion that we had dropped the ball in Cambodia by worrying too much about Lon Nol's neutrality. It was the fault of "career State people" that we had made the same mistake in Hungary in 1956 and later in Czechoslovakia, and Laos by holding up an air strike, and now again "in Cambodia, where we have taken a completely hands-off attitude by protesting to the Senate that we have only a delegation of seven State Department jerks in the embassy, and would not provide any aid of any kind because we were fearful that if we did so it would give them a 'provocation' to come in."[102]

Nixon wrote, "I never had any illusions about the shattering effect a decision to go into Cambodia would have on public opinion at home. I knew that opinions among my major foreign policy advisers [sic] were deeply divided over the issue of widening the war, and I recognized that it could mean personal and political catastrophe for me and my administration."[103]

He made up his mind on April 26 and decided to "go for broke." The Vietnamese Army (ARVN) would enter the "Parrot's Beak" and a joint ARVN–U.S. force would go into the "Fishhook."[104] Secretaries Rogers and Laird tried unsuccessfully to talk the president out of using American troops. Rogers thought the casualties would be out of proportion to any damage done to the enemy. However, Kissinger, Ambassador Bunker, and General Abrams agreed with Nixon; so did George Meany and Chief Justice Berger. However, three of Kissinger's staff resigned to protest over the president's decision.[105] Nixon briefed the Congressional leadership and explained the operation on television, but a reference to "campus arsonists" as "bums" during a visit to the Pentagon was interpreted as applying to the whole antiwar movement and caused great indignation on the campuses, especially after the Kent State University incident. The president was "shocked and disappointed" when "an apparently intentional leak to the press" revealed Secretaries Rogers and Laird had been opposed to his Cambodian decision and he "called Rogers and told him that I felt the Cabinet should get behind a decision once it had been made by the President."[106]

Nixon obviously drew some comfort from a Gallup poll published in *Newsweek* in mid-May:

> It showed that 65 percent approved of his handling of the presidency; 30 percent of these described themselves as 'very satisfied.' Fifty percent approved of my decision to send troops into Cambodia; 39 percent disapproved; and 11 percent had no opinion. In response to the question, 'Who do you think was primarily responsible for the deaths of four students at Kent State?' 58 blamed 'demonstrating students' while only 11 percent blamed the National Guard.[107]

On May 30, Nixon reported on television that the Cambodian operation had been the most successful operation of the Vietnam War, resulting in the capture of "almost as much in enemy arms, equipment, ammunition and food during the past month in Cambodia alone as we had captured in all of Vietnam during all of 1969." At the end of June, he announced the departure of the last American troops from Cambodia, "exactly on schedule and exactly as I had promised." He summed up:

> We had captured enough individual weapons to equip seventy-four full strength North Vietnamese infantry battalions; enough rice to feed all the communist combat battalions estimated to be in South Vietnam for about four months; 143,000 rockets, mortars and recoilless rifle rounds—equivalent to the amount used in about 14 months of fighting; 199,522 antiaircraft rounds, 5,582 mines, 62,022 grenades and 83,000 pounds of explosives; 435 vehicles were captured and 11,688 bunkers and other military structures were destroyed.

The U.S. casualty rate went down to 51 per week in the six months after the operation as compared to 93 per week in the six months before it, and the Port of Sihanoukville remained closed to Soviet and Chinese arms shipments. However, on the day of the previously announced departure from Cambodia, the Senate passed the Cooper–Church amendment, the first restrictive vote ever cast on a president in wartime. "In essence it demanded" wrote Nixon, "that I remove all American troops from Cambodia by July 1. The symbolism of the timing was as serious as the action itself meaningless, since all Americans had already left Cambodia."[108]

On September 7, Kissinger met with the North Vietnamese for the first time since the Cambodian operation had taken place. As Kissinger noted in his book, it was "a week after we had survived the McGovern–Hatfield amendment" which would have set a deadline for American withdrawal on December 31, 1971, while allowing the president to extend the deadline by sixty days in an emergency. Although the amendment was defeated, Kissinger thought the fact 39 senators had voted for it, and that it was reintroduced again and again, gave the communists "another disincentive to negotiate."[109]

Nevertheless, Kissinger encountered no vituperation at the September 7 meeting. However, he soon found nothing had changed. Xuân Thủy even "dismissed our appointment of David Bruce as senior negotiator, despite the fact that at every meeting in February and March Le Duc Tho [sic] had castigated us for failing to replace Henry Cabot Lodge with a man of comparable distinction."[110] On September 17, Madame Nguyễn Thị Bình presented her eight-point peace program in Paris which meant in summary a total and unconditional U.S. withdrawal in nine months, starting immediately, the dumping of the Thiệu–Kỳ–Khiêm Government and the formation of a communist-dominated provisional government which would "negotiate with the Communists to decide South Vietnam's future."[111] On September 27, Kissinger met with Xuân Thủy who put forth his own schedule for American troops, cease-fire between United States and communist forces but not with South Vietnamese forces, and removal of Thiệu–Kỳ–Khiêm, a formula which Kissinger found one for "unconditional surrender and political desertion." Just the same, on October 7, 1970, President Nixon made a speech presenting "a comprehensive program that could well have served as a basis for negotiation except with an opponent bent on total victory." It:

- Offered a standstill cease-fire, including a halt to U.S. bombing throughout Indochina.
- Proposed a peace conference to bring an end to the wars in all the countries of Indochina.
- Expressed readiness to negotiate an agreed timetable for total withdrawal of American forces, in the context of mutual withdrawal.
- Invited Hà Nội to join in a political settlement based on the will of the South Vietnamese people.
- Offered to abide by the outcome of the agreed political process but rejected the "patently unreasonable" demand that we dismantle the organized non-communist forces.
- Called for release by both sides of all prisoners of war.[112]

The president's speech received almost unanimous praise from Congress and the press, but Xuân Thủy rejected the proposal it contained the very next day. Domestic criticism of the administration again began to build, especially after the unproductive raid at Sơn Tây intended to rescue American prisoners. A demand was raised for a unilateral American cease-fire in Vietnam.[113]

Kissinger believed there was a danger by the end of 1970 that our "Vietnam strategy would turn into a debate about the rate of our unilateral withdrawal."

Congressional budgetary pressures and the political requirement to cut the number of men drafted had made it impossible for the president to maintain the flexibility he desired in conducting the troop withdrawals.

As the number of American troops in South Vietnam diminished, the Vietnamese had to reduce their forces in Cambodia, thus making it less difficult for the communists to reestablish their sanctuaries there. Kissinger wrote that he and the president worked out a more practical strategy of American troop withdrawals, the rapid strengthening of South Vietnamese forces, and the progressive weakening of the enemy. "The strategy ... was carried out in essence in 1971 and 1972. And it worked. We managed to withdraw all our forces within little more than a year of the chosen date of the McGovern–Hatfield amendment. And we accomplished this without overthrowing an allied government." He summarized the rest of the story in a footnote: "The one circumstance we could not foresee was the debacle of Watergate. It was that which finally sealed the fate of South Vietnam by the erosion of executive authority, strangulation of South Vietnam by wholesale reductions of aid, and legislated prohibitions against enforcing the peace agreement in the face of unprovoked North Vietnamese violations."[114]

On March 6, 1970, at Key Biscayne, the White House released a presidential statement entitled "Scope of the U.S. Involvement in Laos." It sketched the "highly precarious situation in Laos" which the administration had inherited and the framework of which "had been established by the 1962 accords entered into by the Kennedy administration." It described the communist record of non-compliance with those accords and the presence at that time of some 67,000 North Vietnamese troops in Laos. It outlined the communists' use of the Ho Chi Minh Trail supply route for infiltration of arms and men into South Vietnam and their weakening and subversion of the Royal Lao Government "... to hinder it from interfering with North Vietnamese use of Laotian territory and to pave the way for the eventual establishment of a government more amenable to Communist control."

In his statement, the president set forth his policy as:

- Trying to save American and allied lives in South Vietnam by airstrikes which "have destroyed weapons and supplies over the past 4 years which would have taken thousands of American lives."
- Supporting the independence and neutrality of Laos as set forth in the 1962 Geneva Agreements ... at the request of the legitimate Government of Souvanna Phouma, which the North Vietnamese helped establish ...

- Acting in Laos "to bring about conditions for progress toward peace in the entire Indochinese Peninsula."

Nixon pointed out that what the U.S. did in Laos was "directly related to North Vietnamese violations of the agreements." He said, near the end of his statement, "We desire nothing more in Laos than to see a return to the Geneva Agreements and the withdrawal of North Vietnamese troops, leaving the Lao people to settle their own differences in a peaceful manner."[115]

Against this background, Kissinger wrote it was the pursuit of the strategy which the president and he had devised for withdrawal of U.S. troops from Vietnam that "led us to the Laos operation of 1971."[116] An analysis of the military and political prospects for the next two years, which he asked "the experts in the government and on my staff" to make late in 1970, led him to two conclusions.

- "The enemy had to be prevented from taking over Cambodia and Laos if Vietnamization was to have any chance of success."
- "And the enemy's dry-season logistics buildup would have to be slowed down, or if possible interrupted."

These conclusions suggested the utility of an allied dry season offensive, with the still remaining U.S. troops assuming static security functions and thus freeing South Vietnamese troops for offensive operations. Kissinger first thought of such an operation in connection with Cambodia but action in that area would not have directly addressed the most important danger: "a possible North Vietnamese attack in the Central Highlands and across the Demilitarized Zone." Bunker, Abrams, and Thiệu recommended "a much more daring concept" than Kissinger which would address the key strategic concern. "They proposed to deal with the enemy's logistics buildup in one fell swoop by cutting the Ho Chi Minh Trail in Laos near the DMZ."[117]

General Westmoreland, in his book, wrote that after the closing of Sihanoukville to the communists, the bombing of communist supply depots, and naval blockade of the coast against infiltration by sea, the "North Vietnamese had to depend almost exclusively on the Ho Chi Minh Trail" and raiding the trail was so obviously the next step that the North Vietnamese anticipated it and prepared to meet it. He thought the plan should have been undertaken two years earlier when MACV, which had plans prepared, was at its peak strength.[118]

General Abrams held the view "that if the Ho Chi Minh Trail could be denied to the Communists, or effectively disrupted for even one dry season,

Hanoi's [sic] ability to launch major offensive operations in the South (and Cambodia) would be significantly curtailed, if not eliminated, for an indefinite future." To this end, Abrams proposed a bold plan.[119]

Kissinger wrote that Nixon was determined to involve his key Cabinet officers in every facet of the decision making this time in order to make them take some of the heat from the anticipated critical public reaction. He wrote that Nixon maneuvered to present Secretary Rogers with a "united front of all of his colleagues." Rogers supported the plan as presented by Secretary Laird, "after reassuring himself that there would be no significant increase in casualties," but "insisted that it was crucial that the operation succeed." However, in Kissinger's words, "the government consensus ... began to evaporate as soon as Rogers was exposed to the passionate opposition of his experts." By January 21, it became apparent State was dragging its feet. At WSAG (Washington Special Action Group) meetings, Under Secretary Alex Johnson began to surface objections that did not challenge the decision but would have delayed its implementation indefinitely—a bureaucratic maneuver in which he was superbly skilled. The device to procrastinate was insistence on the prior approval of the Laotian prime minister, Souvanna Phouma.[120] Kissinger wrote that Souvanna Phouma was not about to give more than tacit concurrence on the one hand for fear of provoking the North Vietnamese, nor was he going to be the one who opposed the operation. Kissinger believed the State Department was stalling and that "its objections went beyond the procedural."

In a meeting of the president with Rogers, Laird, Helms, Moorer, Haig, and Kissinger, Secretary Rogers argued the risks of the operation were excessive:

> The enemy had intelligence of our plans. A battle was certain. We were asking the South Vietnamese to conduct an operation that we had refused to undertake when we had 500,000 troops in Vietnam because we thought we were not strong enough. If Saigon [sic] were set back, we would risk all the gains of the previous year and might shake Thieu's [sic] position in the process.

The president was not deterred and, despite press and Congressional criticism stimulated by leaks from official press briefings, ordered the operation, *Lam Son 719*, executed.[121] In Kissinger's words, it "fell far short of our expectations."[122]

General Westmoreland noted in his book that the ARVN made quick gains at first in *Lam Son 719*, getting as far as 25 kilometers inside Laos and reaching all their assigned objectives before the North Vietnamese began heavy counterattacks. During the withdrawal which then became necessary, the weaknesses in the South Vietnamese preparations showed up. Command arrangements were unsound and planning had been done too quickly. The absence of American advisors, to whom ARVN commanders had become accustomed, caused some of the commanders to "fold" and Thiệu had to try to give orders down to the regimental level.[123]

"Between the beginning and the end of the Laotian operation," wrote Kissinger, "no fewer than five Congressional resolutions were introduced, aimed at limiting Presidential discretion in the conduct of military operations, prohibiting expenditures for combat in Cambodia and Laos (which all our studies had shown were pivotal to the war in Vietnam), or fixing a date for unconditional withdrawal." To put it mildly, "both media and Congressional pressures escalated" after the withdrawal from Laos. "Between April 1 and July 1 there were seventeen House or Senate votes seeking to restrict the President's authority to conduct the war or to fix a date for unilateral withdrawal [making a total of 22 for the year]." Senator Mansfield's Sense of the Senate Resolution, adopted 57–42 on June 22, declared "it is the policy of the U.S. to terminate at the earliest practicable date all military operations in Indochina and to provide for the prompt and early withdrawal of all U.S. forces not more than nine months after the bill's enactment subject to the release of American … [prisoners of war]."[124] Antiwar demonstrations in Washington marked April and May, including the one on May Day intended to "bring the government to a halt."

In preparation for resumption of the secret negotiations in Paris, Kissinger prepared a new seven-point peace plan which Nixon agreed to have presented as a "final offer." It offered unilateral American withdrawal contingent on agreement on other issues. The proposal, which Kissinger said marked a turning point in our diplomacy in Vietnam, represented the approach he had recommended in his "Foreign Affairs" article in 1968.[125] Thiệu had accepted it in 1971 and it was assumed he would still welcome it in 1972. Xuân Thủy seemed eager to keep discussion of this proposal alive. On June 22, the Senate passed 57–42 the Mansfield amendment "calling on the President to withdraw all American forces from Vietnam within nine months if Hanoi [sic] agreed to release all our Prisoners." Kissinger thought this action made five of the seven points in the secret negotiations irrelevant. Kissinger met Lê Đức Thọ again on June 26. Lê Đức Thọ presented a nine-point proposal which seemed to be keyed to the McGovern–Hatfield amendment and the Mansfield amendment; "For the first time Hanoi [sic] presented its ideas as a negotiating document and not as a set of preemptory demands." Kissinger was supposed to submit a counterproposal on July 12 "seeking to merge Hanoi's document and ours." However, on July 1, Madame Bình "published a new seven-point plan that partly duplicated Le Duc Tho's [sic] nine points, spelled some of them out in greater detail, omitted others altogether, and added some new ones." Kissinger found Madame Bình's plan "cleverly geared to the American public debate," and noted the North Vietnamese gave several "deceptive interviews to prominent antiwar Americans." "The Congress and media were at one that the administration was passing up yet another unparalleled opportunity for peace." At the same time, "We were constrained from demonstrating that the 'chance' was bogus and at variance with the entire secret—and the public—record of the negotiations."[126]

Kissinger met again with Lê Đức Thọ and Xuân Thủy on July 12 and despite the usual North Vietnamese tactics the meeting did become a real negotiating session. Kissinger believed it "narrowed differences to one issue—the political arrangements in Saigon [sic]." However, at the next meeting on July 26 [they] still insisted that we dump Thieu.[127]

Kissinger next proposed, with Thiệu's agreement, that there could be a new presidential election in South Vietnam within six months of the final agreement's signature. The election would be run by an electoral commission representing all the political forces, including the communists, under international supervision. One month before the election, President Thiệu would resign and his function would be assumed by the president of the senate. At that point, the small residual American force would be withdrawn. We would also shorten our withdrawal deadline from nine months to seven. Nixon approved and the proposal was handed to the North Vietnamese in Paris on October 11. They proposed a meeting for November 17, but later said Lê Đức Thọ was unavailable. Kissinger commented that "the North Vietnamese, in the late stages of planning their major military offensive of 1972, were bending all their energies toward one last test of strength."[128] Kissinger thought that the "biggest single factor" in causing Hà Nội's intransigence was the divisions in America which led them to believe they "could do no worse than a withdrawal-for-prisoners deal." He thought a total collapse of the negotiations was prevented only by a combination of the China announcement, which had overshadowed Madame Bình's seven-point gambit, and the Soviets' announcement on October 12 of Nixon's summit in Moscow. President Nixon finally laid the record of the negotiations before the American people on January 25, 1972.[129]

For a while, about a week, the reaction to the revelation of the administration's record and intentions drew a favorable media reaction.[130] Kissinger found the North Vietnamese had been put "off stride" and "on the defensive." He also found that:

> ... by any normal standards our Vietnam policy early in 1972 was a considerable success. We had withdrawn over 140,000 troops while improving the military position of an ally. We had isolated Hanoi [sic] diplomatically from its main sources of support. At home we had withstood the most bitter assault on a government's policy in this century. We had done all this while fulfilling our global responsibilities by standing on the principle that we did not abandon allies and turn over friendly people to repression.[131]

He thought if we could ride out the expected communist offensive in Vietnam "the President would go to Peking and Moscow with hope that we could begin the construction of a new international order."[132]

The invasion came on March 30, 1972. Nixon saw it as an act of desperation by the North Vietnamese and ordered preparations for a massive bombing in the North, in retaliation.[133] "Three North Vietnamese divisions poured across the demilitarized Zone (DMZ) supported by more than 200 tanks and large numbers of new 130mm recoilless artillery, all furnished by the Soviet Union." Other units were in place to invade the northern part of South Vietnam from Laos along Route 9. Communist forces were concentrating in the Central Highlands and three other North Vietnamese divisions were moving into Military Region 3 in which Sài Gòn was located. "The pretense that the Vietnam conflict was a 'People's war,' a guerrilla uprising in the South, was over; this was an invasion by the North Vietnamese Regular Army in division strength."[134]

The air attacks authorized by the president against military concentrations in North Vietnam (within 25 miles of the DMZ) were handicapped by bad weather which caused many cancellations but, as Kissinger saw it, "Whatever the outcome of the offensive, it could end the war. This was Hanoi's [sic] last throw of the dice. One way or another there would now be serious negotiations." It was important to prevent a South Vietnamese collapse to avoid disastrous consequences to the broader negotiating positions with the Soviet Union and the Chinese and to the United States' relations with its allies.[135]

To make a long story short, General Abrams, foreseeing the communist offensive, had asked for authority to disrupt the communists' operations by air attacks. The White House feared resumption of the attacks would interfere with the president's trip to Peking; the State Department thought it would ruin negotiation prospects. Defense did not want the expense of it. Troop withdrawals continued while airpower was reinforced. "By threatening serious reprisals if Hanoi [sic] challenged us, we did our best to feed the nervousness of Moscow and Peking." In communications through the "private channel," Peking more or less disengaged itself from the issue and its "material support was marginal because of its limited resources." Kissinger warned Dobrynin repeatedly that the Moscow summit would be jeopardized if Hà Nội sought "to force a military decision." Hà Nội had replied to our request for another meeting with Lê Đức Thọ in an "excessively conciliatory tone" so different from their past practice and so contradictory to its military preparations that Kissinger later thought we should have realized Hà Nội was "gearing the resumption of negotiations to the timing of its forthcoming offensive."[136]

When the offensive did start, some civilians in Defense, "much of the State Department," and systems analysis experts thought it should be treated as "the conclusive test of Vietnamization, strengthening South Vietnam's self-defense capacity but not increasing our own effort." However, neither Nixon nor Kissinger was in the mood for such a passive reaction. Kissinger thought that "if we defeated the offensive, we would get a settlement out of it." "Against an intensive bureaucratic opposition," Nixon "ordered repeated augmentation of our air and naval forces in Southeast Asia. He took off all budgetary restraints on air sorties. He directed naval attacks extended 25 miles up the coast of North Vietnam."[137] Including an attack on supply dumps near Vinh, about 150 miles north of the DMZ, "the first use of B-52s in North Vietnam by the Nixon administration,"[138] and later, on the weekend of April 15–16, "a dramatic two-day B-52 attack on fuel store depots in the Hanoi–Haiphong [sic] area together with a shore bombardment by naval gunfire."[139] None of this caused the Soviets to cancel Kissinger's trip to Moscow and he went there on April 20 to prepare for the Nixon–Brezhnev summit.[140]

On April 26, Nixon, in a televised speech, announced the scheduled troop withdrawal of 20,000 men[141]:

> By July 1, we will have withdrawn over 90 percent of our forces that were in Vietnam in 1969. Before the enemy's invasion began, we had cut our air sorties in half. We have offered exceedingly generous terms for peace. The only thing we have refused to do is to accede to the enemy's demand to overthrow the lawfully constituted Government of South Vietnam and to impose a Communist dictatorship in its place.[142]

On May 1, the communists captured the Provincial Capital of Quảng Trị inflicting heavy casualties on South Vietnamese military and civilians.[143]

In the May 2 secret meeting in Paris, Lê Đức Thọ went on the offensive "simply reading its [Hà Nội's] public position to me without explanation, modification or attempt at negotiation." Kissinger concluded that "Now there was no question that we would have to have a showdown. The back of the North Vietnamese offensive had to be broken militarily ... Moscow clearly either could not or would not affect Hanoi's [sic] decisions until the outcome of the offensive was clear."[144]

On May 8, in a televised speech to the nation, Nixon described the military situation and the deadlock in the negotiations and announced that he had ordered:

- The mining of Hải Phòng Harbor and all other North Vietnamese ports (mines to be activated May 11).
- A blockade of North Vietnam.
- Intensified bombing of rail and other lines of communication.
- Continuation of air and naval strikes against military targets in the North.[145]

He also presented a new peace proposal which became the reference point for the terms of the final settlement the following January:

> First, all American prisoners of war must be returned.
>
> Second, there must be an internationally supervised cease-fire throughout Indochina.
>
> Once prisoners of war are released, once the internationally supervised cease-fire has begun, we will stop all acts of force throughout Indochina and at that time we will proceed with a complete withdrawal of all American forces from Vietnam within four months.
>
> Now these terms are generous terms. They are terms which would not require surrender and humiliation on the part of anybody ... They deserve immediate acceptance by North Vietnam.[146]

Kissinger observed:

> The terms were in fact, the most forthcoming we had put forward a standstill cease-fire, release of prisoners, and total American withdrawal within four months. The deadline for withdrawal was the shortest ever. The offer of a standstill cease-fire implied that American bombing would stop and that Hanoi [sic] could keep all the gains made in its offensive. We were pledged to withdraw totally in return for a cease-fire and return of our prisoners.[147]

He wrote that "For the moment, the explanations signals were overwhelmed by Congressional and media outrage," and that "If the critics had paid closer attention to reality and less to personal outrage, they would have noted that the Communist reaction was much more restrained than their own,"[148] "The summit was on. That crisis was over."[149]

Hà Nội's offensive ran down and negotiations were resumed in plenary session on July 13 and in a private meeting on July 19. Certain differences began to emerge between the Americans and General Thiệu. The differences "lay in nuances, in hints whose full import we did not grasp."[150] At the same time there was "significant movement" by Hà Nội and Kissinger thought "We have gotten closer to a negotiated settlement than ever before."[151] Thiệu became more critical on a number of the negotiating documents. Kissinger thought Thiệu was quite right in his desire to convince his people that "An agreement was not a defeat nor a threat to South Vietnam's internal stability," but found Thiệu's "own infuriating negotiating style deprived us of any real insight into his thinking." He eventually grasped that "Thieu [sic] and his government were simply not ready for a negotiated peace."[152]

In a meeting on October 8, "after four years of implacable insistence that we dismantle the political structure of our ally and replace it with a coalition government, Hanoi [sic] had now essentially given up its political demands."[153] "And so it was, Hanoi had finally separated the military and political questions, which I had urged nearly four years earlier as the best way to settle. It had accepted Nixon's May 8 proposal and conceded that the South Vietnamese Government need not be overthrown as the price of a ceasefire. Having ignored our offer of a presidential election, Hanoi even removed the necessity of Thieu's temporary withdrawal before it. The demand for coalition government was dropped; the political structure of South Vietnam was left to the Vietnamese to settle."[154] Kissinger chose "to accept Le Duc Tho's [sic] plan in principle and immediately proceed to negotiate to improve it further."[155]

There still remained the question of Thiệu's reaction and the president was concerned about the possibility he would balk. Kissinger saw Thiệu on October 18 and delivered a letter from Nixon informing him that "... we have no reasonable alternative but to accept this agreement." He also carried a handwritten note from Nixon reading, "Dr. Kissinger, General Haig and I have discussed this proposal at great length. I am personally convinced it is the best we will be able to get and that it meets my absolute condition—that the GVN must survive as a free country. Dr. Kissinger's comments have my backing."[156] Thiệu procrastinated skillfully because of what the American side described as "unwillingness to cut the umbilical cord" to the United States due to his lack of confidence that his government could stand up to the communists alone.[157] As Kissinger put it "Thieu [sic] sought total victory; we, an honorable compromise. By October 1972 these two positions could not be reconciled."[158]

After many discussions in Sài Gòn, Paris, and Washington, during which the North Vietnamese also became very difficult again in order to exploit "the split between Washington and Saigon [sic], the evident division within our own government, and the imminent return of a Congress even more hostile to the administration than its predecessor," Kissinger thought "Hanoi [sic] had in effect made a strategic decision to prolong the war, abort all negotiations, and at the last moment seek unconditional victory once again."[159] Instead they got the "Christmas Bombing," starting December 18 and continuing for 12 days. Thiệu for his part got some tough messages from Nixon including a very tough one on January 16, delivered by General Haig. Kissinger noted it had "required nearly three months, about twenty changes in the text of the agreement and the threat of an American aid cutoff to obtain Thieu's [sic] acquiescence."[160] Negotiations resumed with technical talks on January 2, 1973, and a Lê Đức Thọ–Kissinger meeting on January 8 with a "major breakthrough" on January 9.

At 10 pm on January 23, President Nixon announced a settlement had been reached in Paris and that a cease-fire would begin on January 27.[161]

Marshal Kỳ wrote in his book, "The Vietnam war ended so far as America was concerned, with the cease-fire at midnight on Saturday, January 27, 1973."[162] He added, "In fact the Paris Agreement gave the world an entirely wrong impression. Though it was the end of the war for America, it was never regarded as the end of the war by Hanoi [sic]."[163]

Guenter Lewy commented that the terms of the January 27 agreement were the best terms Kissinger had been able to obtain:

> It was less than a perfect or happy ending to the process of Vietnamization begun some four years earlier—an ending, like the original decision to disengage, strongly influenced by domestic considerations. It was hoped that the agreement would at last put an end to the festering wounds of divisiveness in the U.S. created by the Vietnam conflict.

He went on that "On the face of it, the agreement did look like an abandonment of South Vietnam by its American ally," but added that, "Unknown to all but top policy makers, the Nixon administration had assured the GVN that in case of any major violation of the accords by Hanoi [sic], the U.S. would react forcefully, presumably by resuming the bombing of North Vietnam." On January 23, Nixon had publicly repeated his promise of support for Vietnam. "No sooner had the agreement been signed than North Vietnam started violating its provisions." Kissinger appealed unsuccessfully to Hà Nội to stop these violations. On March 15, Nixon warned the North Vietnamese to stop the violations and resumed aerial reconnaissance flights over North Vietnam. Watergate distracted him and the War Powers Resolution, enacted November 7, 1973, eliminated any threat of the use of U.S. military power to deter a new attack on the South:

> ... the overall balance of forces had shifted decidedly in favor of Hanoi [sic] as a result of the complete American withdrawal and the Congressional prohibition of a reintroduction of American combat forces. Hence in October 1973 the Central Committee of the Lao Dong Party decided that the time had come to assume the strategic offensive, and in the spring of

1974 the NVA General Staff, the General Political Department and the General Logistics Department began formulating plans for large scale offensives to be launched in 1975.[164]

Many diplomatic, military, and organizational lessons have been drawn from the American Vietnam experience, some of them so specific and so vigorously presented as to turn the whole period into what a British historian of the Boer war has called a "war of might have beens."

The one obvious general lesson that emerges is one set by a French statesman three hundred years ago:

> In an era of undisputed autocracy, Richelieu was original also in contending that no policy could succeed unless it had national opinion behind it.[165]

INDOCHINA 1974

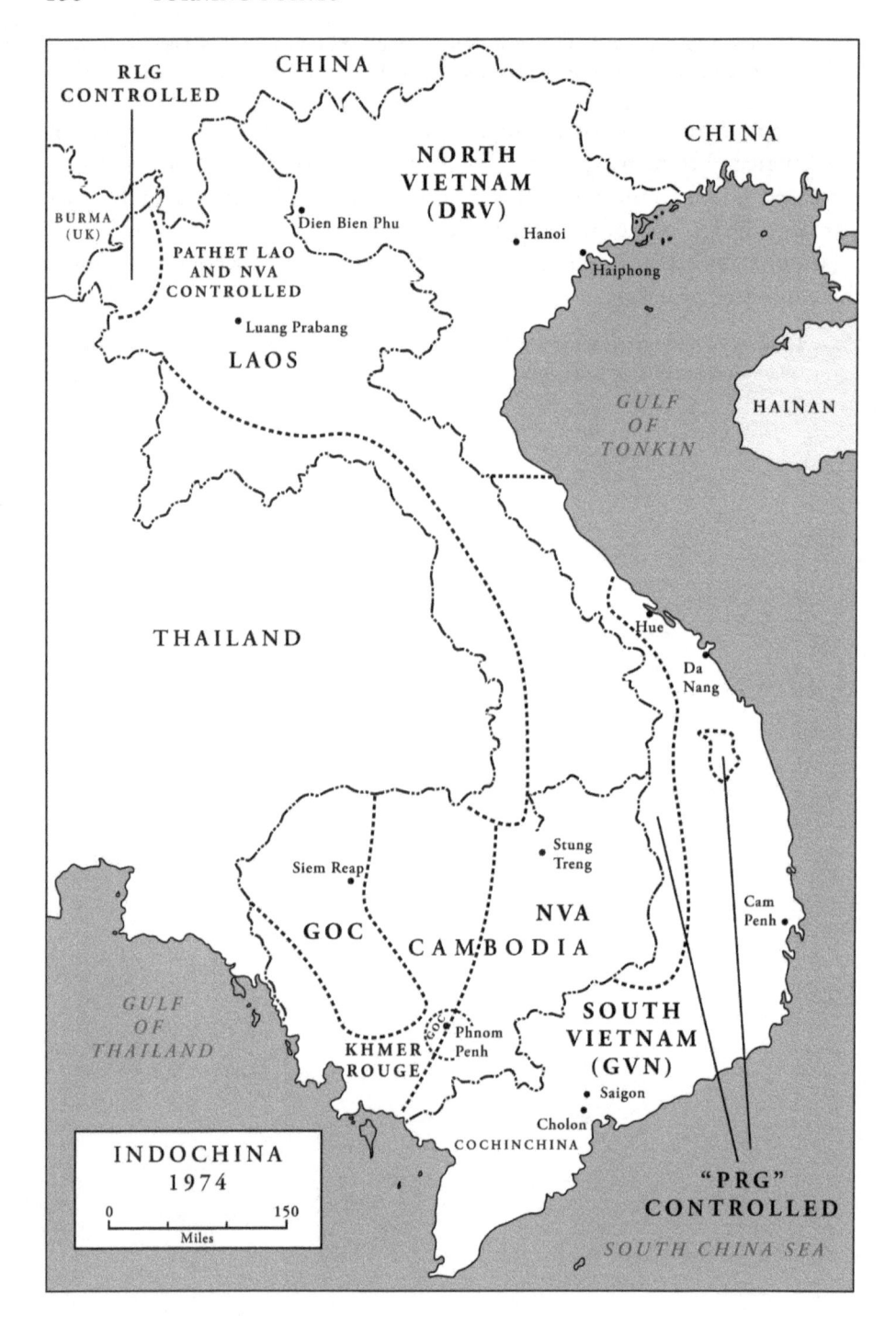

APPENDIX A

The Path to Viet-Nam

A Lesson in Involvement

by William P. Bundy
Assistant Secretary for East Asian and Pacific Affairs[1]

You have asked me to speak this morning on the topic "The Path to Viet-Nam: A Lesson in Involvement." I welcome this opportunity to review the whole history of United States actions with respect to Viet-Nam [*sic*]—speaking personally as to the period up to 1961, during which I had no policy responsibility, and of course necessarily more officially for the period since January of 1961.

Quite apart from the enormous present importance of South Viet-Nam and our actions there, I have often reflected—as one who was tempted to become a professional historian—that the story of Viet-Nam, of Southeast Asia, and of American policy there forms an extraordinarily broad case history involving almost all the major problems that have affected the world as a whole in the past 25 years. For the strands of the Viet-Nam history include the characteristics of French colonial control compared to colonial control elsewhere; the end of the colonial period; the interrelation and competition of nationalism and communism; our relation to the Soviet Union and Communist China and their relationships with each other; our relation to the European colonial power, France; and—at least since 1954—the relation of Viet-Nam to the wider question of national independence and self-determination in Southeast Asia and indeed throughout Asia.

The Viet-Nam story is above all a product of Vietnamese aspirations and decisions. In the early period French decisions were crucial. But I am sure you want me to focus on the American policy role, how and why we became involved, and how we reached the present position. This should not be a purely historical discussion, of course, and I know that you have natural and valid concerns that focus particularly on the decisions of the last 2 years and on the decisions that confront us now and in the future. So, I shall touch briefly on these, fully expecting that your questions will be quite largely in this area.

For our mutual convenience in analysis, I have tried to isolate 10 major American decisions going back to 1945. It is not for me to defend, or necessarily to justify, policy decisions taken before 1961, but it is essential to examine them if one is to understand the present position.

Decisions During French Colonial Era

Our first decisions affecting Viet-Nam were in 1945. President Roosevelt deeply believed that French colonial control in Indochina should not be restored, and this attitude led us in the closing months of the war against militarist Japan to adopt what the French have always considered an obstructive attitude toward their return. Separately, we briefly gave modest assistance to Ho Chi Minh [sic] as an asset against the Japanese. This story, like so much else in the whole record, is best told in Robert Shaplen's thoughtful *The Lost Revolution*.

Second, when the French had returned, we stood aside. In the critical year 1946, and over the next 3 or 4 years, the French first made the Fontainebleau agreement and then broke it, so that major conflict started. It has often been argued, by Shaplen among others, that we could have exerted greater pressure, perhaps even effective pressure, on the French to go through with the Fontainebleau agreement and to set Viet-Nam on the path to early independence. The failure to exert such pressure may thus be construed as a negative policy decision on our part.

I myself am skeptical that we could conceivably have affected the unfortunate course that the French followed in this period. If it is argued that our overwhelming Marshall Plan aid to France should have given us leverage, then it must be pointed out at the same time that the Marshall Plan became operative only early in 1948 and that by then the die was largely cast. Moreover, I doubt very much if the proud and bruised French nation would have responded even if we had tried to act to end the colonial era, as we did to a major extent with the Dutch in Indonesia.

In a very real sense, the tragedy of Viet-Nam derives from the fall of France in 1940 and all the understandable emotions aroused by that event among French leaders, including notably de Gaulle himself. Restored control in Indochina was a badge, however mistaken, for a France that meant to be once again a world power. Although it may be argued that we should at least have tried, I doubt if this deep French attitude could have been shaken by anything we did or said and least of all by anything said or done in connection with the wise and right policy of helping France to get back on her feet.

The third period of American decision began in 1950, just before our involvement in the defense of Korea against Soviet-inspired aggression. The Communists had just taken control in China and entered into the 1950 alliance with the Soviet Union. Communism did then appear to our policymakers as something approaching a monolith, and we came to see the French stand in Indochina as part of a global attempt to repel Communist military adventures. In essence, we acted on two lines of policy between 1950 and 1954: on the one hand, economic and growing military assistance to the French; on the other hand, steady urging that the French proceed rapidly to grant real independence to Indochina, both for its own sake and as the best means of preventing Communist control.

Here it has been argued that we did too much assisting or at least too little urging. I find myself sympathetic to this point of view, as indeed it was expressed at the time by such wise men as Edmund Gullion, who served in Viet-Nam and much later became our distinguished Ambassador in the Congo from 1961 to 1963.

Yet, again I am not sure whether a different United States policy in this period could have brought about the desired result of a France first successfully waging a costly and bloody war to defend Viet-Nam and then granting it independence. Again, French attitudes and actions had deep roots in the still shaky situation of France and in the combination of a valid concern for the Communist threat and a desire to maintain a major French presence and hold in Indochina. Even if the French had acted wisely in every respect in this period, they might have been able to achieve nothing more than a division of the country into Communist and non-Communist areas. The vital difference might have been that valid non-Communist nationalism in Viet-Nam would have had a chance to stand on its feet and develop respected leaders before 1954; and if this had happened the whole later story might have unfolded in a very different way.

As it was, the spring of 1954 brought French defeat, in spirit if not in military terms, and left non-Communist nationalism in Viet-Nam almost bankrupt.

The Period of the Geneva Conference

The period of the Geneva Conference is the fourth period of American decision. That is a complex story, well told from a relatively detached viewpoint by Anthony Eden, now Lord Avon, in his memoirs.

We played a critical backstage role at Geneva. We maintained the possibility of military intervention, which, many observers at the time believe, played a crucial part in inducing the Soviets and the Communist Chinese alike to urge Hanoi [*sic*] to settle for a temporary division of Viet-Nam at the 17th Parallel and for an independent Cambodia and Laos. And we began to lay the groundwork for SEATO [Southeast Asia Treaty Organization], as part of the effort to show strength and to convince Communist China that it would not have a free hand in Southeast Asia.

Yet we were unwilling to participate fully in the framing of the Geneva accords,[2] apparently because our policymakers did not wish to associate themselves in any way with a loss of territory to Communist control. So the Geneva accords were framed largely between Hanoi, Communist China, and the Soviet Union on the one side and the French, who were under the urgent time pressure of their domestic politics, on the other. In the end we confined ourselves to saying two things:[3]

(a) That we would view any aggression in violation of the accords with grave concern and as seriously threatening international peace and security.

(b) That we took the same position on the reunification of Viet-Nam that we took in other "nations now divided against their will"—meaning, then and now, Germany and Korea—and that we would continue to seek unity through free elections supervised by the United Nations. In effect, we thus interpreted the election provision as providing for a free determination by the people of Viet-Nam as to whether they wished reunification and in that sense endorsed it consistent with the similar positions we had taken in Germany and Korea.

All sorts of things could be said about our decisions in that period. Some are of the view that we should have taken military action and tried to nail down at least a clear military division of Viet-Nam, or even to defeat Ho; I myself think that by the spring of 1954 that course would have been untenable.

It may also be argued—and I do not know the contemporary factors—that, involved as we already were by preceding decisions, we should have participated forthrightly in the making of the accords and lent our weight to them from the outset, declaring right then that we meant to stand—with the French if possible, but alone if necessary—in supporting non-Communist nationalism in South Viet-Nam. We would then have acted as we had done for non-Communist nationalism in Korea, although without its being necessary or desirable for us to put continuing forces on the ground as we had to do in the face of the conventional threat to Korea.

At any rate, in July 1954 a new national entity came into being in South Viet-Nam with what appeared at the time to be extraordinarily small chances of survival. At the very end, the French, with a degree of American pressure, installed the staunchly nationalist Diem [*sic*] as Prime Minister, hardly thinking that he would survive and looking rather to a short period in which the French could exit with some semblance of grace and let nature take its course.

Treaty Commitments in Southeast Asia

The fifth set of American decisions came in this setting and indeed overlapped the period of the Geneva Conference. The first aspect of these decisions was our leading role in the formation of the SEATO treaty,[4] signed at Manila in September of 1954 and ratified by our Senate in February 1955 by a vote of 82 to 1. In the SEATO treaty South Viet-Nam and its territory were specifically included as a "protocol state" and the signatories specifically accepted the obligation, if asked by the Government of South Viet-Nam, to take action in response to armed attack against South Viet-Nam and to consult on appropriate measures if South Viet-Nam were subjected to subversive actions. The Geneva accords had, of course, already expressly forbidden aggressive acts from either half of Viet-Nam against the other half, but there had been no obligation for action by the Geneva participating nations. SEATO created a new and serious obligation extending to South Viet-Nam and aimed more widely at the security of the Southeast Asian signatories and the successor states of Indochina.

The second aspect of our decisions at this period was an evolving one. In late 1954 President Eisenhower committed us to furnish economic support for the new regime,[5] in which Diem was already showing himself tougher and more able than anyone had supposed possible. And in early 1955, without any formal statement, we began to take over the job of military assistance to South Viet-Nam, acting within the numerical and equipment limitations stated in the Geneva accords for foreign military aid.

In short, in the 1954–55 period we moved into a major supporting role and undertook a major treaty commitment involving South Viet-Nam.

These decisions, I repeat, are not mine to defend. In the mood of the period, still deeply affected by a not unjustified view of monolithic communism, they were accepted with very wide support in the United States, as the vote and the debate in the Senate abundantly proved. And the Senate documents prove conclusively that there was full understanding of the grave implications of the SEATO obligations, particularly as they related to aggression by means of armed attack.

The important point about these decisions—and a point fervently debated within the administration at the time, according to many participants—is that they reflected a policy not merely toward Viet-Nam but toward the whole of Southeast Asia. In essence, the underlying basic issue was felt, and I think rightly, to be whether the United States should involve itself much more directly in the security of Southeast Asia and the preservation of the largely new nations that had come into being there since World War II.

There could not be the kind of clear-cut policy for Southeast Asia that had by then evolved in Northeast Asia, where we had entered into mutual security treaties individually with Japan, Korea, and the Republic of China. Some of the Southeast Asian countries wished no association with an outside power; others—Malaya, Singapore, and the northern areas of Borneo, which were not then independent—continued to rely on the British and the Commonwealth. So the directly affected area in which policy could operate comprised only Thailand, the Philippines, and the non-Communist successor states of Indochina—South Viet-Nam, Laos, and Cambodia.

Yet it was felt at the time that unless the United States participated in a major way in preserving the independence and security of these nations, they would be subject to progressive pressures by the parallel efforts of North Viet-Nam and Communist China.

The judgment that this threat of aggression was real and valid was the first basis of the policy adopted. Two other judgments that lay behind the policy were:

(a) That a successful takeover by North Viet-Nam or Communist China of any of the directly affected nations would not only be serious in itself but would drastically weaken and in a short time destroy the capacity of the other nations of Southeast Asia, whatever their international postures, to maintain their own independence.

(b) That while we ourselves had no wish for a special position in Southeast Asia, the transfer of the area, or large parts of it, to Communist control achieved by subversion and aggression would mean a major addition to the power status of hostile and aggressive Communist Chinese and North Vietnamese regimes. It was believed that such a situation would not only doom the peoples of the area to conditions of domination and virtual servitude over an indefinite period but would create the very kind of aggressive domination of much of Asia that we had already fought the militarist leaders of Japan to prevent. It was widely and deeply believed that such a situation was profoundly contrary to our national interests.

But there was still a third supporting judgment that, like the others, ran through the calculations of the period. This was that the largely new nations of Southeast Asia were in fact valid national entities and that while their progress might be halting and imperfect both politically and economically, this progress was worth backing. To put it another way, there was a constructive vision of the kind of Southeast Asia that could evolve and a sense that this constructive purpose was worth pursuing as a matter of our own ideals, as a matter of our national interest, and as a realistic hope of the possibilities of progress if external aggression and subversion could be held at bay.

These I believe to have been the bedrock reasons for the position we took in Viet-Nam and Southeast Asia at this time. They were overlaid by what may appear to have been emotional factors in our attitude toward communism in China and Asia. But the degree of support that this major policy undertaking received at the time went far beyond those who held these emotions. And this is why I for one believe that the bedrock reasons I have given were the true and decisive ones.

So the United States became deeply involved in the security of Southeast Asia and, wherever it was welcomed, in the effort to achieve economic progress as well. And the undertaking to support South Viet-Nam economically and militarily and through the protocol to the SEATO treaty must be seen as a part of the wide view that the choice was between fairly deep involvement in Southeast Asia or standing aside in the face of an estimate that to do so would cause Communist Chinese and North Vietnamese power and domination to flow throughout the area.

The Issue of Free Elections

The unfolding of this policy between 1954 and 1961 is a tangled and difficult story. Mistakes, even serious mistakes, were undoubtedly made then and later. Some of these, many believe, were in our economic and particularly in our military assistance policies in Viet-Nam; and it has been argued—to me persuasively—that we should have at least tried harder to counter the growing authoritarian trends of the Diem regime in the political sphere.

What was not a mistake, but the logical corollary of the basic policy, was the handling of the provision in the Geneva accords that called for free elections in 1956. It has been argued that this provision, which was certainly badly drafted, called for a single nationwide election, with reunification assumed. Our interpretation—that what was meant was in effect a plebiscite as to whether reunification was desired—has strong support in reason and the recollections of Geneva participants. What cannot be disputed is that the determination was to be free; the word appears three times in the article of the accords.

Much hindsight nonsense has been written about what took place in 1956 on this issue, and if any of you are planning a thesis subject, I commend to you the examination of the *contemporary* sources and discussion. You will, I think, find clear confirmation that by 1956 two propositions were accepted: first, that South Viet-Nam, contrary to most expectations in 1951, was standing on its own feet and had demonstrated that the makings of a valid non-Communist nationalism existed there; and, second, that North Viet-Nam—which had gone through a period of harsh repression in 1955 and 1956 in which Bernard Fall estimates that nearly 50,000 political opponents were killed outright—would not conceivably have permitted any supervision or any determination that could remotely have been called free.

In the face of these facts, Diem refused to go through with the elections, and we supported him in that refusal. Incidentally, I am told that we urged that he put the monkey on Hanoi's back and force them to refuse supervision or free conditions—as they would surely have done. Diem proudly rejected this advice, which did not change what would have happened but did leave the elements of a propaganda argument that still rages. It is, I repeat, hindsight nonsense, and I would only quote two contemporary statements—one by the then junior senator from Massachusetts, John F. Kennedy, the other by Professor Hans Morgenthau.

Kennedy categorically rejected "an election obviously stacked and subverted in advance, urged upon us by those who have already broken their own pledges under the agreement they now seek to enforce."

And Morgenthau referred to the tremendous change between 1954 and 1956 and the "miracle" of what had been accomplished in South Viet-Nam. He went on to say that the conditions for free elections did not exist in either North or South Viet-Nam and concluded:

> Actually, the provision for free elections which would solve ultimately the problem of Viet-Nam was a device to hide the incompatibility of the Communist and Western positions, neither of which can admit the domination of all of Viet-Nam by the other side. It was a device to disguise the fact that the line of military demarcation was bound to be a line of political division as well.

Unfortunately, the promise of South Viet-Nam in 1956 was not realized in the next 5 years. In the face of Diem's policies, discontent grew—much as it grew in the same period in Korea under Rhee. As in Korea, that discontent might well have led to an internal revolution in a more or less traditional Asian manner. This is not what happened. Despite all that romantics like

[Jean] Lacouture may say, what happened was that Hanoi moved in, from at least 1959 onward (Bernard Fall would say from 1957), and provided a cutting edge of direction, trained men from the North, and supplies that transformed internal discontent into a massive subversive effort guided and supported from the outside in crucial ways.

The realistic view, then and later, has been well summarized by Roger Hilsman in his recent book (with which, incidentally, I have serious factual differences on the period after 1963). Hilsman puts it thus (page 471 of his book):[6]

> Vietnam, in truth, was in the midst of two struggles, not one. The guerrilla warfare was not a spontaneous revolution, as Communist propaganda would have it, but a contrived, deliberate campaign directed and managed from Hanoi. But Vietnam was also in the throes of a true revolution, a social and nationalistic revolution very much akin to the "new nationalisms" that pervaded both the Congo crisis and Indonesia's confrontation with Malaysia. Even while the struggle went on against the Viet Cong [sic], power was in the process of passing from the French-educated mandarin class to representatives of the new nationalism, the Buddhists, the students, and the "young Turks" in the military.

Continued Engagement in Southeast Asia

This, then, was the situation as it confronted the Kennedy Administration in January of 1961. All this is history. Reasonable men can and do differ about what was done. But those who believe that serious mistakes were made, or even that the basic policy was wrong, cannot escape the fact that by 1961 we were, as a practical matter, deeply engaged in Southeast Asia and specifically in the preservation of the independence of South Viet-Nam.

President Kennedy came to office with a subversive effort against South Viet-Nam well underway and with the situation in Laos deteriorating rapidly. And for a time the decisions on Laos overshadowed Viet-Nam, although of course the two were always intimately related.

In Laos, President Kennedy in the spring of 1961 rejected the idea of strong military action in favor of seeking a settlement that would install a neutralist government under Souvanna Phouma, a solution uniquely appropriate to Laos. Under Governor [W. Averell] Harriman's astute handling, the negotiations finally led to the Geneva accords of 1962 for Laos;[7] and the process—a point not adequately noticed—led the United States to a much more explicit and affirmative endorsement of the Geneva accords of 1954, a position we have since consistently maintained as the best basis for peace in Viet-Nam.

In Viet-Nam, the situation at first appeared less critical, and the initial actions of the Kennedy Administration were confined to an increase in our military aid and a small increase of a few hundred men in our military training personnel, a breach—it may be argued—to this extent of the limits of the Geneva accords but fully justified in response to the scale of North Vietnamese violation of the basic noninterference provisions.

Although the details somewhat obscured the broad pattern, I think any fair historian of the future must conclude that as early as the spring of 1961 President Kennedy had in effect taken a seventh United States policy decision: that we would continue to be deeply engaged in Southeast Asia, in South Viet-Nam, and under new ground rules, in Laos as well.

This was not—despite the hindsight straw-man recently erected by Professor [John Kenneth] Galbraith—because President Kennedy believed at all in a monolithic communism. Professor Galbraith forgets a good deal, and notably the Vienna meeting of June 1961 in which President Kennedy set out deliberately to work with the Soviet Union for the Laos settlement—even as at the very same time he dispatched Vice President Johnson to visit Viet-Nam and Thailand and in effect to reaffirm our courses of action there. The total pattern of United States policy toward Communist countries under both President Johnson and President Kennedy belies the Galbraith thesis.

No, neither President Kennedy nor any senior policymaker, then or later, believed the Soviet Union was still united with Communist China and North Viet-Nam in a single sweeping Communist threat to the world. But President Kennedy did believe two other things that had, and still have, a vital bearing on our policy.

First, he believed that a weakening in our basic resolve to help in Southeast Asia would tend to encourage separate Soviet pressures in other areas.

James Reston has stated, on the basis of contemporary conversations with the President, that this concern specifically related to Khrushchev's aggressive designs on Berlin, which were pushed hard all through 1961 and not laid to rest till after the Cuban missile crisis of 1962. At any rate, President Kennedy clearly did believe that failure to keep the high degree of commitment we had in Viet-Nam and Southeast Asia had a bearing on the validity of our commitments elsewhere. As Theodore Sorensen has summarized it (page 651 of *Kennedy*): "… this nation's commitment (in South Viet-Nam) in January, 1961 … was not one that President Kennedy felt he could abandon without undesirable consequences throughout Asia and the world."

Secondly, President Kennedy believed that the Communist Chinese *were* a major threat to dominate Southeast Asia and specifically that a United States "withdrawal in the case of Viet-Nam and in the case of Thailand might mean a collapse in the entire area."[8] Indeed, President Kennedy in one statement expressly supported the "domino theory."[9]

My own view, based on participation and subsequent discussion with others, is that the underlying view of the relation between Viet-Nam and the threat to Southeast Asia was clear and strongly believed throughout the top levels of the Kennedy Administration. We knew, as we have always known, that the action against South Viet-Nam reflected deeply held ambitions by Hanoi to unify Viet-Nam under Communist control and that Hanoi needed and wanted only Chinese aid to this end and wished to be its own master. And we knew, as again we always have, that North Viet-Nam would resist any Communist Chinese trespassing on areas it controlled. But these two propositions were not then, as they are not now, inconsistent with the belief that the aggressive ambitions of Communist China and North Viet-Nam—largely North Vietnamese in old Indochina, overlapping in Thailand, Chinese in the rest of Southeast Asia—would surely feed on each other. In the eyes of the rest of Southeast Asia, certainly, they were part of a common and parallel threat.

So, in effect, the policy of 1954–61 was reaffirmed in the early months of 1961 by the Kennedy Administration. Let me say right here I do not mean to make this a personal analysis of President Kennedy nor to imply any view whatever as to what he might or might not have done had he lived beyond November of 1963. But some untrue things have been said about the 1961 period, and I believe the record totally supports the account of policy, and the reasons for it, that I have given.

Stemming the North Vietnamese Threat

We then come to the eighth period of decision—the fall of 1961. By then, the "guerrilla aggression" (Hilsman's phrase) had assumed truly serious proportions, and morale in South Viet-Nam had been shaken. It seemed highly doubtful that without major additional United States actions the North Vietnamese threat could be stemmed.

President Kennedy took the decision to raise the ante, through a system of advisers [sic], pilots, and supporting military personnel that rose gradually to the level of 25,000 in the next 3 years.

I do not think it is appropriate for me to go into the detail of the discussions that accompanied this decision. Fairly full, but still incomplete, accounts have been given in various of the books on the period. What can be seen, without going into such detail, is that the course of action that was chosen considered and rejected, at least for the time being, the direct introduction of ground combat troops or the bombing of North Viet-Nam, although there was no doubt even then—as Hilsman again makes clear—that the bombing of North Viet-Nam could have been sustained under any reasonable legal view in the face of what North Viet-Nam was doing. Rather, the course of action which was adopted rightly stressed that the South Vietnamese role must remain crucial and primary.

In effect, it was decided that the United States would take those additional actions that appeared clearly required to meet the situation, not knowing for sure whether these actions would in fact prove to be adequate, trying—despite the obvious and always recognized effect of momentum and inertia—not to cross the bridge of still further action, and hoping strongly that what was being undertaken would prove sufficient.

Political Change in South Viet-Nam

This was the policy followed from early 1962 right up to February of 1965. Within this period, however, political deterioration in South Viet-Nam compelled, in the fall of 1963, decisions that I think must be counted as the ninth critical point of United States policy-making. It was decided at that time that while the United States would do everything necessary to support the war, it would no longer adhere to its posture of all-out support of the Diem regime unless that regime made sweeping changes in its method of operation. The record of this period has been described by Robert Shaplen and now by Hilsman. Undoubtedly, our new posture contributed to the overthrow of Diem in November 1963.

I do not myself think that we could in the end have done otherwise, but the important historical point is that our actions tended to deepen our involvement in South Viet-Nam and our commitment to the evolution of non-Communist nationalism, always foreseen to be difficult, that would follow the overthrow of Diem.

Unfortunately, the fall of Diem, while it had overwhelming popular support in South Viet-Nam, failed to produce an effective new government. For a year and a half South Viet-Nam wallowed in political confusion; and power finally passed, with the agreement of civilian political leaders, to the Thieu–Ky [sic] military-led government of June 1965.

This political confusion was disheartening, but it was not surprising. For South Viet-Nam had never been trained by the French to govern itself, and above all, it was faced with steadily rising North Vietnamese and Viet Cong terrorist and military action. Intensification of that action began almost at once after the overthrow of Diem and demonstrated—if it needed demonstrating—that the struggle was not over Diem, despite Communist claims and honest liberal qualms, but was an attempt to destroy non-Communist nationalism of any sort in South Viet-Nam.

In early 1964 President Johnson expressly reaffirmed all the essential elements of the Kennedy Administration policies publicly through every action and through firm internal directives. It is simply not true to say that there was any change in policy in this period toward greater military emphasis, much less major new military actions. Further actions were not excluded—as they had not been in 1954 or 1961—but President Johnson's firm object right up to February 1965 was to make the policy adopted in late 1961 work if it could possibly be done, including the fullest possible emphasis on pacification and the whole political and civilian aspect.

The summer of 1964 did bring a new phase, though not a change in policy. The situation was continuing to decline, and North Viet-Nam may have been emboldened by the trend. Certainly, infiltration was rising steadily and, as we now know more clearly, began to include substantial numbers of native North Vietnamese. But, more dramatically, American naval ships on patrol in the Gulf of Tonkin were attacked, and there were two responding United States attacks on North Vietnamese naval bases.

This led President Johnson to seek, and the Congress to approve overwhelmingly on August 7, 1964, a resolution[10]—drafted in collaboration with congressional leaders—that not only approved such retaliatory attacks but added that:

> The United States regards as vital to its national interest and to world peace the maintenance of international peace and security in southeast Asia. Consonant with the Constitution of the United States and the Charter of the United Nations and in accordance with its obligations under the Southeast Asia Collective Defense Treaty, the United States is, therefore, prepared, as the President determines, to take all necessary steps, including the use of armed force, to assist any member or protocol state of the Southeast Asia Collective Defense Treaty requesting assistance in defense of its freedom.

U.S. Decisions Based on Overall View

So things stood through the election period. But as 1964 drew to a close, the situation was moving steadily downward in every respect, both military and political. A review of policy was undertaken, analyzing three basic choices: to continue the existing policy with every improvement that could be devised within its limits; to take new and major military measures, while adhering to the same basic objectives that had been followed all along; or to move toward withdrawal.

From late November onward, these choices were intensively examined, even as the military threat grew, the political confusion in Saigon deepened, and all the indicators recorded increasingly shaky morale and confidence not only in South Viet-Nam but throughout the deeply concerned countries of Southeast Asia. By late January, it was the clear judgment of all those concerned with policy and familiar with the situation that the first choice was rapidly becoming no choice at all—and not, to use the phrase of one commentator, a "constructive alternative." To "muddle through!" (that commentator's phrase) was almost certainly to muddle out and to accept that South Viet-Nam would be turned over to Communist control achieved through externally backed subversion and aggression.

This was a straight practical judgment. It ran against the grain of every desire of the President and his advisers. But I myself am sure it was a right judgment—accepted at the time by most sophisticated observers and, in the light of reflective examination, now accepted, I believe, by virtually everyone who knows the situation at all at first hand.

There were, in short, only two choices: to move toward withdrawal or to do a lot more, both for its military impact and, at the outset, to prevent a collapse of South Vietnamese morale and will to continue.

And as the deliberations continued within the administration, the matter was brought to a head by a series of sharp attacks on American installations in particular. These attacks were serious in themselves, but above all, they confirmed the overall analysis that North Viet-Nam was supremely confident and was moving for the kill. And as they thus moved, it seemed clear that they would in fact succeed and perhaps in a matter of months.

Let me pause here to clear up another current historical inaccuracy. The basis for the successive decisions—in February to start bombing; in March to introduce small numbers of combat forces; and in July to move to major United States combat forces—was as I have stated it. It depended on an overall view of the situation and on an overall view that what had been going on for years was for all practical purposes aggression—and indeed this term dates from late 1961 or early 1962 in the statements of senior administration spokesmen.

But there is a separate point whether, as has sometimes been asserted, it was the United States alone which unilaterally changed the character of the war in the direction of a conventional conflict. It is alleged that Hanoi was adhering to a tacit agreement that, so long as we did not bomb North Viet-Nam, Hanoi would not send in its regulars, at least in units.

Multiple and conclusive evidence which became available from the spring of 1965 onward seems to me to refute these contentions. As has been repeatedly made public over the past 2 years, we know that one North Vietnamese regiment entered South Viet-Nam by December 1964, and we know that several other regiments entered in the spring of 1965 on timetables of infiltration that can only have reflected command decisions taken in Hanoi prior to the beginning of the bombing.

From the standpoint of the basis for U.S. decisions, this evidence simply reinforces the February picture that Hanoi was moving for the kill. Native North Vietnamese, alone or in regular units, were in themselves no more and no less aggressive than the earlier native South Vietnamese who had gone north and become North Vietnamese nationals. The point is that Hanoi, as we suspected then and later proved, had taken major steps to raise the level of the war before the bombing began.

As to any tacit agreement, these facts alone seem to disprove that there ever was one. Moreover, students of North Vietnamese behavior, and especially of the recent major captured North Vietnamese documents, would in any event find such an allegation hard to credit. Is it not far more reasonable to conclude that Hanoi preferred to conceal its hand but was prepared at all times to put in whatever was necessary to bring about military victory—and that the regular units were simply a part of that policy, introduced after they had run out of native southerners and wanted to maintain and step up the pressure?

But this historical point is less important than the fundamental elements of the situation as it stood at the time. On the one hand, all of what I have earlier described as the bedrock elements still remained: a strong Chinese Communist and North Vietnamese threat to Southeast Asia, a crucial link between the defense of South Viet-Nam and the realization of that threat, and the validity of non-Communist nationalism, whatever its imperfections, in South Viet-Nam and in the other nations of Southeast Asia.

Moreover, the wider implications for our commitments elsewhere appeared no less valid than they had ever been. Viet-Nam still constituted a major, perhaps even a decisive, test case of whether the Communist strategy of "wars of national liberation" or "people's wars" could be met and countered even in the extraordinarily difficult circumstances of South Viet-Nam. Then as now, it has been, I think, rightly judged that a success for Hanoi in South Viet-Nam could only encourage the use of this technique by Hanoi, and over time by the Communist Chinese, and might well have the effect of drawing the Soviets into competition with Peking and Hanoi and away from the otherwise promising trends that have developed in Soviet policy in the past 10 years.

Finally, it was judged from the outset that stronger action by us in Viet-Nam would not operate to bring the Soviet Union and Communist China closer together and that the possibility of major Chinese Communist intervention could be kept to a minimum so long as we made it clear at all times, both by word and deed, that our objective was confined solely to freeing South Viet-Nam from external interference and that we did not threaten Communist China but rather looked to the ultimate hope of what the Manila Declaration,[11] of last fall, called "reconciliation and peace throughout Asia."

On the other hand, it was recognized from the outset that the taking of these new major military measures involved heavy costs and hazards. The South Vietnamese still had to play the crucial role in military security and, above all, in political and economic development and stability. A greater American role was bound to complicate South Vietnamese evolution. It was bound to increase the scale of the war and to cost significantly in lives and very heavily in resources. Even though the casualties and damage of the war remain far below what was suffered in Korea, war is never anything but ugly and brutal.

The balance was struck, after the most careful deliberation, in favor of the course that has since been followed. The key elements in the policy were stated in President Johnson's Baltimore speech of April 1965,[12] and the major combat-force commitment was explained in the President's statement of July 28, 1965.[13] These have been the cornerstones of policy, and they have been elaborated and explained repeatedly and at length by all senior administration spokesmen.

Cornerstones of U.S. Policy

In essence:

(a) Our objective remained solely that of protecting the independence of South Viet-Nam from external interference and force. We declined, and still decline, to threaten the regime in North Viet-Nam itself or the territory and regime of Communist China.

(b) We indicated in April of 1965 that we were prepared for discussions or negotiations without condition, and we have relentlessly pursued our own efforts to enter into meaningful discussions as well as following up on a host of peace initiatives by others. Unfortunately, Hanoi has clung firmly to the objective of insuring a Communist takeover of South Viet-Nam and has refused to enter into any fruitful discussions. Indeed, Hanoi has rejected any discussions whatever—initially unless its basic objective was accepted in advance through the so-called "third point," more recently unless we agreed to a complete cessation of the bombing without any responsive action on their part. Hanoi's philosophy toward negotiation has now become authoritatively available, particularly in the section on "fighting while negotiating" in the captured remarks of one of the North Vietnamese leaders, Comrade Vinh.

(c) We continued to place every possible emphasis on the crucial nonmilitary aspects of the conflict, greatly strengthening our own contribution to the essentially South Vietnamese task of restoring stability and control in the countryside and working for the welfare of the people.

(d) Militarily, our actions were directed to proving to North Viet-Nam that its effort to take over the South by military force must fail and to extending and enlarging the areas in which the vital business of bringing real security and peace to the countryside could go forward with all the strength we could hope to give it. The total effort in the South remained primary, even as the bombing of military targets in the North was carried on—initially to demonstrate resolve but always and basically to make Hanoi's infiltration far more difficult and costly and to prevent levels of new men and equipment that could only, in the arithmetic of guerrilla warfare, multiply many times over, for each addition from North Viet-Nam, the requirement for forces in the South.

(e) We encouraged the South Vietnamese in their own resolve to move to a constitutional basis of government, a process set underway formally by Prime Minister Ky [sic] in January of 1966 and followed since that time in the face of all the difficulties and dangers of attempting to create such a basis in a country without political experience and ravaged by terrorism and by guerrilla and conventional military action.

(f) We encouraged the South Vietnamese at the same time to proceed on the track that has now become reconciliation, the holding out to members of the Viet Cong of the possibility of reentering the political life of their country under peaceful conditions. In essence, we seek and would accept a fair determination of the will of the people of South Viet-Nam along the lines well summarized by Ambassador Goldberg's Chicago speech of May 12, 1967.[14]

These were the South Vietnamese aspects of our policy. But then, as previously, the policy was seen in the wider context of the future of Southeast Asia. So it was that President Johnson lent our strong support in April of 1965 to the development of regional cooperation and of economic projects created through Asian initiative. By this vital element in our policy, we made clear again that our underlying objective was to do what we could to assist in the constructive task of bringing about a Southeast Asia of cooperative and independent nations, whatever their international postures might be.

We had a security job to do in Viet-Nam and were joined over time by five other area nations in supplying military forces to do that job. And we are assisting Thailand against a concerted Chinese Communist and North Vietnamese effort at external subversion, an effort begun—to keep the record straight—as early as 1962 and clearly and definitively by December 1964, before our major decisions in Viet-Nam. Our SEATO and ANZUS undertakings remain firm.

But we looked beyond these, and we must still look beyond these, to the whole question of the future of Southeast Asia and to the role that we can play in assisting the nations of the area to consolidate their national independence and to improve the welfare of their people.

This, then, is a barebones account of "The Path to Viet-Nam." Even within its own terms, it may omit what others would include. And, long as it may seem, it is still incomplete in two respects that it would take far too much time to cover.

First, it is plainly inadequate to focus solely on our policies toward Viet-Nam or even toward Southeast Asia as a whole. Those policies are intimately related to the rest of Asia; to the implications of Asian developments for other areas and, in the last analysis, for our own national security; and to our central world purpose—the creation of an international order of independent states.

Secondly, I have tried to isolate what I consider to have been the major policy decisions. Obviously, policy is not just a matter of single decisions, however fully considered. A vast number of lesser policy decisions have accompanied these basic ones, and the way in which a basic policy is carried out in the end affects its substance. I have not tried to cover, for example, decisions on the balance of effort within South Viet-Nam, decisions on particular negotiating proposals, decisions on the pace and nature of the bombing of North Viet-Nam, or the subtle and difficult problem, over the years, of United States influence toward political progress in the South. I know full well that these are areas in which many of you undoubtedly hold strong views. I welcome discussion of them.

"The Lesson in Involvement"

What, then, is "the lesson in involvement"?

- Is it that we have been trapped into a difficult situation by a series of lesser decisions taken with no clear view of their implications?

- Is it that we should never have become engaged in Southeast Asia?
- Is it that we should never have attempted to support South Viet-Nam?
- Is it that, having supported South Viet-Nam in certain respects (including a treaty) and having become deeply engaged in Southeast Asia, we should nonetheless have decided—or should now decide—to limit the actions we take or even to withdraw entirely?

The first question seems to me both separate and difficult. At some point in the history I have recited we became committed, deliberately and by formal constitutional process, to the support of the freedom of South Viet-Nam from external interference. That commitment included a strong treaty obligation, and that is a clear part of the story. But what is perhaps more to the point is that great powers must face two central points:

(a) As Irving Kristol has pointed out in his recent article in Foreign Affairs, the very definition of a great power is that not only its actions but the cases in which it declines to act have major consequences. At every stage in the Viet-Nam story, it has seemed clear to the leaders of this country that not to act would have the gravest effects. This is the way that successive choices have appeared to four successive Presidents.

(b) The second point that a great power cannot escape is that its actions in themselves affect the stakes. When great powers commit themselves, by treaty and by a total course of conduct extending over many years, an element of reliance comes into being, both within the area and within other areas in which commitments have also been undertaken.

Yet, all this being said, I do not think one can conclude that because we said or did *a*, we must necessarily say or do *b*—in an old phrase of Bismarck's. So I, for one, do not believe that the "lesson in involvement" is that we are the prisoners of history.

Rather, I think we should be focusing on the second, third, and fourth questions I have listed above.

These are big questions, and if I have tried to do anything today it is to stress that the matter has really been looked at for at least the last 13 years in this kind of larger framework. The policies followed today are, as they must be, the policies of this administration. No one can say whether another administration would have done the same. What can be said is that the underlying viewpoint and analysis of factors have been largely similar throughout the last 13 years, if not longer.

This does not prove, of course, that this analysis has been correct. The United States has no divine dispensation from error, and the most that your leaders at any time can do is to exert the best human judgment and moral sense of which they are capable. I, for one, am convinced that this has been done at all stages.

In essence, the question is not capable of geometric proof. Like all policy, it is a judgment. Our bet with history has been that Southeast Asia does matter, that the independence of South Viet-Nam crucially affects Southeast Asia, and that non-Communist nationalism in Southeast Asia and in Viet-Nam has in it the seeds of a peaceful, progressive, and stable area that can take its place in a world at peace.

Independence of Southeast Asia

Other factors enter in, as I have tried to summarize, and despite their variations from time to time remain of major general importance. But it is primarily from the standpoint of Southeast Asia that I would like to close my remarks today. How do the bets I have described look today?

Southeast Asia surely matters more than ever. A region which may have held as few as 30 million inhabitants in 1800—and which is carried under the heading of "peripheral areas" in some textbooks on East Asia—now holds more than 250 million people, more than Latin America and almost as much as the population of Western Europe. The resources of this area are large, and its people, while not yet capable of the kind of dramatic progress we have seen in the northern parts of Asia, have great talent, intelligence, and industry. Its geographical location, while it should not be in the path of great-power collisions, is crucial for trade routes and in other respects.

From the standpoint of our own security and the kind of world in which we wish to live, I believe we must continue to be deeply concerned to do what we can to keep Southeast Asia from falling under external domination and aggression that would contribute to such domination. And I believe also that we have a wider concern in doing what we can, and as we are wanted, to assist sound programs on an individual country or regional basis and to improve the welfare of the peoples of the area. And I do not think that you can do the latter unless the former is achieved.

The second part of our bet is that the independence of South Viet-Nam critically affects Southeast Asia. South Viet-Nam and its 15 million people are important in themselves, but they assume an additional importance if the judgment is accepted that a success for aggression there would drastically weaken the situation in Southeast Asia and indeed beyond. That judgment cannot be defended solely by reference to the dynamics of major aggressive powers and their prospective victims in the past. I myself believe that those parallels have validity, but the question is always what Justice Holmes called "concrete cases." In this concrete case I think the underlying judgment has been valid and remains valid today.

None of us can say categorically that the Communist Chinese would in due course move—if opportunity offered—to dominate wide areas of Southeast Asia through pressure and subversion. But that is what the Chinese and their maps say, and their Communist doctrine appears to add vital additional emphasis. It is what they are doing in Thailand today and, through local Communist allies, in Burma, Cambodia, Malaysia, and Singapore. And it is what they would like to do in Indonesia again. Surely Adlai Stevenson [U.S. Ambassador to the U.N., 1961–65] was right that the threat of Communist China is not so fanciful that it should not serve as a valid assumption of policy. And we can be more categorical that Hanoi intends to dominate at least the successor states of Indochina and would move rapidly to this end if it were to get practical control of South Viet-Nam.

Perhaps the hardest point for some to grasp is the psychological impact of a development such as the fall of South Viet-Nam in this setting. As to Hanoi and Peking, judgment and past experience point to the conclusion that it would greatly encourage them to push further. As to the threatened nations, the view of their leaders is a matter of record. All over Southeast Asia, whatever the posture of the individual nation, the great body of responsible opinion—and I invite you to check this against any firsthand account—accepts the judgment stated only the other day by the independent and nonaligned Prime Minister of Singapore, Mr. Lee Kuan Yew: "I feel the fate of Asia—South and Southeast Asia—will be decided in the next few years by what happens out in Viet-Nam."

I could multiply that quotation 10 times over in public statements and 10 times more in private statements. As Drew Middleton of *The New York Times* reported last June after a trip in the area:

> Despite some misgivings, non-Communist leaders from Tokyo to Tehran largely support United States policies in South and Southeast Asia.

This does not mean that every nation accepts our choice of military actions. Some would have us do more, some less. But it does lead to the clear conclusion that our own view accords with the deep sense in Southeast Asia, and indeed elsewhere in Asia, that the struggle in South Viet-Nam is crucial to the independence and continued ability to work for its people of each and every nation for a wide area.

Lastly, there is the question whether a new Southeast Asia is in fact being built and can be developed. On this point, surely the developments of the last 5 years, and particularly the last 2 years, have been vastly encouraging. Where Indonesia in 1965 was drifting rapidly to Communist control and practical alignment with Peking, it now stands on a staunchly nationalist basis, abandoning the threat to its neighbors and seeking to work out the chaotic economic problems left by Sukarno—with the multilateral help of ourselves and others. Regional cooperation within Southeast Asia, and among Asian nations as a whole, has taken great and historic strides. And it is the widely accepted view in the area—which I share—that these developments would have been far less likely if we had not acted as we did in 1965 and if Communist force had thus taken over in South Viet-Nam.

So all over Southeast Asia there is today a sense of confidence—to which Drew Middleton again testified from his trip. Time has been bought and used. But that confidence is not solid or secure for the future. It would surely be disrupted if we were, in President Johnson's words, to permit a Communist takeover in South Viet-Nam either through withdrawal or "under the cloak of a meaningless agreement."[15] If, on the contrary, we proceed on our present course—with measured military actions and with every possible nonmilitary measure and searching always for an avenue to peace—the prospects for a peaceful and secure Southeast Asia now appear brighter than they have been at any time since the nations of the area were established on an independent basis.

In short, I think the stakes are very grave indeed. The costs are large, and it is clear that we must steel our national capacity and resolve to continue in a tough struggle and still do those things that we must do to meet our problems at home. I find it impossible to believe that we do not have the national capacity and resolve to do both.

Selected Bibliography

Acheson, Dean. *Present at the Creation.* New York: Signet Books, 1970.
Beal, John Robinson. *John Foster Dulles: A Biography.* New York: Harper & Brothers, 1957.
Charlton, Michael, and Anthony Moncrieff. *Many Reasons Why.* New York: Hill and Wang, 1978.
Colby, William, and Peter Forbath. *Honorable Men, My Life in the CIA.* New York: Simon and Schuster, 1978.
Cooper, Chester L. *The Lost Crusade, America in Vietnam.* New York: Dodd, Mead and Company, 1970.
Decoux, Admiral (Jean). *A la Barre de l'Indochine.* Paris: Librairie Plon, 1949.
Devillers, Philippe. *Histoire du Viet-Nam de 1940 à 1952.* Paris: Editions du Seuil, 1952.
Dickens, Charles. *Works.* New York: Avenel Books, 1978.
Dulles, Foster Rhea. *American Foreign Policy Toward Communist China.* New York: Thomas Y. Crowell Company, 1972.
Duncanson, Dennis J. *Government and Revolution in Viet-Nam.* New York: Oxford University Press, 1968.
Eden, Anthony. *Full Circle, The Memoirs of Anthony Eden.* Boston: Houghton Mifflin Company, 1960.
Eisenhower, Dwight D. *Mandate for Change.* New York: Signet Books, 1965.
Fall, Bernard B. *Le Viet Minh, 1945–1960.* Paris: Librairie Armand Colin, 1960.
_____, *The Two Viet-Nams, A Political and Military Analysis.* Revised Edition. New York: Frederick A. Praeger, 1964.
_____, *Street Without Joy, Indochina at War 1946–1954.* Harrisburg, Pennsylvania: The Stackpole Company, 1961.
Halberstam, David. *The Making of a Quagmire.* New York: Random House, 1965.
Hammer, Ellen J. *The Struggle for Indochina.* Stanford: Stanford University Press, 1954.
_____, *Vietnam, Yesterday and Today.* New York: Holt, Rinehart and Winston, Inc., 1966
Historia. (Hors serie 24) *Notre Guerre d'Indochine, Mars 1945–Juillet 1951.* Paris: Librairie Jules Tallandier, 1972.
Imprimerie d'Extreme-Orient. *Conventions Inter-Etats.* Saigon, 1951.
Johnson, Lyndon Baines. *The Vantage Point.* New York: Holt, Rinehart and Winston, 1971
Kissinger, Henry. *White House Years.* Boston: Little Brown & Co., 1979.
Kỳ, Nguyễn Cao. *How We Lost the Vietnam War.* New York: Stein and Day, 1978.
Lansdale, Edward Geary. *In the Midst of Wars, An America's Mission to Southeast Asia.* New York: Harper & Row, 1972.
Lash, Joseph P. *Roosevelt and Churchill, 1939–1941.* New York: W. W. Norton & Company, Inc., 1976.
Lauve, Anita. *On the Question of Communist reprisals in Vietnam.* Anita Lauve Nitt, Consultant to Rand Corporation, Santa Monica, California, which reproduced paper as courtesy to staff member, August 1970.

Lewy, Guenter. *America in Vietnam*. New York: Oxford University Press, 1978.
McClintock, Robert. *The Meaning of Limited War*. Boston: Houghton Mifflin, 1967.
McClellan, David S. *Dean Acheson, The State Department Years*. New York: Dodd, Mead and Company, 1976.
Mecklin, John. *Mission in Torment, An Intimate Account of the U.S. Role in Vietnam*. Garden City, New York: Doubleday & Company Inc., 1965.
Miller, Merle. *Lyndon, An Oral Biography*. New York: G. P. Putnam's Sons, 1980.
New York Times. *The Pentagon Papers*. New York: Bantam Books, 1971.
Nicolson, Harold. *The Evolution of Diplomatic Method*. London: Constable & Co. Ltd., 1954.
Nixon, Richard M. *Memoirs*. (New York: Warner Books, Inc., 1979).
Nolting, Frederick. "The Turning Point." *Foreign Service Journal*, July 1968.
Pike, Douglas. *Viet Cong*. Cambridge, Mass.: Massachusetts Institute of Technology Press, 1966.
Powers, Thomas. *The Man who Kept the Secrets, Richard Helms and the CIA*. New York: Pocket Books, 1981.
Ridgway, Matthew B. *The Korean War*. Garden City, New York: Doubleday & Company Inc., 1967.
Sabattier, General G. *Le Destin de l'Indochine*. Paris: Librairie Plon, 1952.
Schlesinger, Arthur M. Jr. *A Thousand Days, John F. Kennedy in the White House*. New York: Fawcett Premier Books, 1965.
Sisouk Na Champassak. *Storm Over Laos, A Contemporary History*. New York: Frederick A. Praeger, 1961.
Stanton, Edwin F. *Brief Authority*. New York: Harper & Bros., 1956.
Sulzberger, C. L. *An Age of Mediocrity, Memories and Diaries, 1963–1972*. New York: MacMillan Publishing Co., Inc. 1973.
TIME. *Special Report on Indochina*. August 28, 1950.
Tongas, Gerard. *J'ai vecu dans l'enfer Communiste au Nord Viet-Nam*. Paris: Nouvelles Editions Debresse, 1960.
U.S. Department of State. *Program for the Visit to the United States of America of His Excellency Ngo Dinh Diem, President of the Republic of Viet-Nam*, May 1957.
U.S. Department of State. *The Path to Viet-Nam*. Address by William P. Bundy, Assistant Secretary of State for East Asian and Pacific Affairs, prepared for delivery before the 20th annual congress of the National Student Association at College Park, Maryland. Released September 1967.
U.S. Department of State. *Scope of the U.S. Involvement in Laos*. Released March 6, 1970.
U.S. Senate Committee on Foreign Relations. *Background Information relating to Southeast Asia and Viet-Nam* (3d revised Edition). Washington, D.C.: U.S. Government Printing Office, 1967, 79-662 0.
U.S. Senate Select committee to Study Governmental Operations with Respect to Intelligence Activities. *Alleged Assassination Plots Involving Foreign Leaders*. Report No. 94-465. Washington, D.C.: U.S. Government Printing Office, 1975, 61-985 0.
Walt, Lewis W. *Strange War, Strange Strategy*. New York: Funk and Wagnalls, 1970.
Westmoreland, William C. *A Soldier Reports*. New York: Dell Publishing Co. 1980.
Wint, Guy. *The British in Asia*. London: Faber, 1954.
Wolff, Leon. *Little Brown Brother, How the Americans Conquered the Philippines in 1898–1902*. Philippines: Erewhon Press, 1971. Originally published by New York: Doubleday and Co., Inc. and London: Longmans Green and Co., Ltd.

Endnotes

Part I

1. Conversation with Dr. Kenneth P. Landon, October 1980.
2. Robert Aura Smith in *The New York Times Book Review* of the *Struggle for Indochina*, May 1954.
3. Leon Wolff, Little Brown Brother, *How the Americans Conquered the Philippines in 1898–1902* (Philippines: Erewhon Press, 1971), cover and title page.
4. Guy Wint, *The British in Asia* (London: Faber, 1954), 226–28.
5. Bernard B. Fall, *The Two Viet-Nams, A Political and Military Analysis* (New York: Frederick A. Praeger, 1964), 40.
6. Admiral Decoux, *A la Barre de l'Indochine* (Paris: Librairie Plon, 1949), 48.
7. Fall, *Two Viet-Nams*, 40.
8. Decoux, *A la Barre de l'Indochine*, 141.
9. Edwin F. Stanton, *Brief Authority* (New York: Harper & Bros., 1956), 171.
10. Wint, *British in Asia*, 229.
11. Ibid, 230.
12. Ibid.
13. Ibid, 231.
14. Ibid, 233–34.
15. Conversation with Kenneth Landon, October 1980. Editor's note: Identified as the "first" decision of Assistant Secretary Bundy whose enumeration I have borrowed. Department of State Publication 8295, Released September 1967. See Appendix A.
16. Conversation with Kenneth Landon; Hammer, Ellen J. *The Struggle for Indochina* (Stanford: Stanford University Press, 1954), 42–42; U.S. Department of State. *The Path to Viet-Nam*, Released September 1967; Fall, *Two Viet-Nams*, 53.
17. Fall, *Two Viet-Nams*, 51.
18. Ibid, 55–8.
19. Ibid, 53.
20. Ibid.
21. Ibid, 57.
22. Ibid, 69.
23. Conversation with Kenneth Landon, October 1980.
24. Michael Charlton and Anthony Moncrieff, *Many Reasons Why* (New York: Hill and Wang, 1978), 5–6.
25. Ibid, 6–14.
26. Ibid, 17.
27. Bernard B. Fall, *Le Viet Minh, 1945–1960* (Paris: Librairies Armand Colin, 1960), 19–20.
28. Charlton and Moncrieff, *Many Reasons Why*, 17.

29 Ibid, 18.
30 *Historia* (hors Serie 24), *Notre Guerre d'Indochine, Mars 1945–Juillet 1951* (Paris: Libraire Jules Tallandier, 1972), "Leclerc Arrive," Raymond Dronne; Hammer, *Struggle for Indochina*, 110–11.
31 Hammer, *Struggle for Indochina*, 176, 178–81.
32 Ibid, 131; *Historia, Notre Guerre d'Indochine*, "Ho Chi Minh a l'Affut," Jean Laccuture.
33 Conversation with District Chief of Go Vap, 1953.
34 Charlton and Moncrieff, *Many Reasons Why*, 25.
35 Ibid, 25.
36 Ibid.
37 *Historia, Notre Guerre d'Indochine*, "Ho Chi Minh Proclame la Republique," Jean Sainteny.
38 Charlton and Moncrieff, *Many Reasons Why*, Chapter I; Fall, *Two Viet-Nams*, Chapter IV; *Historia*, Sainteny, "Ho Chi Minh," 37; Robert McClintock, *The Meaning of Limited War* (Boston: Houghton Mifflin, 1967), 174.
39 Fall, *Two Viet-Nams*, 107; Hammer, *Struggle for Indochina*, 120; *Historia*, "Leclerc Arrive," 48.
40 *Historia*, Dronne, "Leclerc Arrive," 53.
41 *Historia*, "L'Impromptu de Fontainebleau," Louis Saurel, 59.
42 Hammer, *Struggle for Indochina*, 211; Fall, *Two Viet-Nams*, 73–4.
43 Philippe Devillers, *Histoire du Viet-Nam de 1940 a 1952* (Paris: Editions du Seuil, 1952), 219; Hammer, *Struggle for Indochina*, 147; Fall, *Two Viet-Nams*, 72–3.
44 Fall, *Two Viet-Nams*, 73; Hammer, *Struggle for Indochina*, 153.
45 Hammer, *Struggle for Indochina*, 165–68; *Historia*, Saurel, "L'Impromptu de Fontainebleau," 57–61.
46 Hammer, *The Struggle for Indochina*, 202.
47 Conversation with Kenneth P. Landon, October 1980.
48 Charlton and Moncrieff, *Many Reasons Why*, 27; Historia, Saurel, "L'Impromptu de Fontainebleau," 57; Department of State, *Path to Viet-Nam*, 1–2.
49 David S. McClellan, Dean Acheson, *The State Department Years* (New York: Dodd, Mead and Company, 1976), 259–60; Hammer, *Struggle for Indochina*, 202.
50 Robert McClintock, *The Meaning of Limited War*, Chapter IX.
51 *Historia*, Saurel, 57.
52 Hammer, *Struggle for Indochina*, 149.
53 Ibid, 187–91.
54 Ibid, 191.
55 Ibid, 192.
56 Devillers, *Histoire du Viet-Nam*, 363–64.
57 Hammer, *Struggle for Indochina*, 247 et seq.
58 *Historia*, "L'Autre Solution: Bao Dai chef d'etat,"Philippe Devillers, 89–90.
59 Hammer, *Struggle for Indochina*, 247–48.
60 McClellan, *Dean Acheson*, 239.
61 Ibid, 242.
62 Ibid, 253.
63 Ibid, 262.
64 Ibid.
65 Ibid.
66 Ibid.

67 U.S. Senate, Committee on Foreign Relations, *Background Information relating to Southeast Asia and Viet-Nam*, 3d Revised Edition (Washington, D.C.: U.S. Government Printing Office, 1967, 79-662 0).
68 Hammer, *Struggle for Indochina*, 250–51.
69 Ibid, 267.
70 Dean Acheson, *Present at the Creation* (New York: Signet Books, 1970), 856.
71 Ibid.
72 Ibid, 856; *Background Information*, 44.
73 Devillers, "Histoire du Viet-Nam, Dam chef d'etat," *Historia*, 91.
74 Dean Acheson, *Present at the Creation*, 857.
75 Ibid, 857.
76 McClellan, *Dean Acheson*, 264–65; U.S. Senate, *Background Information*, 4–45.
77 McClellan, *Dean Acheson*, 265, 383.
78 Ibid, 385.
79 Ibid.
80 *Time Magazine*, August 28, 1950, 18–20.
81 Dean Acheson, *Present at the Creation*, 857–58.
82 Ibid, 858.
83 The Pleven Plan was a proposal for an integrated European Army, combining units from several countries.
84 Ibid, 634–40.
85 McClintock, *Limited War*, 178–80.
86 *Historia*, "*Le Roi Jean*," Jean-Pierre Dannaud, 178.
87 Ibid, 179; McClintock, *Limited War*, 161; Acheson, *Present at the Creation*, 861.
88 Hammer, *Struggle for Indochina*, 291; McClintock, *Limited War*, 160, 191; McClellan, *Acheson*, 383.
89 Foster Rhea Dulles, *American Foreign Policy Toward Communist China* (New York: Thomas Y. Crowell Company, 1972), 89–91.
90 Ibid, 91.
91 Ibid.
92 Ibid, 92.
93 Ibid, 92–3.
94 Ibid, 93.
95 Ibid, 94.
96 Ibid, 97.
97 Ibid, 109, 122–23.
98 McClintock, *Limited War*, 173.
99 Dulles, *American Foreign Policy Toward Communist China*, 124.
100 Acheson, *Present at the Creation*, 859.
101 Ibid, 859.
102 Imprimerie d'Extreme-Orient, *Conventions Inter-Etats* (Saigon, 1951).
103 Acheson, *Present at the Creation*, 860.
104 Ibid, 860.
105 Ibid.
106 Ibid.
107 Ibid.
108 Ibid, 860–61.

109 Ibid, 861.
110 Ibid.
111 Ibid, 861–62.
112 Ibid, 862.
113 Ibid.
114 Ibid, 862–63.
115 Writer's recollection.
116 Editor's note: He was also blamed, some thought unjustly, for the Cao Bang disaster of 1950 and his prospects for further advancement in the French Army had vanished.
117 Writer's recollection of conversation with Alessandri in 1953.
118 Dwight D. Eisenhower, *Mandate for Change* (New York: Signet Books, 1965), 215.
119 Ibid, 216.
120 Ibid, 217.
121 Ibid.
122 Ibid.
123 Ibid.
124 Ibid.
125 Ibid, 218.
126 McClintock, *Limited War*, 163; Bernard B. Fall, *Hell in a Very Small Place* (Philadelphia/ New York: J. B. Lippincott Company, 1967), ix, 450 et seq.
127 Eisenhower, *Mandate*, 409–11.
128 Ibid, 412.
129 Ibid.
130 Ibid, 413.
131 Ibid.
132 Ibid, 415.
133 Ibid.
134 Ibid, 416.
135 Ibid, 418.
136 Ibid, 417–18.
137 McClintock, *Limited War*, 167–68.
138 Charlton and Moncrieff, *Many Reasons Why*, 33.
139 McClintock, *Limited War*, 168.
140 Eisenhower, *Mandate*, 426.
141 Ibid, 427.
142 Ibid, 428–29.
143 Ibid, 429.
144 Ibid, 432.
145 Ibid, 433.
146 Ibid, 433–34.
147 Ibid, 437–38.
148 Ibid, 442.
149 Ibid, 443–48.
150 Ibid, 448.
151 McClintock, *Limited War*, 173–74.
152 Ibid, 175.
153 Ibid, 176–77.

154 U.S. Senate Committee, *Background*, 82–91.
155 Acheson, *Present at the Creation*, 859.
156 U.S. Senate Committee, *Background*, 82.
157 155 U.S. Department of State, *The Path to Viet-Nam*.

Part II

1. Dwight D. Eisenhower, *Mandate for Change*. (New York: Signet Books, 1965), 452.
2. Ibid, 539–40.
3. Ibid, 543–44.
4. Ibid, 559–60.
5. Ibid, 575–76.
6. Ibid, 573 note.
7. Ibid, 576.
8. U.S. Senate, Committee on Foreign Relations. *Background Information Relating to Southeast Asian and Vietnam*, 3d Revised Edition "(Washington, D.C.: U.S. Government Printing Office, 1967, 79-662-0), 50–83.
9. Michael Charlton and Anthony Moncrieff, *Many Reasons Why* (New York: Hill and Wang, 1978), 41.
10. Ibid.
11. Ibid, 42.
12. U.S. Department of State, "The Path to Viet-Nam." Released September 1967, 4–5.
13. John Robinson Beal, *John Foster Dulles: A Biography*. (New York: Harper & Brothers, 1957), 239.
14. Ibid, 240.
15. Ibid.
16. Ibid, 243.
17. Ibid, 241–43.
18. Chester L. Cooper, *The Lost Crusade, America in Vietnam*. (New York: Dodd, Mead and Company, 1970), 129, 130.
19. Charlton and Moncrieff, *Many Reasons Why*, 42.
20. Ibid, 43.
21. Dennis J. Duncanson, *Government and Revolution in Viet-Nam*. (New York: Oxford University Press, 1968), 202.
22. Charlton and Moncrieff, *Many Reasons Why*, 43–6.
23. Ibid, 49.
24. Ibid, 50.
25. Ibid, 52–3.
26. Ibid, 50.
27. Ibid, 53.
28. Ibid, 54–5.
29. Ibid, 37–8.
30. Ibid, 57.
31. Cooper, *The Lost Crusade*, 129.
32. Ibid, 128.
33. Ibid, 129.
34. Ibid, 131–33.

35 Ibid, 134.
36 U.S. Senate Committee, *Background*, 89.
37 Cooper, *The Lost Crusade*, 136.
38 Nguyễn Cao Kỳ, *How We Lost the Vietnam War* (New York: Stein and Day, 1978), 34.
39 Edward Geary Lansdale, *In the Midst of Wars, An American's Mission to Southeast Asia* (New York: Harper and Row, 1972), 176.
40 U.S. Senate Committee, *Background*, 80.
41 Cooper, *The Lost Crusade*, 137.
42 Ibid, 137.
43 New York Times, *The Pentagon Papers* (New York: Bantam Books, 1971), 62–4.
44 Cooper, *The Lost Crusade*, 137–38.
45 Ibid, 138.
46 Philippe Devillers, *Histoire du Viet-Nam de 1940 à 1952* (Paris: Editions du Seuil, 1952), 68, 89, 91.
47 Cooper, *The Lost Crusade*, 139.
48 Robert McClintock, *The Meaning of Limited War* (Boston: Houghton, Mifflin, 1967), 160.
49 Lansdale, *In the Midst of Wars*, 245–47.
50 Ibid, 244.
51 Ibid, 244–45.
52 Cooper, *The Lost Crusade*, 140–43; Lansdale, *In the Midst of Wars*, Chapters 14–6.
53 Cooper, *The Lost Crusade*, 146.
54 Ibid, 148.
55 Ibid, 149.
56 Ibid.
57 Ibid, 149–50.
58 U.S. Department of State, "Path to Viet-Nam," 5.
59 Ibid, 5.
60 Guenter Lewy, *America in Vietnam*. (New York: Oxford University Press, 1978), 7.
61 Ibid, 7–8.
62 Ibid, 9.
63 Bernard B. Fall, *The Two Viet-Nams, A Political and Military Analysis*, Revised Edition (New York: Frederick A. Praeger, 1964), 156–7.
64 Anita Lauve, *On the Question of communist Reprisals in Vietnam* (Reproduced by Rand Corporation, Santa Monica, California, August 1970), 3.
65 Fall, *Two Viet-Nams*, 155.
66 Lauve, *Communist Reprisals*, 4 (quoting Hoang Van Chi).
67 Lauve, *Communist Reprisals*, 4 (quoting DRV Government Decree No. 473 TTG, March 1, 1955).
68 Lauve, *Communist Reprisals*, 4.
69 Fall, *Two Viet-Nams*, 155–56.
70 Gerard Tongas, *J'ai vecu dans l'enfer Communiste au Nord Viet-Nam*. (Paris: Nouvelles Editions Debresse, 1960), 122.
71 Lauve, *Communist Reprisals*, 8–9.
72 Ibid, 9–10.
73 Tongas, *l'Enfer Communiste*, 448.
74 Lauve, *Communist Reprisals*, 11–2.
75 Ibid, 15.

76   U.S. Department of State, "Path to Viet-Nam," 5.
77   Ibid, 5–6.
78   Lewy, *America in Vietnam*, 15–6.
79   Ibid, 16–17.
80   Cooper, *The Lost Crusade*, 158; Lewy, *America in Vietnam*, 17 et seq.
81   Lewy, *America in Vietnam*, 17.
82   Ibid, 18.
83   William Colby, *Honorable Men, My Life in the CIA*. (New York: Simon and Schuster, 1978), 145–46.
84   Cooper, *The Lost Crusade*, 161.
85   Ibid, 153. U.S. Department of State. *Program for the Visit to the United States of America of His Excellency Ngo Dinh Diem, President of the Republic of Viet-Nam*, May 1957.
86   Cooper, *The Lost Crusade*, 154.
87   Duncanson, *Government and Revolution in Viet-Nam*, 229.
88   Ibid, 21.
89   U.S. Senate committee, *Background*, 95–6.
90   Ibid, 97.
91   Duncanson, Government and Revolution, 273–76.
92   Ibid, 277–82.
93   Douglas Pike, Viet Cong. (Cambridge, Mass.: Massachusetts Institute of Technology Press, 1966), 72–3.
94   John Mecklin, Mission in Torment, An Intimate Account of the U.S. Role in Vietnam. (Garden City, New York: Doubleday and Company Inc., 1965), 38–9.
95   New York Times, *Pentagon Papers*, 115.
96   Ibid, 117–18.
97   Ibid, 118.
98   Fall, *Two Viet-Nams*, 121.
99   Sisouk Na Champassak, *Storm Over Laos, A Contemporary History* (New York: Frederick A, Praeger, 1961), 31.
100 U.S. Senate committee, Background, 75.
101 Ibid, 75.
102 Sisouk, Storm Over Laos, 59–60.
103 Ibid, 65.
104 Ibid.
105 Ibid, 67.
106 Ibid, 74.
107 Ibid, 92.
108 Ibid, 127.
109 Ibid, 136.
110 Ibid, 157–71.
111 Arthur W, Schlesinger, Jr., *A Thousand Days, John F. Kennedy in the White House* (New York: Fawcett Premier Books, 1965), 156.
112 Ibid, 308.
113 Ibid, 309.
114 Ibid, 310.
115 Ibid, 311–13.
116 Cooper, *The Lost Crusade*, 163–4.

117 Mecklin, *Mission in Torment*, 105.
118 Colby, *Honorable Men*, 192–95.
119 Cooper, *The Lost Crusade*, 167.
120 Ibid, 169.
121 David Halberstam, *The Making of a Quagmire*. (New York: Random House, 1965), 161.
122 Cooper, *The Lost Crusade*, 169.
123 Charlton and Moncrieff, *Many Reasons Why*, 64–6.
124 Ibid, 70.
125 Ibid, 70–1.
126 Ibid, 71.
127 New York Times, *Pentagon Papers*, 79.
128 Ibid, 79.
129 Ibid, 79–83.
130 U.S. Department of State, "Path to Viet-Nam," 6.
131 Ibid.
132 Ibid, 7.
133 Ibid, 7–8.
134 New York Times, *Pentagon Papers*, 83–84.
135 Charlton and Moncrieff, *Many Reasons Why*, 76–7.
136 Mecklin, *Mission in Torment*, 157.
137 Ibid, 162.
138 Ibid, 99.
139 Ibid, 107.
140 Ibid, 164.
141 Colby, *Honorable Men*, 205–7.
142 Mecklin, *Mission in Torment*, 180–81.
143 Ibid, 183, 184, 189, 192–93.
144 New York Times, *Pentagon Papers*, 158.
145 Schlesinger, *A Thousand Days*, 909.
146 U.S. Senate Select Committee to Study Governmental Operations with Respect to Intelligence Activities, *Alleged Assassination Plots Involving Foreign Leaders*, Report No. 94-465 (Washington, D.C.: U.S. Government Printing Office, 1975, 61-985 0).
147 Ibid, 261–62.
148 New York Times, *Pentagon Papers*, 158–59.
149 Charlton and Moncrieff, *Many Reasons Why*, 101.

Part III

1 Lyndon Baines Johnson, *The Vantage Point* (New York: Holt, Rinehart and Winston, 1971), 42.
2 Ibid, 43
3 Merle Miller, *Lyndon, An Oral Biography* (New York: G. P. Putnam's Sons, 1980), 349.
4 Thomas Powers, *The Man who Kept the Secrets, Richard Helms and the CIA* (New York: Pocket Books, 1981), 152.
5 C. L. Sulzberger, *An Age of Mediocrity, Memories and Diaries, 1963–1972* (New York: Macmillan Publishing Co. Inc. 1973), 232.
6 Johnson, *Vantage Point*, 44.

7   Ibid.
8   Ibid.
9   Ibid, 44–5.
10 Ibid, 45.
11 Ibid, 45–6.
12 Powers, *Man Who Kept the Secrets*, 219.
13 Johnson, *Vantage Point*, 46.
14 Ibid.
15 Ibid, 54; see also U.S. Senate, Committee on Foreign Relations. *Background Information Relating to Southeast Asia and Vietnam*. 3d Revised Edition (Washington, D.C.: U.S. Government Printing Office, 1967, 79-662 0), 98–9.
16 Johnson, *Vantage Point*, 54.
17 Ibid, 62–3.
18 Ibid, 63–4.
19 Ibid, 64.
20 U.S. Department of State, "The Path to Viet-Nam," Released September 1967, 8.
21 Frederick Nolting, "The Turning Point," *Foreign Service Journal*, July 1968, 18–20.
22 Charles Dickens, *Works* (New York: Avenel Books, 1978), 572–74.
23 Ellen Hammer, *Vietnam, Yesterday and Today* (New York: Holt, Rinehart and Winston, Inc. 1966), 170.
24 Ibid, 179.
25 Ibid.
26 Guenter Lewy, *America in Vietnam*. (New York: Oxford University Press, 1978), 28.
27 Hammer, *Vietnam, Yesterday and Today*, 179.
28 Ibid, 180. See also "The Path to Viet-Nam," 8.
29 Johnson, *Vantage Point*, 64.
30 Ibid, 65.
31 Nguyễn Cao Kỳ, *How We Lost the Vietnam War* (New York: Stein and Day, 1978), 45–6.
32 Ibid, 65.
33 Ibid, 66.
34 Ibid.
35 Ibid.
36 Ibid, 66–7.
37 Ibid, 67.
38 U.S. Department of State, "The Path to Viet-Nam," 8.
39 Ibid.
40 Ibid.
41 Michael Charlton and Anthony Moncrieff, *Many Reasons Why* (New York: Hill and Wang, 1978), 116.
42 Johnson, *Vantage Point*, 67.
43 Ibid.
44 Ibid, 67–8.
45 Ibid, 68.
46 New York Times, *The Pentagon Papers* (New York: Bantam Books, 1971), 234.
47 Ibid.
48 Ibid, 235.
49 Ibid.

50 Ibid, 240.
51 Johnson, *Vantage Point*, 112–15.
52 DESOTO patrols gathered signals (and other) intelligence in hostile waters and were performed by U.S. Navy destroyers. The "De Haven" component of the acronym was because USS *De Haven*, an Allen M. Sumner-class destroyer built in World War II, carried out the first such patrol off China in April 1962. The patrols were a response to China massively expanding their offshore territorial claims.
53 Johnson, *Vantage Point*, 118.
54 Merle Miller, *Lyndon*, 384–85.
55 Johnson, *Vantage Point*, 118–19.
56 Charlton and Moncrieff, *Reasons Why*, 113–14.
57 U.S. Department of State, "The Path to Viet-Nam," 8; see also U.S. Senate, *Background Information on Indochina*, 126.
58 Lewy, *America in Vietnam*, 35.
59 *Pentagon Papers*, 307.
60 Ibid, 310.
61 Ibid, 312.
62 Ibid.
63 Ibid.
64 Johnson, *Vantage Point*, 119.
65 Ibid, 119.
66 Ibid, 119–20.
67 Ibid, 120.
68 *Pentagon Papers*, 315.
69 Ibid, 315–16.
70 Johnson, *Vantage Point*, 121–22.
71 U.S. Department of State, "The Path to Viet-Nam," 9.
72 Ibid.
73 Johnson, *Vantage Point*, 122–23.
74 Ibid, 123–24.
75 Ibid, 124.
76 Ibid.
77 Ibid.
78 Ibid, 125.
79 Ibid; see also Nguyễn Cao Kỳ, *How We Lost the War*, 56–7.
80 Johnson, *Vantage Point*, 126–27.
81 Ibid, 128.
82 Ibid, 129.
83 Ibid, 131.
84 Ibid, 132.
85 Ibid.
86 Lewy, *America in Vietnam*, 39.
87 Ibid, 39–40.
88 Ibid, 40.
89 U.S. Senate, *Background Information on Indochina*, 145–48.
90 Johnson, *Vantage Point*, 132.
91 Ibid, 132.

92 Ibid, 133–34; see also U.S. Senate, *Background Information on Indochina*, 148–83 for speech text.
93 Johnson, *Vantage Point*, 134; see also U.S. Senate, *Background Information on Indochina*, 153–56 for U.S. Reply and text of 17 Nation Appeal.
94 Johnson, *Vantage Point*, 135–36.
95 Ibid, 137.
96 William C. Westmoreland, *A Soldier Reports* (New York: Dell Publishing Co. 1980), 133.
97 Johnson, *Vantage Point*, 138.
98 Lewy, *America in Vietnam*, 42.
99 Ibid, 42–3.
100 Johnson, *Vantage Point*, 139.
101 Ibid, 139.
102 Ibid, 140.
103 Ibid, 140–41.
104 Ibid, 141.
105 Ibid, 142.
106 Ibid, 142–43.
107 Ibid, 143.
108 Ibid.
109 Ibid, 143–44.
110 Nguyễn Cao Kỳ, *How We Lost the War*, 78–80.
111 Johnson, *Vantage Point*, 144.
112 Ibid, 145.
113 Ibid, 145–46.
114 Ibid, 146.
115 Ibid, 147.
116 Ibid.
117 Ibid, 149.
118 Ibid, 151.
119 Ibid, 153.
120 Ibid.
121 Ibid, 232–33.
122 Charlton and Moncrieff, *Reasons Why*, 119.
123 Ibid.
124 Ibid, 121.
125 Ibid.
126 Ibid, 167.
127 Johnson, *Vantage Point*, 233.
128 Ibid, 233–34.
129 Ibid, 234.
130 Ibid, 235.
131 Ibid.
132 Ibid, 236–37.
133 Ibid, 238.
134 Ibid, 238–39.
135 Ibid, 241.
136 Ibid, 243–41.

137 Nguyễn Cao Kỳ, *How We Lost the War*, 92.
138 Writer's recollection.
139 *Washington Star*, February 20, 1968, A-1, A-6.
140 Nguyễn Cao Kỳ, *How We Lost the War*, 92–3.
141 Ibid, Chapter 8; Lewis W. Walt, *Strange War, Strange Strategy*, Chapters 10, 11 (New York: Funk and Wagnalls, 1970); William C. Westmoreland, *A Soldier Reports*, 220–29.
142 Westmoreland, *A Soldier Reports*, 229.
143 Johnson, *Vantage Point*, 248.
144 Ibid.
145 Ibid, 249.
146 Ibid, 259–63.
147 Ibid, 265.
148 Ibid, 267.
149 Ibid, 579–91.
150 Charlton and Moncrieff, *Reasons Why*, 126–27.
151 Ibid, 128.
152 Johnson, *Vantage Point*, 384.
153 Ibid, 435.
154 Ibid, 507.

Part IV

1 Richard M. Nixon, *Memoirs* (New York: Warner Books, Inc., 1979), 368, Vol. 1.
2 Ibid, 380–81.
3 Ibid, 398–400.
4 Ibid, 402–3.
5 Ibid, 404.
6 Ibid, 405.
7 Ibid, 406–7.
8 Ibid, 416–17.
9 Ibid, 420.
10 Ibid, 421.
11 Ibid, 421–23.
12 Ibid, 443.
13 Henry Kissinger, *White House Years* (Boston: Little Brown & Co., 1979), 26.
14 Ibid, 27.
15 Ibid, 27–8.
16 Ibid, 29.
17 Ibid.
18 Ibid, 30.
19 Ibid, 43.
20 Ibid.
21 Ibid, 42.
22 Ibid, 45.
23 Ibid, 47.
24 Ibid, 47–8.

25 Charlton and Anthony Moncrieff, *Many Reasons Why* (New York: Hill and Wang, 1978), 187–88.
26 Ibid, 189.
27 Ibid, 189–90.
28 Ibid, 190–91.
29 Ibid, 191.
30 Ibid, 192–93.
31 Ibid, 193.
32 Ibid, 196–97.
33 Ibid, 197–98.
34 Ibid, 198.
35 Ibid, 198–99.
36 Nixon, *Memoirs*, Vol. I, 428–29.
37 Ibid, 430.
38 Ibid.
39 Ibid, 431.
40 Ibid.
41 Ibid, 432.
42 Ibid.
43 Ibid, 423–33.
44 Ibid, 433–34.
45 Ibid, 435.
46 Ibid, 441.
47 Ibid, 457.
48 Ibid, 462–63.
49 Ibid, 470–71.
50 Ibid, 471–72.
51 Ibid, 472.
52 Ibid, 478–82.
53 Ibid, 482.
54 Ibid, 483.
55 Ibid.
56 Ibid, 484.
57 Ibid, 484–85.
58 Ibid, 485.
59 Nguyễn Cao Kỳ, *How We Lost the War* (New York: Stein and Day, 1978), 171.
60 Ibid, 172.
61 Ibid, 173.
62 Ibid, 174–75.
63 Lewy, *America in Vietnam*, 162.
64 Ibid, 163.
65 Ibid, 164–66.
66 Ibid, 166.
67 Ibid, 167.
68 Ibid.
69 Ibid, 166.
70 Ibid, 168.

71 Ibid, 170–71.
72 Ibid, 175.
73 Nixon, *Memoirs*, Vol. I, 485, 465k.
74 Ibid, 486, 465k.
75 Ibid.
76 Ibid, 487, 465k.
77 Ibid, 487–488, 468k.
78 Kissinger, *White House Years*, 279.
79 Ibid, 259.
80 Ibid, 259–64.
81 Ibid, 264.
82 Ibid, 281–82.
83 Ibid, 304.
84 Ibid.
85 Ibid.
86 Ibid, 305.
87 Nixon, *Memoirs*, Vol. I, 496–97, 476k.
88 Ibid, 503.
89 Ibid, 504.
90 Ibid, 507.
91 Ibid.
92 Ibid, 507–8.
93 Ibid, 510.
94 Ibid, 512.
95 Kissinger, *White House Years*, 306.
96 Ibid, 308.
97 Nixon, *Memoirs*, Vol. I, 534.
98 Ibid, 535–36.
99 Ibid, 551–53.
100 Kissinger, *White House Years*, 447.
101 Nixon, *Memoirs*, Vol. I, 553.
102 Ibid, 555–56.
103 Ibid, 556.
104 These two places were so-called from their appearance on the map. The French had always called the former the *Bec du Canard* (Duck's Bill) but the U.S. Army, for its own ornithological reasons, had changed the name.
105 Ibid, 558.
106 Ibid, 566.
107 Ibid, 578.
108 Ibid, 578–79.
109 Kissinger, *White House Years*, 971.
110 Ibid, 976.
111 Ibid, 978.
112 Ibid, 980–81.
113 Ibid, 983–84.
114 Ibid, 986.
115 U.S. Department of State. *Scope of the U.S. Involvement in Laos*, Released March 6, 1970, 3, 4, 5.

116 Kissinger, *White House Years*, 986.
117 Ibid, 990–91.
118 William C. Westmoreland, *A Soldier Reports* (New York: Dell Publishing Co. 1980), 514–15.
119 Kissinger, *White House Years*, 991.
120 Ibid, 997.
121 Ibid, 999–1002.
122 Ibid, 1009.
123 Westmoreland, *A Soldier Reports*, 515.
124 Kissinger, *White House Years*, 1012.
125 Ibid, 1018.
126 Ibid, 1022–25.
127 Ibid, 1031.
128 Ibid, 1039–41.
129 Ibid, 1043.
130 Ibid, 1044.
131 Ibid, 1045–46.
132 Ibid, 1046.
133 Nixon, *Memoirs*, Vol. 2, 60–61.
134 Kissinger, *White House Years*, 1097.
135 Ibid, 1098.
136 Nixon, *Memoirs*, Vol. 2, 64, 70.
137 Kissinger, *White House Years*, 1109.
138 Ibid, 1118.
139 Ibid, 1121.
140 Ibid, 1124.
141 Ibid, 1167.
142 Nixon, *Memoirs*, Vol. 2, 70.
143 Kissinger, *White House Years*, 1167.
144 Ibid, 1173–74.
145 Nixon, *Memoirs*, Vol. 2, 83–4.
146 Ibid, 84.
147 Kissinger, *White House Years*, 1189.
148 Ibid, 1190–91.
149 Ibid, 1194.
150 Ibid, 1311.
151 Ibid, 1318–19.
152 Ibid, 1322–23.
153 Ibid, 1344.
154 Ibid, 1345.
155 Ibid, 1349.
156 Ibid, 1368–69.
157 Ibid, 1367.
158 Ibid, 1393.
159 Ibid, 1446.
160 Ibid, 1467.
161 Nixon, *Memoirs*, Vol. 2, 269.
162 Nguyễn Cao Kỳ, *How We Lost the Vietnam War*, 189.

163 Ibid, 192.
164 Lewy, *America in Vietnam*, 202–5.
165 Harold Nicolson, *The Evolution of Diplomatic Method* (London: Constable & Co. Ltd., 1954).

Appendix 1

1. Address prepared for delivery before the 20th annual congress of the National Student Association at College Park, Md., on Aug. 15 (press release 177). Because of time limitations, Mr. Bundy read excerpts from the address, and the complete text was made available to the audience. For additional remarks made by Mr. Bundy on this occasion, see Department of State press release 177-A dated Aug. 15.
2. For texts, see *American Foreign Policy, 1950–1955, Basic Documents, vol. I*, Department of State publication 6446, 750.
3. For background, *see Bulletin* of Aug. 2, 1954, 162.
4. For text of the Southeast Asia Collective Defense Treaty and protocol, see Ibid, Sept. 20, 1954, 898.
5. For text of President Eisenhower's letter, see Ibid, Nov. 15, 1954, 785.
6. Roger Hilsman, *To Move a Nation: the politics of foreign policy in the administration of John F. Kennedy* (Doubleday, Garden City, N.Y., 1967).
7. For texts, see BULLETIN of Aug. 13, 1962, 259.
8. A reply by President Kennedy during his press conference on June 14, 1962.
9. For transcript of an NBC interview with President Kennedy on Sept. 9, 1963, see BULLETIN of Sept. 30, 1963, 499.
10. Public Law 88-408; for text, see BULLETIN of Aug. 24, 1964. 268.
11. For text, see Ibid, Nov. 14, 1966, 734.
12. For text, see Ibid, Apr. 26, 1965, 606.
13. For text, see Ibid, Aug. 16, 1965, 264.
14. For text, see Ibid, June 5, 1967, 838.
15. Ibid, Apr. 26, 1965, 606.

Index

17th Parallel, 40, 57, 121, 125, 170

Abrams, General Creighton, 2–3, 125, 142, 152, 156–60
Acheson, Dean, 14–19, 23–28
Agency for International Development, 94
aggression, v, 16–18, 23–25, 37, 41, 65, 72, 79, 87–88, 103–4, 107–10, 118–19, 124–5, 169–73, 177, 180, 186–7
Agnew, Spiro, 142, 149
Air Force, 5, 32, 46, 102,
    South Vietnamese Air Force, 106
    United States Air Force, 32, 102
air strike, 32, 35, 102, 106, 107, 152
Alessandri, General Marcel, 28
ammunition, 5, 23, 53, 73, 128, 143–4, 153
Anglo-Saxon, 2
antiwar protest, 140, 152
ANZUS, 31, 36, 184
Argentina, 71
Armistice, 2, 36, 57
arms, 5, 10, 11, 19–22, 28, 65–73, 103, 106, 110, 136, 139, 143, 153–5
Army
    173rd Airborne Brigade, 115–16
    British Indian forces, 7
    Expeditionary Corps, 13, 27, 39
    First Division, 123–4
    Imperial Guard, 54
    Lao National Army, 28
    Military Assistance Command, Vietnam (MACV), 86, 101, 108, 125, 143, 156
    National Guard, 117, 153
    North Vietnamese Army, 48, 103, 135, 139
    paratroopers, 73
    Pathet Lao Fighting Units, 69
    People's Liberation Armed Forces (PLAF), 23, 62
    Republic of Vietnam Armed Forces (RVNAF), 144
    Royal Army, 71–72
    South Vietnamese Army, 39, 48, 95, 115, 144
    Special Forces, 78, 124
    Vietnamese National Army (ARVN), 18, 28, 152, 157–8
artillery, 28, 33, 128, 136, 144, 160
assassination, 9, 62, 70, 82, 87
Associated States, 15–19, 21–26, 29–31, 34, 36–41
asylum, 81
Atlee, Clement, 7
atomic weapons, 14, 34, *see also* nuclear weapons
Australia, 35, 37, 72, 81, 113, 115–16, 123

B-52, 139, 147, 161
BBC, 5, 6, 8, 34, 45–49, 76, 77, 79–82, 95, 100, 119, 120, 125, 132–6
Berlin, 14, 32, 33, 102, 136, 176
Bidault, Georges, 29, 32, 33, 38
Bình, Madame Nguyên Thi, 12, 154, 158–9
Blum, Léon, 12, 13
bombing, 97, 101–9, 112–19, 120–9, 133, 137, 139, 140–5, 150, 154, 156, 160, 162, 164, 178, 180–4
    halt, 112, 120, 121, 127–9, 145
Borneo, 172
Buddhism, 52, 61, 66, 67, 80–81, 90, 92, 123–4, 174
Bundy, William P., vii, 41–42, 55, 61–62, 78–79, 85–86, 89, 95, 98, 100–7, 119–21, 167

Bunker, Ellsworth, 125, 139, 142, 152, 153, 156
bureaucracy, 50, 129, 132, 147, 150
Burma, 6, 8, 11, 74, 187
Buttinger, Joseph, 50

Cambodia, v, 15, 52, 73–74, 89, 112, 125, 135, 137, 139, 140, 150–8, 170, 172, 187
Canada, xi, 46, 57, 60, 95, 96
Cao Đài, 52–53
Catholicism, 52, 92, 93
Catroux, General, 2
cease-fire, 13, 34, 36, 39, 44, 56, 58, 60, 74, 75, 128, 149, 154, 162
Ceausescu, Nicolae, 146
Ceylon, 6, 8, 110
Chennault, General Claire, 5
Cherne, Leo, 50
China, 1, 2–13, 15–19, 26, 35, 40–42, 69, 74, 96, 101, 106, 143, 159, 167, 169–73, 176–7, 181–2, 187
Chinese Communists, 3, 23, 32, 35, 65, 69, 96, 112, 117
Churchill, Winston, 6, 38
CIA, vii, 21, 32, 48–50, 75–78, 80–82, 85–86, 89, 94, 101–6, 114, 131, 140, 151
Clifford, Clark, 121, 129
Cochinchina, 8–12
Colby, William, 48–49, 62–63, 80, 135
Cold War, 8, 22, 66
colonialism, 1, 3, 8, 11, 12, 15, 17, 49, 58, 66
colonial power, 4, 8, 49, 57, 167
Commander in Chief, Pacific Fleet (CINCPAC), 114, 121
Commander U.S. Military Assistance Command, Vietnam (COMUSMACV), 101, 125
Committee for Defense of National Interests (CDIN), 70
communism, vi, 14, 17–18, 22–23, 36, 42, 48, 50, 54, 60, 70–81, 87, 88, 90–96, 100–12, 117, 120–8, 130–9, 141–53, 167, 169–73, 176, 179, 180–8
Confucianism, 52, 91
Congress, viii, 17, 20, 26–30, 32–37, 48, 62–63, 107, 111, 115, 118, 120, 128, 138–9, 145–6, 149, 154–9, 162–4, 179

coup de force, 6–7
coup d'état, 6, 7, 68, 72–73, 82, 89, 91–93, 151
Cuba, 75, 176
Cuban missile crisis, 176

Dalat Conference, 10
d'Argenlieu, Admiral, 9, 12–13
de Gaulle, General Charles, 8, 10, 11, 88–89, 139, 168
DeHaven Special Operations off Tsingtao (DESOTO), 97–98, 103
de Lattre de Tassigny, General, 18, 20
Demilitarized Zone (DMZ), 122, 125, 128, 139, 141, 156, 160–1
democracy, 9, 15, 58–59, 81, 86, 122, 123, 137
Dewey, Lieutenant Colonel Peter, 7–9
Dewey, Thomas, 20
dictatorship, 55, 63, 77, 92, 161
Diệm, Ngô Đình, vii, 45–46, 51, 55, 63, 65–68, 76–79 80–86, 90, 95, 171, 173–4, 178
Điện Biên Phủ, vi, 22, 28, 30–36, 39, 41, 44, 46, 50
Dobrynin, Anatoly, 131, 141, 146–8, 160
Durbrow, Elbridge, 67–68, 76

Eden, Anthony, 4, 25, 27, 34, 36, 38, 47, 169
Eisenhower Administration, vii, 39, 41, 51, 74, 78, 132
Eisenhower, Dwight D., 20, 22, 28–30, 32–44, 51–53, 63–65, 68, 74–77, 99, 108, 110, 129, 132, 140, 171
election, vii, 8, 44–48, 54–57, 64, 70–73, 96, 124–5, 128–9, 134–6, 141, 145, 159, 163, 170–4, 179
elite, 63, 70, 92, 149
Embassy, 48, 50, 52, 68, 71, 76, 81, 82, 93, 113, 121, 152
European Defense Community, 21, 24, 29, 32, 37

Fall, Bernard, 2, 58, 61, 69, 174–5
Far East, 1–3, 23, 32, 105, 107–8
financial aid, 14, 64, 66
Final Declaration, 38, 46, 47, 54, 56
Fontainebleau Conference, 9, 10, 12

Ford, Gerald, 107, 120
Formosa, 23, 43–44, 99
France, 2, 4, 7–12, 15–26, 30, 32, 36–40, 45, 53, 167–9
Free World, 22, 31, 34, 37, 44, 133
French colonialism, 8, 12, 168
French Colonial War, 11
French Communist Party, vi, 7
French National Assembly, 22, 24, 26, 37
French Union, 9–12, 15–18, 24, 29, 31, 36–38, 43, 47, 51
Fulbright, Senator William, 48, 100, 120

Geneva, 33, 35, 38, 39, 44, 75, 90, 96, 174
  Accords/Agreements, vi, vii, 17, 40, 43, 44, 46, 48, 54, 58–60, 66, 69, 76, 109–10, 121, 155, 156, 170, 173, 175, 176
  Conference, 32, 35, 36, 38, 56, 57, 72, 74, 169, 171
Giáp, Võ Nguyên, 5, 9, 10, 12, 21, 62, 69
Goodpaster, General Andrew J., 107, 132
Gracey, General Douglas D., 7–8
Great Britain, 8, 35, 145
Gromyko, Andrei, 75
guerrilla warfare, 30, 36, 46–47, 49, 53, 61, 65, 68, 71, 76, 79–80, 86, 94, 97, 101, 102, 105, 112, 117, 124–5, 135, 160, 175, 177, 183
Gulf of Tonkin, vii, 95, 97, 102, 179
Gullion, Edmund, 169

Hải Phòng, 12, 53, 122, 137, 161–2
  Harbor, 137, 162
Hạ Long Bay Agreement, 13
Hammarskjöld, Dag, 71–72
Hawaii, 81
helicopter, 74, 105, 113, 143–4
Hòa Hảo, 52–53
Hoover, Herbert, 20
Hoover, J. Edgar, 140
Hitler, Adolf, 2
Ho Chi Minh, 5, 16, 63, 90, 91, 95, 131, 168
  Trail, vii, viii, 90, 112, 122, 155–6
House Appropriations bill, 35
House of Representatives, 63, 87, 149

Hull, Cordell, 2, 8–9
Humphrey, Hubert, 85, 108, 122–3, 128–9
Hungary, 57, 152

imperialism, 16, 36, 58, 62
Inauguration, 76, 131–2
Indochina, vi, 1–20, 22–27, 29–34, 35–41, 44, 47, 49, 76, 78, 143, 154, 158, 162, 168–9, 171–2, 177, 187
  War, 7, 13, 14, 20–21, 29, 34, 49
Indonesia, 6–8, 11, 19, 61, 112, 145, 168, 175, 187–8
insurgency, vi, 6, 55–56, 61–62, 80, 93–94, 96, 109, 124, 144
International Commission for Supervision and Control, 47, 57
International Control Commission (ICC), 57–60, 69, 71, 74, 95, 110
International Rescue Committee, 50
Italy, 71

Japan, 1–8, 28, 42, 49, 72, 168, 172
Johns Hopkins University, 110
Johnson, Lyndon Baines, vii, 51, 78, 82, 85–90, 92–99, 101–29, 132–3, 136, 138–40, 142, 144–6, 150, 176, 179, 182–3, 188

Kennedy, John F., 48, 51, 55, 74–79, 81–82, 85–86, 88–90, 92, 95, 112, 130, 133, 138, 155, 174–7
Kent State affair, 135, 152–3
Khrushchev, Nikita, 44, 75–76, 176
Kissinger, Henry, vi, viii, 128–32, 134, 136, 138–41, 145–64
Koh Chang, 2
Komer, Robert W., 123, 125, 143
Kong Le, 73, 112
Korean War, vi, 17, 19, 23
Kuomintang (KMT), 3, 7, 10

Laird, Melvin, 139–41, 147, 148, 150–2, 157
Lam Son 719, 157
landownership, 58
land reform, 54, 58–59
Lansdale, Colonel Edward, 46–47, 50, 52–53, 76

Lansdale Group, 52
Lao People's Democratic Republic, 69
Laos, v, 10, 15, 17, 21, 27–29, 36, 38, 40–41, 65, 69–78, 89–90, 96–97, 103, 112, 115, 125, 137, 150, 152, 155–8, 160, 170, 172, 175–6
Laotian People's Rally, 70
Lawton Collins, General J., 40, 51
Leclerc, General, 9–10
Lenin, Vladimir, 49, 64, 150
Letourneau, Jean, 26–27
liberation front, 62, 96, 112, 122
Lodge, Henry Cabot, x, 67, 81–82, 85–89, 94, 101, 121, 125, 154
Luang Prabang, 21, 71, 73

MacArthur, General, 19, 23, 24
Maddox, USS, 97–98, 100
Magsaysay, Ramon, 46
Malaya, 6, 8, 11, 48, 172
Manila, 28, 34, 124, 171, 182
  Pact, 34, 40, 43, 171, 182
Mansfield, Senator Michael, 48, 50–51, 55, 106–7, 118, 120, 145–6, 149, 158
Mao Tse-tung, 91, 136
March 6 Accord, 10–12
Marshall Plan, 11, 14, 39, 74, 168
McCarthyism, 22, 48, 120
McCone, John, 85, 89, 98, 101–5, 114
McGovern–Hatfield amendment, 153, 155, 158
McNaughton, John T., 102, 106
media 139, 158–9, 162, *see also* press
Mekong, 74, 87
Mendès, Pierre, 21–22, 38, 40
Middle East, the, 99, 102, 136, 138, 140
Military Assistance Advisory Group, 28, 32, 66, 75
modus vivendi, 10, 35
Molotov, Vyacheslav, 38, 44
Moscow, 15, 22, 74, 76, 89, 106, 108, 111–12, 122, 127, 151, 159–61

National Assembly, 22, 24, 26, 37, 64, 68–70, 91
nationalism, 3, 7, 12, 15–18, 55, 61, 63, 70, 79, 90, 95, 167, 169–70, 174–5, 178–9, 181, 186

National Liberation Front, 62, 96, 122
national security, vii, 15, 22, 41, 52, 67, 85–86, 94, 103, 111, 125, 129–33, 140, 184
National Security Action Memorandum (NSAM), 86, 103
Navarre, General, 22, 31, 33
Navarre Plan, 31
Navy, 5, 28, 102, 144
  French Navy, 5, 28
  Marine Corps, 74, 101, 102, 113–16, 124
  Seventh Fleet, 23, 74
  Third Marine Amphibious Brigade, 115
  Vietnamese Navy, 98
Neo Lao Hak Sat (NLHS), 70, 73
neutralization, 74–75, 88–9
New Zealand, 35, 37, 124
Nixon, Richard, v, vi, viii, 22, 35, 51, 127–38, 139–54, 156–64
Nolting, Frederick, 67, 76–79, 81, 89–91
North Atlantic Treaty Organization (NATO), 15, 28–29, 34–35, 38–40, 47, 88, 139
Northeast Frontier Agency, 71
North Korea, 3, 19, 22–23, 108, 112
Nosavan, Phoumi, 71, 73
nuclear weapons, 14, 33–34, 43, 137
Nutter, Warren, 133–4, 136

Office of Strategic Services (OSS), 5–7
oil, 99

pacification, 52–53, 95, 101, 108, 122–3, 134–5, 144, 179
Pakistan, 74, 145
Paris, 17–18, 21, 24–28, 32, 38, 40, 45, 72–73, 126, 133, 136, 139, 141–2, 144–7, 151, 154, 158–9, 161, 163–4
"Path to Vietnam" speech, 89, 95, 100, 103
Patti, Major Archimedes L. A., 5–6
peace, vii, viii, 3, 13–16, 21–23, 35–39, 46, 55, 64, 70, 72, 76, 81, 86, 95–96, 105–6, 110–12, 117–25, 127, 129, 138, 141, 144–9, 154–9, 161–3, 170, 175, 179, 182–3, 186, 188
  treaty, 3, 14
Pearl Harbor, 88
peasant, 13, 63–64, 68
Peking, 14, 23, 25, 27, 71, 77, 89, 106, 108, 111, 127, 136, 151, 160, 181, 187–8

Pentagon Papers, 68, 78, 82, 96, 100, 101, 103
People's Revolutionary Party (PRP), 62
Pescadores, the, 43–44
Philippines, the, 1–3, 5, 11, 37, 41, 46, 74, 145, 172
Phnom Penh, xi, 73, 152
Phouma, Prince Souvanna, 69–75, 78, 108, 112, 155, 157, 175
Plaine des Jarres, 69, 71–72
plebiscite, 55, 173
Poland, 46
police, 52 53, 58, 81, 123, 135
policy maker, vi, 79, 91, 130, 164, 178
Politburo, 136, 144, 151
population, 8, 29, 35, 46, 52, 56, 58–61, 67, 81, 91, 125, 146, 186
Population Classification Decree, 58
postcolonialism, 2
press, vii, viii, 11, 35, 39, 53, 57, 63, 66–68, 74, 77, 80–81, 89–90, 93, 101, 118, 123, 126, 129, 131, 140, 148, 150–2, 154, 157, *see also* media
prime minister, 7, 22, 28, 40, 45, 69, 70, 73, 91–93, 116, 124, 139, 157, 171, 183, 187
prisoners of war, 137, 154, 158, 162
Program Evaluation Office, 75
propaganda, 3, 23, 46, 61, 72–73, 96, 108–9, 174–5

Queen Elizabeth II, 139

Radio Hanoi, 122–3, 148
rearmament, 17, 20
reconnaissance, 103, 164
Reinhardt, Ambassador Frederick, 54, 67
resistance, 9, 11, 15, 26, 28, 29, 58, 60, 69, 80, 91, 121
reunification, 55, 62, 170, 173
Robertson, Walter S., 45, 54
Rogers, William, viii, 129–31, 139–40, 146–52, 157
Roosevelt, Franklin D., 4–9, 120, 168
Rusk, Dean, 6–8, 47, 74, 76–77, 84–86, 91, 98–102, 105, 107, 111, 113, 118, 120–2, 127, 129

Sài Gòn, xi, 7–8, 13, 17–21, 25–28, 30, 50–54, 67, 71, 75–76, 80–82, 86–88, 92–95, 101–7, 113–16, 123, 146, 151, 160, 163
Sainteny, Jean, 5, 8–12, 136, 138, 145, 147
San Antonio formula, 125
San Francisco Peace Treaty, 3
Santiphab, 70, 73
Savannakhet, 73
Schuman, Maurice, 9, 15–18, 22, 25, 27, 37
Seaborn, Blair, 95–96
secret ballot, 44–47, 56
Sihanoukville, 110, 112, 151, 153, 156
Singapore, 2, 172, 187
Smith, Bedell, 22, 29, 32, 38
Somsanith Government, 73
Souphanouvong, 69, 72–74
South China Sea, 74
Southeast Asia Treaty Organization (SEATO), 38, 41, 47–48, 55, 85, 100, 170–3, 184
    Treaty Protocol, 41, 55, 85, 100, 171, 173
South Korea, 3, 19, 23, 37, 99, 114–15, 117, 119
South Vietnamese Government, 60, 77, 101, 103, 106, 124, 163
Soviet Union, 3–4, 14, 32, 40, 75, 111, 148, 160, 167–70, 176, 181
Special Technical and Economic Mission (STEM), 17
Stalin, Joseph, 8, 15, 22
Stassen, Harold, 20
subversion, 26, 41, 60–66, 70, 104–5, 110, 155, 172–3, 180, 184, 187
suicide, 80, 92

Taiwan, 3, 23, 44, 93
tanks, 99, 136, 160
task force, 39, 40, 144
Taylor, General Maxwell, 90, 93, 101–8, 111, 113, 114, 116
Taylor/Rostow Mission, 77, 79–80
Tet Offensive, 125–6, 134, 143–4
Thailand, 3, 35, 37, 41, 74, 76, 112, 124, 145, 172–7, 184, 187
Thiệu, Nguyễn Văn, 92, 137, 142, 151, 157, 159, 163–4, 178
Tho, Le Duc, 144, 147, 151, 154, 158–9, 161, 164
Thompson, Llewellyn, 105, 108
Thompson, Sir Robert, 49, 134–5, 148

Thúy, Xuân, 145–7, 151, 154, 157–9
Tibet, 23
Tonkin Gulf Resolution, 100, 119
Training Relations and Instruction Mission (TRIM), 52–53
Trí Quảng, Thích, 81, 123
truce, 13, 22, 30, 53, 121
Truman Administration, 22, 39, 41
Truman, Harry S., vi, 6, 14–19, 22–23, 29, 39, 41, 48, 99, 119

unification, vii, 54–56, 62, 64, 88, 170, 173
United Nations, 3, 16, 19, 21, 23, 29, 31, 37–38, 64, 71–72, 107, 170, 179
   Charter, 16, 64, 109–12
   General Assembly, 30
   Security Council, 23
United States Declaration, 38
United States Department of Defense, vii
United States Information Agency (USIS), 81
United States State Department, v–xi, 24, 72, 74, 81–82, 88, 90–91, 116, 129–32, 141, 146–7, 150, 152, 157, 160–1

Vance, Cyrus, 105, 146
Văn Hinh, General Nguyễn, 46, 51
Việt Minh, vi, 11, 21, 54, 57, 61, 64,
Vietnam, 5, 10, 11–17, 20–27, 29, 38–40, 44–46, 49–51, 54–58, 66–69, 71, 74, 76, 80–82, 85–88, 90–95, 97–99, 100–105, 110–15, 119–28, 129–30, 132–9, 142, 145, 148–50, 154–8, 164, 165, 167, 175
   Democratic Republic of, 7, 10, 14, 23, 40, 59, 97
   Free, 40, 54, 65, 68
   North, vii, vii, ix, 5, 41, 44, 47, 53, 58–61, 69–72, 75, 76, 78, 90, 95–99, 100–9, 110–15, 116, 120, 122, 125–8, 135–9, 145–7, 149–50, 153, 155–9, 160–1, 164, 172–3, 176–9, 181, 183–4
   South, v, vii, ix, 5, 41, 47, 53, 58–61, 65, 76–79, 85–88, 90–95, 97, 99, 100–7, 109, 110–16, 119, 122, 123, 125–8, 133–9, 140, 143, 145, 148–50, 154–8, 160–1, 164, 178, 180, 182–4
   War, v, vii, viii, ix, 82, 127, 139, 153, 154, 164
Vietnamization, 17, 133–6, 141–4, 148–50, 156, 161, 164
V-J Day, 7
Voice of America (VOA), 81, 98

Washington, xi, 18, 25, 29, 35–39, 51–53, 63–64, 70, 73–77, 81, 86–87, 91–4, 98–102, 113, 114, 123, 140, 147, 149, 150, 163
   Special Action Group (WSAG), 157
Watergate, viii, 155, 164
Westmoreland, General William C., 86, 101, 104–6, 113, 115, 118, 121–5, 142–3, 156–7
Wheeler, General Earle, 102, 105, 129, 139
White House, 25, 40, 54, 87, 90, 97, 99, 101, 113, 116, 118, 128–32, 136, 144–5, 149–50, 155, 160
White Paper, 109
Wilson, Harold, 139
World War II, vi, 1–2, 4–7, 24, 40, 49, 67, 85, 87, 133, 172

Yalta, xi, 4, 8
Yugoslavia, 14, 23, 111